Thoughts on *Planet Backpacker:*

I wonder how many readers have been as inspired as I have by Robert Downes' globe-circling prowls through the underbelly of the third world's teeming cities. You have to visit some of these places to appreciate that his sort of seat-of-the-pants travel, flopping in two-star hostelries and assorted *caravanserai*, dining on peasant fare and mixing it up with the locals, is a daunting experience even for twenty-somethings. And Downes has more than a few miles on him.

-- *James R. McCormick • Mideast peace activist*

I couldn't agree more with Robert Downes' sentiments. There aren't enough Americans who get off the "beaten path." I do meet an occasional one here in India, but most are embassy workers or inves- tors or here on some cushy job or another. There aren't too many real travelers, and I agree that it's because we fear much of the world. I often have the very same conversation with my fellow travelers: Why are there so few Americans out there exploring?

What Downes says is true: most locals are overjoyed to meet an American, especially after spending their days listening to our music, and watching our movies and TV shows. They want to know what we're really like; they want to compare the messages and images we spread across the world to the real thing. To wit, some of my best friends here in Delhi are Baghdad-born-and-raised. An American Jew and Iraqi Muslims? Sounds like a joke; but it's not. It's just how things really work out here in the world.

-- *Adam Fivenson • American traveler • Delhi, India, 2007-'08*

In *Planet Backpacker* Robert Downes captures the romanticism and realities of backpacking around the world. This is not a 'what to pack' or 'what kind of gear to buy' book, rather *Planet Backpacker* explores the human experience of the journey by blending humor- ous incidents and anecdotes. This book will serve as an inspiration to anyone who has ever considered such an adventure -- start putting in for a leave of absence now."

-- *Richard A. Coates, author of The Glovebox Guide series.*

What readers are saying:

"I just finished it about an hour ago and thought it was freaking amazing."

-- *Peter A. Richards, backpacker*

"*Planet Backpacker* is the kind of book you can't stop reading -- I couldn't put it down. Downes has a soul that's a mile wide."

-- *Mark Staycer, www.imaginelennon.com*

"Being a teacher, I don't often read a lot of books between September and May, but I must say I had a hard time putting your book down, and had it finished in three days. What a cool adventure!"

-- *Bill Leahy -- Midland, MI*

"Bob's style of writing is sensationally descriptive and as fun as listening to a great storyteller. I'm loving it!"

-- *Charlotte Beals, Horizon Books*

"Your book is - hands-down - one of the best reads I've had in a while... Thanks for sharing your stories."

-- *Laura Merrifield Oblinger, Traverse City, MI*

*To John
Happy Travels!
Robert
Downes*

Planet
Backpacker

Across Europe by Mountain Bike

& Backpacking on Through Egypt, India

& Southeast Asia... Around the World

Robert Downes

The Wandering

PRESS

Traverse City, Michigan
Revised 2009

Published by
The Wandering Press
P.O. Box 1262
Traverse City, Michigan, 49685

First edition published by The Wandering Press in 2008
Completely Revised 2009
Printed in the United States of America

Planet Backpacker is available at a discount when purchased in bulk
for educational or fundraising use, or by organizations.
For details, write: P.O. Box 1262, Traverse City, MI 49685
Or, email bob@planetbackpacker.net

Cataloging-in-Publication Data

Downes, Robert, 1952-
     Planet backpacker : across Europe by mountain bike &
     backpacking on through Egypt, India and Southeast Asia--
     around the world / Robert Downes. -- Rev. [ed.].
     p. cm.
     LCCN 2008938682
     ISBN-13: 978-0-9821344-1-2
     ISBN-10: 0-9821344-1-2

     1. Downes, Robert, 1952---Travel. 2. Backpacking--
Eurasia. 3. Eurasia--Description and travel.
4. Voyages around the world.   I. Title.

GV199.44.E83D69 2009   915.04'3
                              QBI09-600002

www.planetbackpacker.net

For Jeannette

My Thanks

No trip around the world is a solo endeavor, and neither is the writing of a book. Angels smooth your path and keep you from crashing on the rocks along the way.

Two of those at the top of my list to thank are my wife, Jeannette, for being so brave and generous in allowing me to pursue a dream. And to my best friend and business partner, George Foster, whose wisdom, enterprise and instinct for success brought the *Northern Express Weekly* to life -- a platform which put me on this road years ago.

Other people remembered with fondness include Intrepid Travel group leaders Esam Abd Elsalam in Egypt, Vinit Nair in South India and Bill Raymond in Vietnam for their insights and humor. Jim Moore, for inspiring the idea of a lone journey, and Dave Dewey, both my brothers in music. Peg Muzzall and her gift of a light which guided many journeys in the darkness, and Kristi Kates for holding down the fort at *Northern Express* in my absence, along with the gift of a pen that scribbled the notes that went into this book. Bill Brown, Larry Munsey and Bob Perkins for their loyalty in reading my daily travel blog. To my *Northern Express* colleagues in print: Rick Coates, Anne Stanton, Colleen Zanotti (who created the fine maps in this edition), Kyra Cross, Kristen Rivard, Jamie Kauffold, Lynn Gerow, Matt Malpass, Jan Staycer and Kathy Johnson. My brother Mike, who was my first partner in adventure, and all the kids: Nathan, Chloe, Nicole, Brian, Erin and the grand kids, Emily, Anna, Benjamin, Luke, and those who will travel on without us in their time. And to Mom & Dad, great travelers who will always be with me in spirit.

Also, good travels to all of the friends I met on the road, mentioned in this book. And to readers of my blog and columns in *Northern Express*, who kept my spirits up on the far side of the world -- thank you.

***

Any errors in this book are entirely my own, although in my defense, a traveler often hears tales which turn out to be the exact opposite of the truth. I tried to sort that out the best I could.

Contents

The Monkey God

"To be young, really young, takes a very long time."

-- Pablo Picasso

On the plane from Goa to Bombay, I look out the window and find a gigantic flying monkey shaking his fist at me with his fangs bared. His eyes are filled with a kingly contempt. The monkey bats at the wing, toying with the plane, and then gives it a mighty swat. People are screaming their brains out as the jet goes into a skittering dive, spiralling down to its fatal rendezvous with the green hills of India.

Oh, dear me...

At least, that's what I fear, for while trying to be funny, I inadvertently wrote some unfriendly shit on my travel blog about Hanuman, the monkey god of the Hindus, who can fly like the wind with the power of a hurricane. Too late, I realize that he may not have much of a sense of humor. Even though I later went back and deleted the "Bring me the head of the monkey god" comment from my blog, I'm superstitious enough to believe that this flying monster might try fiddling with my flight, especially here on his home turf in India.

Back home, I'm not much of a believer in sympathetic magic -- like where poking a pin in a rag doll can give someone a pain in the rear. But here in the world I call Planet Backpacker, things like voodoo, evil eyes and dancing gods with six arms seem to have more currency. It's a magic world, after all, and certainly a place riven with myth, mayhem and chance.

And it's not wise to cross Hanuman. In Indian mythology he is a fearless, implacable foe -- a regular badass monkey monster, if you will. Clever and cunning, he is devoted to Lord Rama, one of the chief gods of the Hindu pantheon.

Long ago, in a war against the demon king Ravana on the isle of Sri Lanka, the monkey god was sent to the Himalayas to find a magic plant growing on the side of a mountain which could help win the war. Unable to find the plant, Hanuman simply tore a Himalayan peak from the earth and carried the mountain back to Lord Rama.

So, I certainly hope the monkey god doesn't have an internet connection, much less an interest in reading my blog.

As it happens, the plane lands just fine and the worst of it is navigating the abysmally bad airport in Bombay (aka Mumbai), where a bored customs officer insists on tearing through all of the gifts I bought in India.

"What's this?" he says, fingering two small brass cymbals connected by a length of rawhide. Purchased from a Chinese peddler at a flea market in Goa, the cymbals are rimmed with the signs of the zodiac.

"They're for playing music," I say, demonstrating. I give the cymbals a gentle rap and the ringing hum of a vibration fills the air.

Big mistake, because the officer spends the next five minutes enchanting his colleagues with his skill at clinging the cymbals. The steam of an intolerable pressure starts building in my brain, wondering when this idiot is going to let me go so I can catch the next plane to Delhi.

But here on Planet Backpacker, you don't mess with customs officers or airport security men unless you wish bring down a world of hurt and hassle.

"You are musician, eh?" he says at last, pointing to the half-size guitar on my shoulder.

"Yes. I use these cymbals to start the show," I reply. "You cling them together and then you start to play."

He gazes at the cymbals in his hands -- obviously, he'd love to have them, and if no one was crowding over my shoulder, perhaps he would. But by now the long line behind me has grown restive and he hands them back with a sad sense of resignation. "Go," he waves. "And have a good trip. Come back to India someday, yes?"

Yes, yes I will, I think, walking away. But I cross my psychic fingers with the promise because there's so much of the world to see. Other gods, other people... Who can say? It could be Latvia next, or Mauritania or Japan. For all I know, India will have to do without me.

The *Daemon's* Call

It's been said that at any given moment, there are 100,000 backpackers traveling around the world. But who knows? Maybe there are a few hundred who make it the 24,902 miles around the whole show each year. It's not like we register with a global Vagabond Department.

Whatever the case, in the fall of 2007, I was one of those living the dream of a lifetime: to travel around the world with no strings attached. Just me, a sawed-off guitar and an old mountain bike.

But getting the trip together was anything but speedy.

Everyone has a dream, and mine had burned in my breast for decades. All my life I had wanted to travel around the world -- not piecemeal, one trip at a time -- but straight through like the sailors of the 18th century, who earned a gold hoop through an earlobe for making it all the way around. That hoop would pay for a proper funeral if they kicked off.

Backpacking around the world is one of the few 'epic' adventures that are still possible for the average person to achieve.

Adventure magazines such as *Outside* spin endless tales of mountain climbers taking on K2; or amateur explorers skiing to the North Pole; or sailors going solo around the world. These seem to be the "big 3" adventures. Curiously, they all involve long stretches of monotony and plowing through vast wastelands of water or snow.

For me, however, mountain climbing has all the appeal of trudging on a Stairmaster outdoors for the month of January. And it often seems that the climbers in the adventure magazines tend to be wealthy physicians with financial resources on par with Mt. Everest.

As for sailing around the world or a polar trek, that also sounds expensive, not to mention lonely. And you have to dedicate your life to 'learning the ropes' of sailing, unless a trip to Davy Jones' locker is part of the plan.

But going around the world offers the target range dummies of Mystery, Exotica and Thrills popping up around every corner. Plus, backpacking through Africa, Southeast Asia and India offers a stew of sensations at affordable rates -- an epic adventure within the grasp of Everyman or Everywoman.

And those are the people you meet on the global highway: backpackers of modest means who don't have to swallow steroids or train for six months -- they're just regular folks who have the gumption to go.

Ideally, such a trip should be made under the age of 25 when you're an unjaded *naif* and too much of a bother to be hassled by locals overseas. But at that time in my life, I was rat-house poor. As a pauper undergrad, I lived for a time in a $25-a-month basement room in Detroit's inner city, just trying to trudge through university. Nights there were often filled with the sound of police helicopters, sirens and even gunshots. I wanted out. More poverty on the roads of the world was not on my radar when I graduated.

Yet, as the years went by, the barrier of being broke was replaced by the barrier of success. My dream of circumnavigating the earth got buried beneath a mountain of responsibilities that included a marriage and family, a mortgage, and a career as editor and co-publisher of the alternative *Northern Express Weekly* in northern Michigan. And, in their final years, I was committed to watching over my parents, Edwin and Ila, whose own love of travel inspired many hours of conversation.

But even mountains can be moved. Hanuman the monkey god managed it when he tore the mountain from the earth and flew it to a faraway land. Then there's the example of Islam: "If the mountain will not come to Muhammad, then Muhammad will come to the mountain." Whatever that means.

So there came a rare time in life when the mountain of my responsibilities drifted away and evaporated like the morning mist. The kids grew up, my parents passed away, and the business grew successful enough to run itself. All that remained was a promise and a dare.

And, of course, my wife Jeannette.

Not many wives would allow their husband to go rambling around the world for months on end. I had always imagined that Jeannette and I would make the trip together, being kindred spirits who've enjoyed the sights of China, Peru, Europe and Greece. I had saved for five years, planning a trip for two.

But on our daily walks as I blabbered on for the 1,000th time about itineraries -- whether to go to Russia, Ethiopia or Crete, while Jeannette said not a word in reply -- it slowly dawned on me that my wife's dream lay with her family, and not on the road. And unlike me, she still had responsibilities she couldn't dodge. Going around the world would mean giving up her daycare business and dropping the ball on clients who were counting on her. She also wanted to keep watch on our daughter, who was in her first year of college. Unlike me, the time was not right for her to go.

But how could I go without Jeannette -- my rock, security blanket and wing man? I'd be lost without her. The fun of travel comes from sharing, and I wanted to see the world with her.

But gradually, I realized that it's wrong to impose your dream on someone you love, or to even try. I began wrestling with the idea of going alone. It was scary thought, like a knock on the door in the dead of night. "Alone" is, after all, a rather lonely word, especially adrift out in the wide world.

Today, I would never encourage anyone to travel around the world -- alone or otherwise -- because if you're cut out for such a trip, you don't need any spurs to your backside. There's already a beast within you -- your own private tiki god clawing at the door to get out -- a compulsion you can't resist.

World travelers are driven by a spirit which the Greeks called a *daemon*. Wanderlust, travelin' bone, travelin' jones -- call it what you like -- but it's something that beats at your breast from the inside. Your *daemon* demands that you slave joyfully at the altar of your passion, be it music, art, writing, hunting, running, cooking, or grafted to the joystick of a Playstation. Every hardcore traveler burns with this spirit -- money doesn't matter, and neither do the rough spots -- it's making the trip that counts.

I had traveled alone before for periods of up to a month and knew that it could be a lonely, depressing experience. A few years back, I spent three dismal weeks bumming around Spain, Portugal and Morocco. It was a drag traveling by myself, dealing with the generally unfriendly people of the Iberian peninsula (the French are Valentine sweethearts by contrast). How could I go it alone for months on end in some of the strangest and most difficult countries on earth?

On the other hand, I kept imagining myself on my deathbed some-day, thinking -- *Damn, I never did the one thing that I really wanted to do in life...* followed by a ghastly *urk!* And wasn't it true that I'd grown to enjoy my own company through the years, sort of like a bottle of old wine or a good guitar that grows more resonant with age? At least, I'd learned to put up with myself. Perhaps I could tough it out and accept loneliness as the price of admission to my dream. The trip would certainly be cheaper: I could camp out part of the way and stay in hostels. Perhaps Jeannette could meet me somewhere, midway through the trip...

My *daemon* grumbled that it was time to go it alone.

And I listened.

American Quest

Every journey needs a quest -- it's not enough to just bum around gawking at the sights.

Some travelers search for the source of the Nile, others reach for the Sea of Tranquility. Some go upriver to the heart of darkness, others head down a private Mississippi to freedom. Some seek a golden fleece, the holy grail, or PeeWee Herman's bicycle. There are those who crave enlightenment at a monastery in the Himalayas, and those who seek a spanking in a Tokyo fetish bar. Some search the world over for love, and manage to write volumes about their glandular urges.

But as my trip unfolded, I found that my quest was hunting down those whimsical critters known as my countrymen -- or rather, the lack of them.

Mostly when you travel overseas, you could care less if you meet another traveler from the States, but in the Third World, you crave confirmation that you're not alone.

Where are all of the friggin' Americans? I wondered on my way through the developing world. Over and over, I found the Middle East and Asia brimming with backpackers from Australia, France, Germany, Sweden, New Zealand, Brazil, Holland, Russia, Britain... but amazingly few Americans. I'd scan the registries of guest houses and hostels, finding pages filled with visitors from other countries, but few signatures from the U.S.A.

There were hordes of us milling around Europe, but once past the touristy squares of Vienna and Prague, it was as if the folks from Iowa, Delaware and Alabama literally dropped off the map.

Some might say that my informal research in hotels, hostels and backpacker hangouts was too anecdotal to be valid. I'm sure that one could use statistics to "prove" that the developing world is brimming with American travelers, even though you're not likely to find any sitting next to you at dinner in the fish market.

For instance, according to an "Adventure Travel Report" cited by the Travel Industry Association, "Adventure travelers are everywhere. One-half of U.S. adults, or 98 million people, have taken an adventure trip in the past five years. This includes 31 million adults who engaged in hard adventure activities like whitewater rafting, scuba diving and mountain biking."

But that doesn't mean that any of them are mountain biking in Borneo. More likely, they're rafting in Ohio. And just because the *New York Times* travel section plugs Swaziland or Ulan Bator to more than a million readers, that doesn't mean you'll find any of them rubbing elbows with other Western backpackers over yonder. Odd too, that many of the travelers in the *Times'* "Why We Travel" photo feature each Sunday tend to be of Europeans or Australians poking around the rough spots of the world, and not the paper's American readership.

So, who cares? I did, just because it bugged me that my countrymen weren't part of the action out in the great beyond. When you're lost on the streets of a Third World city, nothing is sweeter than hearing an American accent; it's as friendly as a glass of ice tea. I yearned to hear those voices on the beaches of southern India and the streets of Cairo and Bombay.

As months passed by, it made me wonder if Americans are simply afraid to travel in the Third World, imagining terrorists hiding behind every espresso machine outside our borders.

I'm hardly the first to notice that Americans tend to avoid scruffy places overseas. You find them gravitating to all-inclusive resorts in Cancun or wearing matching hats on guided bus tours of Europe.

In his book, *Smile When You're Lying*, travel writer Chuck Thompson reports hearing from Latin Americans that *norteamericanos* are afraid to visit most countries south of the border. That has been my experience there as well. You're more likely to meet a French Canadian, a German, or a Scandinavian traveling on a bus in Mexico, Central America or South America than a gringo from the nearby States. (Costa Rica and the touristy parts of Guatemala are the exceptions with maybe 30-50% American travelers.)

I'm sure there are travel statistics which show that there are plenty of Americans visiting places such as Southeast Asia each year. But their style of travel -- in guided bus tours or gated, all-inclusive resorts -- tends to keep them at a distance from the people who live there.

They're missing all the fun, not to mention the enlightening experience that can only come from traveling with a backpack among the people who live in the lands you're traveling through.

Compared to their backpacking cousins from Europe or Australia, Americans are groping in the dark when it comes to understanding what the world is really like. We lack the kind of personal travel experience that no amount of reading, web-surfing or trolling the Discovery Channel can replace. Millions of couch spuds in America have seduced themselves into believing that the stagey episodes of *Survivor* -- which don't involve an ounce of risk -- are actual adventures.

So when the average American knows no more about our planet than what can be learned at Disney's EPCOT Center or from the scaremeisters of FOX News, then the world truly becomes a more dangerous place, if only because uninformed people are easily manipulated. Every Arab and Islamic person becomes a scary target, even those with hands extended in friendship.

Even the idea of traveling overseas seems over the top to some: "When I told people back home that I was going to visit Vietnam, most of them said: 'What do you want to go *there* for?' -- like I was crazy or something. They just assumed that Vietnam was a dangerous place," said Katie Snow, a potter from Oregon, who I met while backpacking between Hanoi and Ho Chi Minh City.

On the other hand, it's true that you feel a chill from some Westerners overseas when you tell them you're an American. In 2002, the Pew Research Center conducted surveys of 38,000 people in 44 countries and found that "favorable opinions of the U.S. had plummeted."

And that was the good news, because in subsequent studies, contempt for America went off the deep end. In a "Eurobarometer" survey in 2003, Europeans considered the United States a threat to world peace on par with North Korea and Iran -- only Israel scored higher as a troublemaker.

If Americans had contempt for the French in 2004 for not supporting our bogus war plans in Iraq, rest assured, the feeling was mutual.

It probably wasn't the smartest idea, backpacking around the world in 2007. It's not like there was a love-fest for America that year, considering our war in Iraq, torture scandals, secret prisons, closed borders, and the unilateral arrogance shipped by the Bush administration in the wake of 9/11. We were the uncool kids at the party.

In Lincoln's words, we had always been "the last best hope of mankind"; but America had lost its way, and the world was in a foul mood at having that feel-good myth punctured.

There's a scene in the film *Casablanca* where a group of uniformed German officers are singing one of their fight songs in Rick's American Cafè. Outraged by their arrogance, good-guy Victor Lazlo stands up and leads a a group of tear-streaked French refugees in a rousing round of the "Marseillaise."

I got the impression overseas that some western Europeans and Canadians think of Americans in the same way as the Nazis in Rick's Cafè -- tolerated, but barely, and then only because they have to. Perhaps that's part of the reason Americans are so timid about traveling these days -- we're not stupid -- we catch that vibe.

Fortunately, these drama queens tend to be few and far between, and you can always tell them to stuff it, reminding them of the nasty deeds committed by their own governments in the colonial days.

And the backpacking gig is something of an antidote for anti-Americanism. It forces people in other lands to deal with you as a person, rather than ranting about the policies of whatever president or political party is in power back in the U.S.A. Your presence knocks the people you encounter out of their own particular brand of mindlock, be they from France, Egypt, Denmark, India or wherever. I had a good time serving as a citizen ambassador in many strange places, able to catch an earful of opinions and give as good as I got in return.

And who knows? Maybe it's not fear that keeps Americans from vagabonding through the Third World, but simply a trend back to our tradition of isolationism. Perhaps it's just the twilight of the Pax

Americana and the Yanks are retreating from the peaceful, prosperous world they created, like Tolkien's elves departing Middle Earth. Like: "Our time here is done, Mr. Frodo -- see you at the Grey Havens."

Yeah, maybe that's it.

Whatever the case, my accidental story took on an accidental quest: To find out why Americans are so glaringly absent from the backpacking world when it's brimming with other Westerner travelers. And to share the news that it's a pretty darned good time out there, freestyling around the Earth.

Some might say, why write a book about backpacking at a time when the wheels seem to be coming off America and few of us have the money to travel?

Short answer: it's a hell of a lot cheaper to travel via the backpacking route than it is the traditional vacation, where you're pumping out cash like water through a fire hose. And you see more too.

Diogenes wandered around with a lantern in broad daylight, looking for an honest man. For me, it was a flashlight, walking home from the beach bars at night on the far side of the world, wondering why I felt so alone.

An Accidental Story

I didn't set out to write a book about backpacking around the world. This was an accidental account that took shape one dashed-off entry at a time. It was written in more than 100 internet cafés located down the side streets and back alleys of the world. Most were dingy, dim holes with the sticky black gum of ten thousand fingers imbedded on the keyboards of their antique computers. If some of that grime gets on your hands reading this book, blame it on Cairo or wherever...

Even the weblog that led to this story was an afterthought. Two weeks before leaving home in Traverse City, Michigan, I was sitting in a coffee house and mentioned to owner Shayne Daley that I was heading off on a long trip.

"You should set up a travel blog," said Shayne, who had just returned from motorcycling around Mexico. "That way, you don't have to repeat yourself every time someone emails you to ask how the trip is going. It's a good way to keep in touch with your family and friends."

Somewhere in my head, a light went on. I secured a blog account on livejournal.com and passed out my handle -- bobdownes52.livejournal.com -- on the eve of my departure.

As the days and weeks of the trip unfolded, I was elated to learn that my online scribbles had grown popular with folks back home. Friends passed on my blog to others and the positive feedback spurred me to expand upon the tales from the road.

Blog. It sounds like a monster, doesn't it? Something that eats things in a lusty manner -- like a lunch of traditional prose, perhaps. With the blog monster in hot pursuit, my words were hot off the trail, typed in a fever in scores of internet cafès, sometimes within minutes of my experiences. Next to me would be some guy from Britain or Germany, yakking over a webcam connection to folks back home, with a guy from India or Vietnam on my other elbow, locked in mortal combat in a World of Warcraft web game.

My online dispatches were written in a charged atmosphere that crackled with international suspense -- or more likely, my version of a game of "Where's Waldo?" Perhaps I was just a Walter Mitty, the milquetoast created by James Thurber, who daydreams a life of der-ring-do, but in my own mind, when I walked into an internet cafè, I was transformed into Secret Agent Man, filing my reports from loca-tions rife with intrigue.

I felt electrified by the voltaic chemistry of travel and the inspiration it brings to writing. Is it any wonder that some of our greatest writers dating back to Homer, Cervantes, Stevenson, Twain, Melville, London and Hemingway were also fierce travelers? They were struck by the lightning.

On the road, my blog had the episodic, cliffhanging quality of the magazine serials of Dickens in another age. I became adept at tramp-ing the back streets and alleys of every town in search of a keyboard (internet cafès are never on the main drag -- they don't rake in enough cash to afford posh digs). I became addicted to mainlining my words onto the 'net, craving online cribs with a junkie's fever. Pathetic, but it kept my head together in strange places.

It all got a little silly at times, but the search for cafès led me down miles of obscure lanes that I never would have seen otherwise.

As the miles of Ireland and England rolled by beneath the wheels of my mountain bike, it dawned on me that I was writing a nascent book online. I felt the muse of Jack Kerouac, whose *On the Road* began as a collection of notes scribbled down while he was hitchhiking around America in the late '40s. I vowed to keep the final cut rough -- simi-lar to Kerouac's stream-of-consciousness style. And always with the small "i" of a person of no consequence, drifting with the current.

The blog became the armature around which the story was sculpted. Gradually, it morphed into a remix, like the jam of a wandering MC.

The Parallel World

"It is not down in any map; true places never are."

-- Herman Melville

This was a "return to forever" experience for me, going full circle back to how the modern backpacking movement got started. And that, it turns out, was quite a long time ago.

At the age of 17, overwhelmed by wanderlust and the spirit of the times, I hitchhiked 3,000 miles round-trip from Detroit to California in 1970 to see what was left of the hippie experiment in San Francisco. The scene was mostly dead, but LSD was still being dished out like after-dinner mints and there was a reefer haze and the hormonal whiff of free love lingering in the air of the Haight-Ashbury neighborhood, which was still years away from being turned into the marketing emporium of navel rings, rasta hats, designer bongs, tattoo parlors and Grateful Dead t-shirts that is is today.

It was the golden age of hitchhiking and thousands of us were criss-crossing the country, making up the adventure travel scene as we went along. Many were searching for Jack Kerouac's romanticized vision of living "On the Road."

It was on that trip that I first became aware that there is an alternative world of gypsy travelers paralleling our own. You would seldom -- if ever -- meet them in the ordinary, workaday world, but as soon as you hit the road, the portals would open, revealing the oddest people, along with young adventurers heading for distant horizons.

My first ride on the road to California, for instance, was with an old man in a rusted Chevy station wagon that was packed with wary animals -- a raccoon, possum, badger, various dogs and cats -- there must have been at least a dozen peering out of small cages or loose in the car. The driver looked like a wizard with filthy grayish-brown hair that rolled past his shoulders. The car reeked of shit and was a tussle of dirty clothes, cracker boxes, dog food, soda bottles and the old-timer's sleeping bag. A nervous-looking monkey rode his shoulder as we drove along, looking at me. In fact, I got the impression that all of the animals were looking at me with imploring eyes, begging me to help them. I think the wizard and I talked a bit about Jesus, and although I put in a word for the animals, there was no chance of him letting them go.

You'd be unlikely to meet such a Dr. Doolittle in the 'real' world -- but he was sure to surface in the parallel land that I came to call

Planet Backpacker. It's not a Twilight Zone or a parallel dimension, but an actual world that escapes the notice of those who stay put. It's an 'other' reality.

I thought of myself as a teenage anthropologist, going to investigate the ruins of what was by then considered a dead phenomenon, even though the hippie scene of the Summer of Love was only three years in the grave.

Ten months before I hit the road, members of Charles Manson's creepy Family had carved up pregnant actress Sharon Tate and a party of her friends at a suburban home in L.A. And that December of '69, the Rolling Stones gaped helplessly onstage while their Hells Angels bodyguards stabbed concert-goer Meredith Hunter to death before their eyes at the Altamont rock festival. Then too, four students were shot down by members of the Ohio National Guard at Kent State University in May, 1970, just weeks before I left home. Those events marked the death of the '60s and the hippie dream.

But the implosion of the hippie myth generated the supernova of the 'human potential' movement of environmentalism, the running boom, New Age therapies, the back-to-the land craze, and a new breed of backpacking college kids who were mesmerized by what the world had to offer.

By the time I thumbed my way to San Francisco, most of the artificial love vibes in the Haight had evaporated, but there were still some crash pads around where a brother or sister (ie: any young drifter) could stay for free, smoke weed, and read the *Mr. Natural* comics of R. Crumb.

On the road to 'Frisco with two other young travelers, I met an aging hippie -- 26 years old -- who'd been fasting and meditating for a week in the hills of Big Sur. A dead-ringer for Jesus with a red-gold beard, Jack had come up with a simple plan to save the world and jump-start the comatose Age of Aquarius: he would simply invent a cure for cancer and then use the hundreds of millions in profits to make the world a better place.

We thought his idea was brilliant.

We got to his place in the Haight -- a big Victorian home across from Golden Gate Park. Jack walked in and found another newcomer -- a runaway girl with long dark hair parted in the middle, wearing a frumpy peasant blouse, jeans and sandals, yet ripe with a plain-spoken pulchritude. "Want to ball tonight?" he asked, as casual as a cat, even though he looked to be 10 years older than her. "I guess so," she giggled -- it would have been uncool to have refused -- and sure enough, the bunk next to mine was rocking that night with proof that free love, at least, still lived.

I'm not sure you'd find the same scenario going down in the average hostel in London or Amsterdam today, but who knows? There were certainly some wishful thinkers among my dorm mates.

In those seminal days, we drifters carried our gear in old army surplus or Boy Scout rucksacks -- which were cheap, khaki canvas bags with shoulder straps. The contents of my knapsack were a sleeping bag, a plastic sheet, a jar of peanut butter, a spoon, and a can of spray-on dry shampoo with a brush to clean my long hair. Even teenage backpackers have a sense of vanity.

The plastic sheet served as both tent and groundcover. And at the time, few of us had a clue about sleeping pads, such as a ThermaRest; you just flopped your sleeping bag down on the cold, hard ground and took pride in acquiring the spartan ability to sleep on the hardpan of the earth.

One morning in July, I woke up in the tall prairie grass outside Cheyenne, Wyoming, soaked to the bone with my teeth chattering from the morning dew. A car full of longhairs had picked me up downtown near midnight on "Rodeo Day" -- and said the drunken cowboys in town would surely stomp the shit out of me if they caught me. Such was the prevailing attitude Bob Seger sang about in "Turn the Page," when he described catcalls of "Is that a woman or a man?" from his tours in the late '60s-early-'70s.

We didn't have any of today's high-tech backpacking equipment back then, but even so, we thumb-trippers had a network. You made friends in the space of an hour or two and lost them just as fast -- the same as today's backpacking brotherhood.

By chance during that trip, I hooked up with a dozen hitchhikers on the way home along the California coast, with all of us waiting to catch a ride on a quiet stretch of road. One hitcher was only 16-years-old, barefoot, and wearing a bowler hat. He'd had an argument with his 'old man' back in New Jersey -- something about refusing to mow the lawn -- and had run off to California that very instant, without even taking his shoes. A van roared up, blasting "Whole Lotta' Love" by Led Zeppelin from its 8-track cassette -- the soundtrack of the summer for freaks on the road.

Everyone stopped to admire the new external frame backpack of a guy who was headed for Nevada. We'd never seen anything like it: it was bright orange and wonderfully balanced to carry heavy loads. I couldn't believe how light it seemed when I tried it on, even though it was full of gear.

Those packs became the camels of a new nomadic lifestyle. Not in the sense that some nylon webbing cobbled together with aluminum tubes made that much of a difference, but by virtue of the fact that we had crossed into a realm of new possibilities. Advances in jet travel and discounted standby tickets, for instance, which could take you overseas and back for a little over $200. The magical appearance of youth hostels and rail passes. The *Let's Go* guides, written by Harvard students, which presaged *Lonely Planet* and the *Rough Guides*. By 1972, backpackers were swarming across Europe in what *Life* magazine called "an American invasion" of college kids out to see the world.

The new lightweight gear took us to places which had once required full-on expeditions with porters -- from the wilds of Alaska to the fabled Hippie Trail to India. There was even a Magic Bus full of backpackers that made regular trips from Amsterdam to Afghanistan. Then came magazines such as *Outside* and *Mariah* in the late '70s, and trekking companies which dabbled in faraway places. And the rise of the affluent American middle class allowed the young to travel as never before. The throttle yawned wide open on adventure travel.

Suddenly, the world was ours to explore in a way that had been impossible only a few years before. You no longer needed a guide in a pith helmet and a long line of porters to take you on safari to Borneo, or a dogsled to get you through the Yukon. All you needed was a backpack, a Eurail pass, and enough daring to take you into the heart of your dreams.

***

Anyway -- here's where the wheels hit the road and the story begins, with the first entry of my blog. Some might say this is a rehash of *The Odyssey*: a man in search of his youth on the way around the world. But that would be untrue -- this is a story about the world itself, and refusing to grow old in order to see it.

Before kissing Jeannette goodbye and leaving her teary-eyed in our driveway, I dashed up to our bedroom and placed a photo of our sunburned faces on her pillow. It would be something for her to find that night when she went to bed, alone for one of the few times in our 11-year marriage.

"Jeannette," I wrote on the back of the photo, *"I love you always and forever. I'll think of you every night and fall asleep with a smile on my face. - Love, Bob"*

Ireland

Dublin Daze
Sept. 7, 2007
Dublin, Ireland

   Saw my first Irish palm tree while riding my bike into town from the airport. The ride was pretty hairy -- my bike was literally a box of 20-year-old junk that I put together on the curb at the airport. One of the pedals was almost completely stripped. It soon fell off and only a sincere prayer and some heavy wrenching fixed it by the side of a freeway. On such events are great adventures made... I guess!

   At the airport, I debated loading my boxed-up bike, duffel bag and guitar onto a bus and assembling it all in town. Fresh off the plane, I feel very much the 'gentleman traveler' -- uncertain and on the preppy side -- a long way from getting my hands dirty in my new role as a gritty globetrotter.

In fact, I already have a sick feeling, because it's not like I can spend a couple of weeks over here in Europe and then chicken out and run home to my wife and friends with some shameful excuse. This is it -- the wide world is my home for the next few months, with all its predators, hubbub and dark corners...

"Can I get a ride with this stuff?" I ask Joe Friendly Irish bus driver. Fuck no (drives off). Okay -- I needed that -- there are months of going it alone ahead of me, so I may as well get used to winging it from the get-go. This is it -- the show's underway -- time to be a brave little soldier.

My old, black, beater mountain bike rises to the challenge. I roll downhill into downtown Dublin, off and on the sidewalks, mingling with other bikes, pedestrians and the flow of traffic -- feeling my way with the load of heavy gear hanging off the bike. Onboard are two panniers with my clothes and camping gear, a sleeping pad strapped to the handlebars and a backpack for later. Oh yeah, and a half-size acoustic backpacker guitar.

Prior to this, my only test ride with this stuff was circling the block once back home. My gear and I float down the street and along the Liffey River like a lazy bumblebee.

I check into a hostel in downtown Dublin and find five other bunkmates in my room. Haven't slept in a bunkbed since I was eight years old. It's a novel experience for me... and the bedbugs, I'm sure.

Gotta' check out the brew tonight -- have heard it runs about $10 a pint -- kind of expensive if you're trying to be a carefree backpacker on a budget. Speaking of which, I've already been robbed... by the Exchange Rate Bandit. The dollar is worth only 65 cents against the Euro and I hear it's even worse in England.

The pedal falling off my bike seems like a bad omen. Back home, a bike mechanic told me that the old junker would never make it across Europe. "I wouldn't try going very far on that thing," he said. "You'd be better off buying a new bike."

"Well, I'm only going to ride about 1,000 miles across Europe and down the Danube," I said. "Then I plan to give it away to some homeless street person in Budapest. So I don't want to take along some fancy bike that I can't afford to ship home."

"Well good luck, because you're going to need it," he scoffed.

No Snoring Please...
Sept. 8, 2007
Dublin, Ireland

Did I mention that my five roommates are both male and female and from many other countries? I wake up and gaze into the cornflower blue eyes of a blonde in the bunk next to mine. She's about 20 years old with a complexion of pink roses and peach cream, and has been moaning all morning because some guy a bunk over has been snoring all night, keeping her awake. Plus, the room is about the size of a mini-van... I tiptoe around, trying not to wake anyone. This will definitely limit my late-night beer drinking, because who wants to stumble in and out of a hostel dorm in the early hours to take a pee?

In Dublin, I find the template for virtually every hostel the world over: There's a common room where a slack bunch of mostly-young people from many lands sit on cast-off furniture, gaping at an animated film (we used to call them 'cartoons') on TV, or reading left-behind paperbacks. A fair number of the books are in German, Swedish or Russian.

Some of the guests spend much of their time haunting the hostel's couch -- too overdosed on travel to endure more tramping out on the streets. The common room includes a shelf of well-thumbed travel guides from every destination you can imagine: Cambodia, Slovenia, Turkey, Malaysia... Then there's a kitchen spilling over with old pans, mismatched plates and dinnerware; it's plastered with hand-lettered signs spelling out the rules on cleaning up. And often, a little bar down by the reception area, where travelers raise a pint at exorbitant prices and trade tall tales and info on destinations down the line.

Just off the bar is a handful of gummy old PCs, one of which invariably has a sign taped on it reading "Out of Order." These are important artifacts because they tend to be among the slowest-running computers in the world.

***

My new 'job' as a backpacker is to hack away at the sights from one end of the world to the other. I get with it.

Kilmainham Goal is an old prison just a beer bottle toss away from the Guinness factory. It's a dank, dreary place with doors of iron that are three inches thick, punctuated by windows no bigger than a vent. It's the place where the rebels of the 1916 uprising against the British were incarcerated, only to be shot a few days later in the courtyard. One guy had to be tied up and shot while seated in a chair because he was too wounded to stand.

It was a time when thousands of British troops were stationed in Dublin to maintain control of a country which had been under their heel for centuries.

Most of the Irish weren't sympathetic to the rebellion, which destroyed central Dublin. British gunboats shelled the town and their troops burned the rebels out of the central post office, which the Irish had been using as a fortress and headquarters.

But after the Brits shot down the leaders with a firing squad, public opinion turned and there was a revolution that freed Ireland. The caveat was that the British kept Northern Ireland, which was mostly Protestant. This keepsake has been the bone of contention in the Emerald Isle ever since.

During the Potato Famine of the 1840s, starving people used to commit petty crimes so they could be tossed into this prison for a daily cup of gruel. But there was a price to pay: prisoners were required to maintain absolute silence in the dismal, damp, freezing cells -- if you started going nuts and couldn't keep yourself from talking, the guards tossed you into a jet-black basement dungeon for God knows how long. The emphasis on complete silence was considered state-of-the-art rehabilitation for prisoners back then.

Hard labor here on a starvation diet meant piling rocks all day in a courtyard until a pyramid was made, then hauling them to the other end of Stonebreakers Yard in a ceaseless toil worthy of Sysphus. Kind of like my endless walk around town.

My Catholic ancestors would have loved seeing all of the sights of Dublin: St. Patrick's well of baptism, St. Valentine's grave, the Viking quarter of town and a bunch of rusty old writer stuff like memorials to James Joyce and such... yawn..

I'm probably the only American to ever visit Dublin who didn't visit the sprawling Guinness factory for a 'free' beer. I learn that it costs 13 euros to take the tour (about $20 U.S.) and reflect that I've already seen the old Stroh's Brewery in Detroit years ago on a tour that didn't cost a dime.

Moving on...
Sept. 10, 2007
Killarney, Ireland

Ah, the Dublin nightlife -- hundreds of young people in their 20s parade up and down the Temple Bar district, packed with pubs. The Irish girls are lusty, busty-looking lasses with broad smiles and a twinkle to their eyes -- very pleasant to look at. Yet, as an aging drifter, I am completely invisible to the young merrymakers.

But I did make a visit to Ireland's oldest pub, a place called the Brazen Head, established in 1198. I had hoped to hear some traditional Irish music, but it's the same Eagles and John Mellencamp crap you hear in the bars back home, and the place is packed with package tourists. Begorrah...

Mostly, I get me jollies playing a few slide guitar blues licks on the banks of the Liffey River. I meet some skanky homeless people on the benches along the river, including a teenager who appears to be high on either glue or heroin. There are a lot of down-and-outers in Dublin.

The kid offers some mumbling conversation. "I used to play drums, but I had to sell them," he says.

"You should keep at it -- playing drums will make you strong."

"I needed the money," he shrugs, nodding off.

"Are you messed up on something?" I ask.

"I'm okay... it's just..." he fades out and looks down at his shoes as a couple of cops stroll by, rousting druggers along the riverbank.

"Where do you live?" I ask. A look on the edge of tears crosses his kitten face. "Out here," he shrugs. Soon he drifts off to a druggy sleep and I tip-toe off.

***

But that all seems long ago now, because since then, I've caught the train west out of Dublin with the intention of biking up the west coast of Ireland. I've biked the lakes of Killarney and am now on the Dingle peninsula, which is Ireland's version on Hanalei in Kauai.

It's as wet and misty as Hawaii here, with sheep dotting every hillock, instead of palm trees. The dew makes for interesting camping. I just plan to stay wet all day --- it makes it easier to do the laundry.

Ireland is supposed to be a cycling paradise but that's bosh. The roads are about as wide as an American bike path and you have trucks and buses passing you constantly at 50 mph. Plus, there's no shoulder on the road to flee to -- just miles and miles of prickly hedge that looms eight feet high and runs right to the edge of the highway.

To a safety squirrel like me, it's an all-day white-knuckle ride from Killarney to Dingle, clenching the handlebars with a shiver as each car or truck goes whizzing by, close enough for me to knock on their windows.

The route passes through the town where the "Wild Colonial Boy" came from in the Irish ballad:

"There was a wild colonial boy, Jack Dugan was his name
He was born and bred in Ireland in a house called Castle Maine
He was his father's only son, his mother's pride and joy
and dearly did his parents love the wild colonial boy
At the early age of 16 years, he left his native home
And to Australia's sunny land he was inclined to roam."

The wild colonial boy takes on the mantle of Robin Hood in Australia, robbing the rich and helping the poor, until "a bullet pierced his brave young heart," and he died, half a world away from his hometown.

Thankfully, I have no such plans.

The good news is that it's been raining sheets all summer in Ireland, but has let up in the past two weeks -- just for me! It's sunny enough to get a tan. Fortune loves a fool, so perhaps the heavy rain will stay away a wee bit longer. They say it only rains once a week in Ireland: from Monday through Sunday.

Speaking of luck, my bike, Dulcinea, broke two spokes on her back wheel, a near-fatal wound with all the heavy gear I'm hauling. A mechanic in Killarney says the bike is too much of a hopeless junker to fix, owing to some problems with the rear sprocket and the absence of any spokes that will fit the old rambler.

"Do you think I should buy a used bike?" I ask, imagining the cycle trip getting nixed from the get-go. "I'm planning to ride up Ireland, across England and down the Danube -- it's a long way."

The mechanic purses his lips and gives Dulcinea an appraising eye.

"Oh nooo," he drawls, nodding his head at the bike in appreciation. "Tha's quality. Just pedal on. Pedal on and see how looong tha' wheel will last."

Aye-aye, cap'n...

Wet & Wild
Sept. 11, 2007
Dingle Peninsula, Ireland

Woke up in a pool of water this morning after breaking a cardinal rule of camping -- never let your ground cover peek out from under your tent in the rain. The water rolls down the rain fly where it collects in the vinyl and floods your tent. Oh well, nothing like an early morning swim.

I ditch my heavy gear and bike 30 miles around the cliffs and pastures of the Dingle Peninsula. I breath in the heather, the cowshit and the peat fires of the local cottages and feel far more in touch with the land than the tourists passing by in monster buses.

There are old graveyards along the route, thick with moss and Celtic crosses. Is it safe to photograph them, or will the spirits hex my trip? I take a couple of cautious shots but don't push my luck. Don't want to provoke that shrieking spook known as the banshee...

For the first time in weeks, my chronically-aching back isn't killing me -- I thought it might do me in on this trip, but it seems to be getting better with all the heavy riding and walking. This confirms my belief that nothing is worse for a bad back than sitting in a chair, which is what I do all day in my editing job back home.

The hostel in Dingle has camping in the front yard and that evening I sit on the front porch, twanging on my guitar as the sun goes down. Gretchen, a woman in her late 40s, settles in to hear my fumbling blues. It turns out she's from southern Germany and is looking for a new home in Ireland.

"Why do you want to move to Ireland?" I ask. It seems odd that someone would want to move to a country with a different language, even though she speaks good English. And western Ireland seems a pretty obscure place.

"I don't like Germany anymore," Gretchen says. "It's changed. All the German people think about now is buying new things, and they are never happy unless they have the most expensive car or TV or clothes."

"We have that in America too. We call it 'keeping up with the Jones's.'"

"Yes, just like that," Gretchen says. "If their neighbor gets something new, they're unhappy unless they get something even better."

Gretchen owns a couple of horses and plans to bring them to western Ireland, where the riding is superb on the broad fields along the coast. "I think my horses and I will like it here."

"But what about a job?" I ask. "Are there many places to work in western Ireland?

"I will find something," she says with a dreamy gaze toward the sunset.

The River Shannon
Sept. 13, 2007
Kilkee, Ireland

I camped by the broad River Shannon last night. Got off the ferry late and there was no campground, so I hustled behind an embankment when no one was looking and bandit-camped by the river. There's a glimmering light on the river, which is wide as a bay, and it strikes me that the light is shining from America, 3,000 miles away. It was the light of freedom for many of the old Irish emigrants.

As the sun went down, I wondered if my ancestor, Michael Downes, passed this way on his journey to America back in 1850. Perhaps he saw much the same sunset.

It feels like the good old days of my backpacking youth, when my lodgings were often a snug hollow under a bush or a freeway overpass. Once, back when, I slept in a cemetery in Chicago, and on another trip in a garbage dump outside of Copenhagen. I slept beneath a volcano in Sicily and under a freeway overpass during a lightning storm in the mountains of Tennessee. It's a satisfying feeling, bandit camping, since there are virtually no public parks in Ireland and hardly any road-side parks. If you need to take a leak while traveling through the old sod, you are SOL, as we say. We have it so lucky in America -- here it is all pay, pay, pay...

It was a tough ride yesterday and I needed all the help of St. Patrick, Mother Mary, Mother McCree and all the saints of Ireland to get down 60 miles of wicked, narrow roads in heavy traffic. Lots of prayers, along with my St. Christopher medal, lucky travel shirt, lucky travel hat and a magic Irish coin got me through in one piece. But there were a couple of close calls, I assure you, and if the roads are this skinny in England, I'm going to "Plan B."

The day starts with a steep 4.5-mile climb up the infamous Connor Pass over the spine of western Ireland. Not as tough as climbing a volcano in the middle of Lake Nicaragua earlier this year with my friends George Foster and Bob Perkins, but on that order.

Halfway up the hill and gasping like a lungfish, I decide to throw out my backpack and some clothes, deeming them to be too much weight. But after agonizing over what to ditch, only a pair of bluejeans get tossed -- good material for a bird's nest, I hope. I reason that my old bike could go kabonkers at any time, in which case I'll need my backpack.

That's one of the problems of planning a trip around the world that involves both cycling and backpacking. There are two sets of gear required, neither of which are expendable. And, oh, by the way, some genius decided to bring a guitar along as well. It's a lot of junk to haul around on a bike.

I spend much of the day composing angry letters in my head and cursing Robin Krause, the author of *Ireland by Bike*, which induced me to ride these narrow lanes. The book regales the wonders of biking in Ireland, but says little about the narrow roads and murderous traffic. I assume that Krause wrote it before a new round of prosperity hit Ireland and every drunk on the island ran out and bought a car. One driver nearly takes my head off during a stop to adjust a pannier -- he goes speeding past a line of six cars at around 60 mph, missing me by a foot.

Had another tough climb today, cranking 800 feet up the Cliffs of Moher. Very impressive looking out over the sea from the top of these green cliffs which cut a knife's edge along the coast of western Ireland -- like the north shore of Kauai. This is also the number one spot for suicides in Ireland -- a place of terrible beauty -- ideal for launching oneself into the infinite.

There was a shrine to St. Bridget on the way up the hill -- the site of an old Celtic well of worship which is now filled with hundreds of statues of the Virgin Mary, along with the favorite saints of passersby. It's a holy cave, aglow with candles and the watchful eyes of ikons. Deliciously creepy.

I make it to the top of the cliffs without having to walk my bike, but my legs are startin' to quiver and I've definitely got sore knees.

In a small town north of Moher, I get the first of what could be many flaming earfuls about "George Boosh" from a stocky Albanian chap wearing a black baseball cap. He's got a visa to work in Ireland for several months as a builder.

"Why do George Boosh and America want to kill so many people?" he demands. "Why not peace like Cleenton? What would you think if soldiers were coming to kill your family for no fucking reason? For terrorists? What terrorists? That was in 2001; there are no terrorists now!"

Blah, blah, blah -- you're preaching to the choir, dude. I explain that many people in America hate the war in Iraq and think that George Bush sucks, but basically, this guy just wants to vent.

"Well, you know, the American people did kick the Republicans out of office in the last election," I point out, somewhat defensively. "That was our way of saying we don't support what President Bush did in Iraq."

"Yes, well I think you should come to Albania," he wags a finger at me. "You will see, there is no terrorist there."

"Well, I'm sure that's true."

"No terrorists -- just people trying to get by. Just living. People who want peace."

"Right. I'm definitely planning to go to Albania someday," I say, anxious for the lecture to end. "I have heard many good things about Albania."

International relations are restored and I ride off with a wave, but it does make me wonder what sort of reception an 'ugly American' will get farther along the road, especially in the Muslim countries.

The Dog in the Road
Sept. 13, 2007
Tralee, Ireland

Here's a vignette about those 'courteous Irish drivers' I've been dodging. I was leaving Tralee with warm feelings in my heart after talking to blessed, beautiful wife J'nette over a Skype.com connection when I saw a little white Irish terrier straying into the busy road. Cute little dog.

Surely the driver will stop as we do for ducks crossing the street back home, I thought, but then the car ran right over the dog with a horrible crack.

I was utterly shocked -- it happened right before my eyes.

"You fucking idiot!" I yelled, shaking a fist. But the car sped away without a pause, and no one stopped. The little dog was howling in pain and bleeding from its head. He was going to get hit again at any second.

Seeing a break in traffic, I dumped my bike at the curb, ran over and cradled the dog as tenderly as possible. A cop had told me once that you should never touch a dog that's been hit by a car because they tend to bite instinctively in their distress, but the dog had gone unconscious in a matter of seconds. Still wearing my bike helmet, I carried him to a garage across the street and began yelling for help. Miraculously, the dog roused himself and started pushing blindly into some old tires.

A young mechanic peeked from around the door at the dog howling in pain while I babbled on about trying to find the owner.

"Cud ya taak 'im oover thure?" he said with a brogue as thick as a truck tire, pointing to a fringe of grass alongside a fence outside the garage.

"What?"

"Cud ya taak 'im oover thure? A'hm afreud of doogs."

I couldn't believe this oaf was afraid of the pitiful small terrier who seemed to be keening his last breath. I stared at him dumbstruck.

Then a dark, middle-aged man turned up with a quizzical look on his face and and asked if anyone had seen an Irish terrier? I was too angry to respond. I turned on my heel and stomped off -- furious at the driver and the dumb-shit mechanic and the horrible Irish traffic -- more conscious than ever of the cars whooshing by.

Don't know if the little guy made it.

The Isles of Aran
Sept. 14, 2007
Off the coast of Ireland

Rolling, rolling, rolling... the traffic lessens after crossing the Shannon and I wander through worn farmland down quiet lanes by the sea. I'm an anonymous soul, pedaling through the Irish towns -- no one pays a lone American rider a lick of attention. Fine. Roll on, roll on...

Here is Spanish Beach, a cold stretch of sand pounded by the North Atlantic. It's named after a party of Spanish sailors who were shipwrecked here in 1588 after the failed invasion of England.

The Spanish Armada of 132 ships carried 21,621 soldiers and 8,066 sailors, hellbent on removing Elizabeth I from the English throne. But the fleet was smashed in an attack by English fireships, followed by a naval battle in the North Sea and a howling storm. Some of the survivors made their way around northern Scotland and Ireland, trying to get home. For their troubles, the shipwrecked sailors had their heads removed with a broad axe, courtesy of the local Irish mayor.

Twenty-four ships were wrecked along the western coast of Ireland in 1588, with 5,000 Spaniards put to death on the Emerald Isle.

***

The Aran Islands are the real dear old Ireland -- spines of stone fences criss-cross the hills -- bleak, gray and peaceful as the grave. The boat to the island rocks with a lunatic violence on the crossing, and every roll feels like we're going to tip & flip beneath the waves.

But once we land, I find a spooky campsite by the sea with what looks to be an old abandoned bathhouse. Yet inside is a free hot shower and bathroom -- it's a suite at the Hobo Ritz. And boy, do I need that shower.

Above the camp is an ancient ring fort -- 2,000 years old, with a 15th

On the streets of Galway: There's always someone playing a guitar in Ireland.

century castle plunked in the center. Man, this is the real shit, I think. The good part of the stay though, is hanging out at the pub that night, watching rugby on the telly, listening to the buttery Gaelic language of the locals, and chatting with a local musician.

Seamus invites me outside for a smoke and we talk shop. I mention that I like the song, "The Hills of Athenry," about a young man who is transported to Australia on a prison ship for stealing crops to save his baby from starvation. I have played it myself at open mics back home, and have even had tears well up in my eyes when singing it.

"By a lonely castle wall, I heard a young girl calling:
Michael, they are taking you away.
For you stole Trevalyn's corn,
So our babe might see the morn.
Now a prison ship is waiting on the bay."

Seamus gives me a hard stare. "I hate that fookin' song," he says. "Everyone here plays it to death."

I guess it's the "Margaritaville" of Ireland. He isn't too keen on Irish music in general.

"Irish music is full of self-pity and sad songs about what the British did to us," he says. "It's time to get over it -- it's time to move on."

It's a tough bunch of people on these islands. The men do whatever work they can find -- fishing, construction, playing guitar in the pubs. Half the battle must be staving off cabin fever.

Fifteen hundred years ago, this was literally the End of the World. No one knew what was over the sea beyond the Aran Isles until the Vikings discovered Iceland. Perhaps they saw the smoke of volcanic eruptions hundreds of miles to the northwest and surmised there was land there -- that's how the Polynesians found Tahiti.

The Africans of Galway

Made it back to the mainland and an endless 25-mile ride to Galway. It seemed to take forever because I rode on a skinny trail by the side of the road to avoid traffic. Going into the trip, I always felt that placid Ireland would be the most dangerous destination on the planet because of having to bike on the roads.

Other than Dublin, Galway is a must-do destination for backpackers in search of Ireland's party scene. After wandering around the maze of the town, I find a hostel near the train station and lug my bike and all its gear up to the second floor at the behest of the desk clerk-- a royal pain in the ass.

Galway is a pleasant tourist town with a pedestrian walkway lined with shops. On the waterfront, there's an old Spanish Gate of stone, harkening back to a time when the Irish did a lively trade with Spain (when they weren't chopping their heads off, that is).

Walking back to the hostel late at night, I'm shadowed by a sexy blonde in a short skirt with knee-high black leather boots. Naturally, I'm suspicious, because attractive women simply don't pursue men, especially by lamplight. Sure enough, I catch a glimpse of the hooker's face in the dim light of a plaza at the center of town and notice that it's vaguely masculine. Spooky.

At the hostel's kitchen, it becomes clear as to how far I have to go to fit into the backpacking lifestyle. Many travelers have brought food from the market -- a young woman with her hair tied in a bandanna is stir-frying a huge pan of zucchini, veggies and sausage for her lucky boyfriend. I sneak in and make my wretched meal of Ramen noodles and coffee, quiet as a mouse.

At the table, a brotherhood of backpackers are creating a pyramid of beer bottles. I sense that they're intimidated by my age -- there are no Americans on the hostel's register, as was also the case in Dublin and Doolin -- and certainly no one my age is bumming around with the kids. Oh well, screw 'em if they can't handle it. I snuggle in a corner and delve into the wifi on my PDA -- a Nokia N800 internet tablet that has been something of a flop so far. I had expected there would be free wifi internet all over hip, technologically-enlightened Europe, but it turns out you have to pay for everything here, including a pee in a public restroom.

In terms of being connected to the Web, America is definitely a hipper place, since I can easily find free wifi in my home town.

A group of Africans are huddled in the street next to my hostel -- their skin a dark chocolate and their accents a lumbering, thick rumble. They smell of the musk of weeks of not bathing. What are their lives like? I wonder. They all look stone broke with one set of clothes on their backs -- how do they make it as strangers in this strange land?

The Africans are the travelers I admire the most. How alone they must feel, trying to make it in the world. With a wave of my hand, I could be in a taxi to the airport and home within a day from anywhere in the world. I have at least $50,000 in my pocket in the form of deep credit lines on my three credit cards. I have the internet to communicate with family and friends every day. What do the Africans have? I observe that they have a network of countrymen -- some guy from Zambia or Ghana or Zimbabwe who's established a beachhead in Ireland helps them with transportation, menial jobs and a place to stay -- perhaps 10 to a room (at a painful price, no doubt), inching their way into a new culture. Tough bunch.

Dear Old Ireland
Sept. 15, 2008
The train from Galway to Dublin

Have you ever been to Moyvore? Not many people have. It's a tiny village in County Westmeath in the center of Ireland. It's not on any tourist route -- there's nothing much to do there. It's an anonymous place of lumpy fields, populated mostly by sheep and cows.

Yet it is was from here in 1850 that my great, great grandfather, Michael Downes, emigrated to the United States. I am his 259th descendant.

If you have more than a dash of Irish blood in ye, chances are that someday you'll travel to the Emerald Isle in search of your roots. The place is teeming with American visitors, packed into tour buses.

We Americans mob Ireland searching for clues to our past in picturesque pubs, which are as lacquered and ornate as antique music boxes. We look hopefully to the heather, the occasional thatched-roof cottage, and the rocky walls of the old country, seeking signs of our roots. It's an impulse we Irish-Americans have, similar to the need of every good Muslim to visit the holy city of Mecca at least once in a lifetime, or the expectation of every American parent to take their kids to Disneyworld.

Perhaps we have that inbred, instinctual need to return because there is so much pain in Ireland's past. When Michael Downes left Ireland in 1850 as a man still in his 20s, it was at the tail end of the five-year Potato Famine that killed one million people, with another million fleeing the country.

Ireland's British overlords actually shipped large amounts of food out of the country during the famine so as not to 'coddle' a starving people they considered to be lazy, and even subhuman.

Many peasant farmers were also evicted from their homes so that the land could be used to raise profitable cattle -- the tenants were tossed out like unwanted cats with nowhere to go. Thus, satirist Jonathan Swift wrote that the roads across Ireland were strewn with corpses, their mouths stained green from trying to survive by eating grass.

It was a form of ethnic cleansing from which Ireland has never fully recovered. The scenes of countless crumbling stone houses which we find so charming today once housed scenes of utter desperation. How many of these green fields are riddled with bones?

Needless to say, I'm grateful that my distant kin chose to bail on Ireland for a new land. He arrived on American shores in a "coffin ship," risking cholera, typhus and drowning, and worked on a river boat on the Grand River in western Michigan before finding a job on a farm outside Grand Rapids (an area which looks much like Westmeath, by the way). His brother, James, made it to Buenos Aires in Argentina, where today I have a relative named Juan Downes.

My brother Mike and I are still in touch with our ancestor's legacy. Our grandfather, James Downes, was a streetcar conductor in Grand Rapids at the turn of the 20th century. James bought a 190-acre farm 20 miles west of town in 1909, and today, we still own 90 acres of its woods and a small lake.

The Irish who emigrated to America were scorned and reviled by many in their new homeland, the same as Mexican migrants are today. They were considered lazy, shiftless, ignorant Micks. They were persecuted by an anti-Catholic, nativist political party called the Know Nothings.

And no different than the Mexicans today, they were given the dirty, dangerous, scut work -- they were cowboys, miners, canal diggers, farm workers, factory hands and soldiers, flooding America with a million immigrants. No doubt, some of the ancestors of those persecuted immigrants look down their noses at the Mexican migrant workers today.

Thirty years ago, African-American writer Alex Haley celebrated his own beginnings with the publication of *Roots*, accompanied by a television miniseries. Haley had spent 10 years researching his slave past, and even journeyed to a village in Gambia, where his ancestor Kunta Kinte had been abducted in the 1750s. Apparently, there was quite a celebration when he showed up.

I'm sorry to say that I didn't share my own Alex Haley moment with a return to Moyvore. After a week of bike-camping along the hideously narrow roads of western Ireland, I took the coward's way out and elected to forgo dodging more cars and trucks on the extra 50-mile trip to my ancestors' homestead.

I had hoped to ambush my distant relatives with a write-up of what happened to their lost kin Michael and James -- the internet tells me there are still family members in the town.

Instead, I contented myself with the scenery, passing by a few miles to the south on the train from Galway to Dublin. Moyvore -- maybe I'll see you next time around.

Moving on, I'm taking only one souvenir with me from this green land of rocks and rain: the name of *Ireland*, scrawled on my Lucky Travel Hat.

England

The Wobbly Wheel
Sept. 17, 2007
Whitehaven, England

What a thrill it is, rolling into the mouth of a mammoth ferry in the Port of Dublin at the head of hundreds of cars and trucks, being waved on deep into the bowels of a ship by the sailors and mechanics with smart salutes and snappy waves. The ferry looks to be the length of two football fields. I feel like George Boosh, landing on the deck of that aircraft carrier -- Mission Accomplished!

But at 1 a.m., shivering on the far side of the Irish Sea, I make sure to be the last one off the ship so as not to be run over by an avalanche of steel. I find my way to a railway station by 2 in the morning, along with superb accommodations -- a clean spot on the tile floor, under a counter. I roll out my ThermaRest and take a blessed sleep.

Before getting on the ferry, I had whiled away a few pleasant hours, practicing the blues on my backpack guitar -- so happy I brought it along -- besides being lots of fun and a time-killer, it's a great conversation-starter and I've met a number of people while playing. Instead of being just a suspicious middle-aged weirdo traveling around, people surmise that I'm a free-spirited, guitar-playing, middle-aged weirdo -- there's a difference!

Anyway, I finally figure out Robert Johnson's "Rolling and Tumbling," which has eluded me all these years, and I've got a good thing going with Willy Dixon's "Hoochee Coochee Man." I've also brought along my lucky brass slide -- a tube that fits over the pinkie finger of my left hand -- and a jumbo C harmonica and harp rack.

"Excuse me, would you like to busk with me?"

I look up to find that a street urchin out of a Dickens novel has joined me in the parking lot.

"What?"

"Would you like to busk with me until the boat leaves? I play the penny whistle."

Blossom, as I call her, is a little under five feet tall and has the pinched face of a wren and thin little brown British teeth, bespeaking a childhood of malnutrition. She wears a big green floppy hat straight out of faeryland, knee-high lace-up boots, and a purple wool skirt and leggins -- the perfect picture of a retro medieval troubadour.

"Thanks, but I just play for fun," is my lame reply. Truth to tell, I don't think I've got the chops to make it as a busker on my tinny backpacker guitar, which frankly, sounds like crap. There are lots of street musicians in Ireland though, and every pub has some poor slave playing guitar.

"Well, can you help me out then? I'm stranded here in Ireland," Blossom begins her sad tale. "I came to protest the construction of a freeway and now I can't get home, and if I could only get hold of my 15-year-old daughter, she'd send the money, but no one will lend me the cash."

It's hard to imagine a mother leaving 15-year-old to mind the homefront while going off penniless to protest a road project across the sea, but I keep these thoughts to myself. Some moms, after all, are more on the order of alley cats.

Blossom spends the afternoon begging for money to pay for a ferry ticket home. She's a great beggar, playing the sad violin of pinched need with great skill for all who'll listen.

And they do. Fortune loves a fool, so Blossom eventually scores enough cash to make the fare after a sustained fit of histrionics.

The Land of Cymru

The ferry across the Irish Sea lands in Wales, which is known as Cymru in the country's native tongue. It's a beautiful land of distant, shining mountains; broad, shimmering rivers; and vast castles built in the 1200s by Edward I.

Once, there was a lively slave trade by the Vikings between Ireland and Wales, back when Dublin was the slave capital of Western Europe in the 11th century. Irish bondsmen were sold in England and on the continent. Even 200 years ago, Moorish pirates sailed the coasts of Ireland, scooping up Christian slaves to suffer to the end of their lives at the oars of their galleys. The Irish were considered to be a sub-race of savages, and therefore, fair game.

But it's kind of a quiet place now though, and I imagine the only slavery in Wales these days is that which comes from boredom.

My train runs through Llanfairpwllgwyngyllgogerychwyrndrob-wllllantysiliogogogoch, the Welsh town with the longest name in the world. It is translated as "The church of St. Mary in the hollow of white hazel trees near the rapid whirlpool by St. Tysilio's of the red cave."

Like the Gaelic people of western Ireland, those of Cymru have their own antique language which sounds like ancient elvish to the ears. But to speak modern Irish, Welsh or British, you just add some variant of 'fook, fooker, or fooking' to every other word, usually in a loud voice in a cafe or sooch so that all can hear. Such as, "'At fooking fooker fooked up me fooking day wit 'is fooking foolishness."

American Invasion, Part II

Whitehaven is a sleepy seaside town that's not quite making it as a resort, located up near the Scottish border in northwestern England. The town marks the start of the C2C Trail, a bike path which runs across the country to the North Sea.

It was here in 1778 that commander John Paul Jones attempted to seize the harbor and burn a British fleet during the American Revolution. But some of his crew got a bit tipsy while reconnoitering the town and the raid was something of a flop.

Jones was a Scotsman who apprenticed as a seaman in Whitehaven before moving on to America and the Revolution. His raid was the only successful invasion of Britain since 1066, and though the English pooh-pooh it now, apparently it gave them a pretty good scare back in the day.

Last night was a bit of hell, arriving here after 10 p.m. from Carlisle with my bike broken down in order to stuff it into the cargo hold of a bus (which served as the final link of the train trip from Wales). I assembled it in the dark and rode up and down the waterfront along the Irish Sea in the cold rain, looking for a campsite. No go, Joe -- so I had to resort to paying the big bucks (about $40) for an old hotel. I feel like a traitor to the spirit of roughing it for staying in a hotel instead of a campsite or a park bench. But not enough to hazard a night in the chill sheets of rain by the sea.

Today I will pedal through the Lake District, which inspired poets such as William 'Lonely as a Cloud' Wordsworth. These romantic brooders on the heath invented a form of poetry which has been a mainstay of high school poets ever since.

The Mountains of Cumbria
Sept. 18, 2007
Keswick, England

With a third spoke blown, it looks like curtains for Dulcinea, yet the bike makes it over a tough pass in the mountains of Cumbria (so tough that I had to get off and push) and we roll into the village of Keswick.

Named after Don Quixote's unrequited love, Dulcinea is 20 years old -- I got her back in 1987 and spent that summer riding 800 miles up from Seattle and around Vancouver Island and back. She still has the 'moosehead' handle bars of the earliest mountain bikes and provides a comfortable ride. But her glory days are long gone and she's basically a clunker and a junker now, with a skipping chain rattling out her final cruise.

Although mechanics back home and in Killarney had told me the bike was unfixable due to the worn metal signature of 20 years of wear on the chain and sprocket, a mechanic in Keswick had the flywheel off and a new rim on in under half an hour. The trip is saved!

Keswick, the world-famed home of the Cumberland Pencil Factory, has the look of a town you might expect to find in Switzerland. Quaint shops overlook a broad pedestrian mall that's packed with tourists visiting the Lake District.

At a campground on the lake outside town, I meet a swarthy long-haired Scotsman who is backpacking across Britain with a huge army pack that dwarfs his five-foot-tall body. Since my tent is next to his, I give him a shout-out and am then completely mystified by his cartoon language, which doesn't sound a lick like English.

"Kerflugely blooey bodola pooty snade," he says, or something on that order, nodding with animation. "Yar flagel berf snagger ma jock-le." At first, I think he's spoofing me, but manage to understand every ninth word or so and deduce that he is indeed speaking our shared tongue.

Later, I learn that the Scots from the northern end of the country speak an English dialect with an accent as thick as axle grease that is incomprehensible to the untrained ear. This is probably why I didn't understand a word of the hit film, *Trainspotting*, starring Ewan Mc-Gregor, and would also appreciate subtitles on British films such as *Lock, Stock and Two Smoking Barrels*. The Brits just don't know how to speak English.

The C2C Trail is luvly, as we say here in England -- no cars for much of it -- it runs mostly along bike paths through storybook scenery that conjures thoughts of Robin Hood, knights and highwaymen. It's like riding through a fairy tale.

On the other hand, it's quite cold here -- in the 30s at night, and I had to get up at 4 a.m. to put all my clothes on. Not that it helps much, with my shivering knees banging together. One stretch, through Britain's only mountain forest, was very much like the trails of dark, rainy Alaska.

Pooped in the Pennines
Sept. 18, 2007
Northern Pennines, Britain

So there I was on my bike, chasing a large pink sheep lumbering down a mountain path -- just a typical sight on the way across England and around the world.

Other interesting stuff today: I rode past the castle of the REAL Lord Greystoke. If you grew up reading Tarzan books like I did, you realize this is a very big deal. Who could forget Tarzan's visit to Pelucidar in *Tarzan at the Earth's Core*, or his hellish night of temptation by the super sexy Queen of Opar in her peekaboo gown in which the Lord of the Jungle remained as chaste as a daisy? Or what about that bizarre entomological encounter in *Tarzan and the Antmen*? Anyway, only got a glimpse of m'lord's castle, which is hidden behind high walls and rows of trees. Didn't see Cheetah anywhere... probably a butler now.

Four American women fly by me on touring bikes -- a group of friends from Florida who are cycling across England with day packs. They're not a very friendly bunch, but they are on a 'ladies only' trip, after all.

Other sights along the way include quizzical squirrels as big as cats with tufted ears and scarlet coats, like something out of Narnia; also shaggy cows with long curling horns that look to be relics of the Ice Age.

Crossing the bike path are faint trails through the heather, with small, weathered wooden signs marking the Coast to Coast hiking trail. It looks like it would be a very wet mash indeed, wading through those knee-deep weeds, which are soaked with dew.

The 190-mile Coast to Coast Trail was charted in 1972 by Alfred Wainwright, a "fellwalker" who mapped the route from St. Bees in Cumbria to Robin Hood Bay on the Yorkshire coast. The script of his hand-written manuscript was published as one of his seven *Pictorial Guides*, which are still used to steer hikers across England today.

The Coast to Coast is one of 15 national trails which crisscross England, including the Yorkshire Dales Trail, The Pennine Way, and Hadrian's Walk. Happily, an outfit called SUSTRANS (Sustainable Transportation) got the idea to create bicycle routes paralleling the foot trails, making it possible to journey the same route on two wheels. I've taken the easy way out by biking the alternative C2C.

The Druid's Ring

At a lonely corner with the iron sky hanging low and dark over the land and the mountains of Scotland shining a sword-metal blue in the distance, I take a side path to an ancient Druids' circle of stone.

Set on a high hill north of village of Little Salkeld, this is the circle of Long Meg and her Daughters, which dates back to the Bronze Age. It's either the second or third largest stone ring in England, with 65 boulders surrounding an area the size of a football field.

There's a woman pressing both hands into the biggest rock at the site -- the 12-foot-tall monolith of red sandstone known as Long Meg. The spiral markings on this rock are said to date back 4,500 years. The woman seems to be trying to channel the spirit world through the stone. Hope the spooks don't eat her brain. My uncle Alvin was psychic, and his belief was that it's unwise to invite visits from creepy dead things on the 'other side.'

Legend has it that Long Meg was a witch who danced on the moor with her wild daughters. They were turned into stone for profaning the Sabbath.

Long Meg and her daughters were turned to stone...

I count 65 stones at the site, but later read differing accounts of their number -- 62, 63, 64... And no wonder, because the circle is said to be filled with a magic that makes it impossible to count the same number of stones twice.

More than 2,000 years ago, the Druid priestesses and priests danced here under the moon for the blue-painted Picts and mysterious Celts.

The Druids were students of nature and the dispensers of justice -- they were so powerful that it was not unknown for a Druid priest to stand between two armies and stop a battle. Their cardinal belief was in the indestructible nature of the soul, which is reincarnated in others -- sometimes years after one's death.

It took up to 20 years to become a Druid priest because the course of study involved memorizing all of their knowledge in the form of verse. When the Romans stamped out their last band in the 70s A.D., all of their oral teachings of the stars, naturopathy, and what they knew about the size of the earth and the universe died with them.

They're celebrated now by new-agers, but back then, the Celts enjoyed burning people alive and head-hunting.

It's a spooky, atmospheric place, and you can almost hear the echo and drum of ghosts in what was once a Sacred Grove. I saw an ancient tree cut down next to the druid's circle, with countless rings zeroing back to those days. Wonder how many human sacrifices fed its roots with their blood? That old time religion...

Speaking of the good old days, it turns out that some of the ancestors of us white folks weren't so nice. In *The Gallic Wars*, written by Julius Caesar during his conquest of Europe from 58-51 B.C., the Roman conqueror notes that the tribes of northern Europe were "greatly devoted" to human sacrifice.

Here's one of the nuggets he left us on what our Celtic ancestors were up to back then:

"Others use figures of immense size, whose arms and legs, woven out of twigs, they fill with living men and set on fire, and the men perish in a sheet of flame. They believe that the execution of those who have been caught in the act of theft or robbery or some crime is more pleasing to the immortal gods; but when the supply of such fails they resort to the execution even of the innocent."

It's a little something for you hippies to think about at the next Celtic music concert.

Misty Mountain Hop

Oops, forgot I have to climb Britain's highest mountain range -- the Pennines. I spend more time walking than riding and reach the top of the highest pass at the limit of my strength. Several times I remind myself that a number of people my age have dropped dead back home recently, and that I should take it easy riding on the uphills.

No worries there, though, because it's all I can do to wrestle my bike and heavy gear on foot over these passes.

After one particularly long struggle, I find darkness descending on the moors and the closest town still far away. I ride seven miles down a mountain pass in the darkness and pouring rain, gripping my brakes to the limit the entire way as the pads slide ineffectually on the slick hubs of my wheels.

In Alston, I find a hostel at the pricey rate of $40 -- more than twice what I expected to pay out in the sticks of northern England. Apparently, the days of the $10 hostel are long gone. But it has free internet, friendly folks, and it's good to be out of the rain. Sharing the place are a group of English cyclists who looked to be in their 60s and 70s. They're riding with daypacks, with their gear trucked on ahead.

"Did you enjoy your ride over the passes?" asks a woman rider who appears to be in her mid 60s.

"I would have, but I had to walk over most of them," I reply. "Didn't you?"

"Oh no, although I did have to put my bike in an easier gear."

Great, after an intense summer of long rides and weight-training to prepare for this trip, I'm being skunked by septuagenarians. Back in my "used-to-be" days as a triathlete, cycling was my best event in the race, and I prided myself as being pretty strong in the saddle.

I console myself that the oldies aren't lugging 50 lbs. of camping gear on a heavy 15-speed antique of a mountain bike, but it's small comfort.

Across the Moors
Sept. 20, 2007
Sunderland, Britain

It's raining when I set out the next day, but fortunately, I have an expensive, high-tech rain suit that 'wicks' the water away. Needless to say, within an hour I'm drenched to the bone inside and out. Never have seen any of this 'breathable' rain gear that works, especially when you're sweating buckets, pushing 90 lbs. of bike and gear up a mountain. At least it keeps the wind off...

Pedaling on through the dreary moors, I can see why English literature is so in awe of these wastelands. They are a mix of Alaska's tundra and the western prairie -- a sea of marshland that's covered in fog and swept by high winds.

I ride past the forlorn rock outposts of Roman legionnaires from 1,500 years ago, and the ruins of a ghastly old lead-mining operation from the 19th century. The miners used to send kids down into the flue of the lead delivery pipes to scrape at the metal which built up on the walls. The children breathed in those toxic fumes all day for who knows what horrible fate.

To get lost on the moors in the old days was most likely a death sentence, and everyone knows they are home to ghosts and goblins. The Hound of the Baskervilles lived out on the moors -- a big brute who loved to get the jump on lost souls. Plus, you could stumble onto one of the invisible fairy roads that criss-cross England and wind up in the Kingdom of Faery, never to return.

This is also the land of the reivers (raiders), bandit families who raided farms on both sides of the Scottish border for several hundred years. Those who lived in this lonely wasteland turned their homes into miniature castles, complete with towers which served both as a lookouts and as sanctuaries to hide in if the reivers showed up at your door, bent on rape, pillage, murder and fire.

I get a taste of the moors by taking an alternate, off-road track for 10 miles or so, pushing my bike up a steep mountain path on a rocky trail. At the top, the wind nearly blows me off the bike several times, but the sun begins to shine and I get a big grin thinking about how much fun it is bumping along a rocky trail high up on the moors. Then I get to thinking it wouldn't be too cool to break a leg out here in this chilly wasteland, and pedal on more cautiously.

Once over the mountains, it's 30 miles downhill, and I speed across the rest of England like a rocket. I camp in a public park outside Tynemouth -- strollers give me funny looks as the sun goes down, but there's nowhere else to pitch my tent.

My ride across England ends with a three-mile walk to a cycle shop -- I blow a tire out the side of the rim of my bike and it's impossible to fix, even with duct tape, that indispensable cure-all which belongs in every traveler's kit.

I dip my front tire in the North Sea, just as I did in the Irish Sea, to formally complete the C2C Trail. Damn! I forgot to register for my official 'I did it' certificate, drummed up for bike weenies to be signed at the end of the trail, suitable for framing. Oh well, at least Dulcinea knows we made it.

The ride across England has gone so well that I decide to cycle an extra 200 miles north to Scotland on the Castles & Coast Trail. It's supposed to be lousy with ancient fortresses and scenery.

But less than 15 minutes after deciding to head for Scotland, I round a quay into the full force of the North Atlantic wind, and know in an instant that not even a lunatic would try pushing against it for 200 miles in late September. It's like trying to shut a bank vault door with three guys on the other side pushing against you.

The front pack blows off my bike -- a tattered mess, and where will I stash my scant food supply now? Bike camping is awash with such petty concerns. I spend the rest of the day getting lost in the maze of streets, alleys and public parkways leading into the city of Newcastle.

So, defeated, I catch a train to London, tucking Scotland away for another time.

London Calling
Sept. 23, 2007
London, England

It's a thrill mountain biking around the busy streets of London, rolling down the same lanes where Shakespeare strolled and Henry VIII rambled. You float in the bloodstream of the city as a speeding cell, trailing in the wake of red, amoeboid, double-decker buses and a swarm of corpuscular taxis.

London -- many backpackers disparage the place, but I find it the most thrilling city in the world (sorry New York, apologies, Vegas), packed with history, theatre and a cool vibe. Okay, truth or dare: Manhattan and Lost Wages may have an edge on the excitement factor, but the former is frenetic and the latter full of squares, while London maintains a steady hum that for lack of a better word is best described as "groovy."

There are tens of thousands of people marching down the streets, all laughing and talking (when they're not huddled miserably under their umbrellas in draperies of rain, that is). Riding the Tube, you're sure to hear a half-dozen languages, and the people-watching is spectacular: The young London women dress to kill in the Elizabeth Hurley mode and you see folks from all over the world: India, Africa, the Arab countries. It's fun just getting lost and stumbling upon unexpected locales, such as a street of antique booksellers, the gypsy vibe of Camden Market, or the square at Covent Garden -- occupied by street musicians good enough to be international stars.

But it's expensive here -- everything costs twice what you'd pay in the States: cuppa' coffee: $3-$4. Sandwich or burger: $10. Small slice of pizza: $3. Coke: $2. Apartment overlooking the river: $1-$4 million. And people aren't smoking their brains out here, like in Dublin, perhaps because ciggies are $13 a pack and have SMOKING KILLS in big block letters covering the whole pack.

Strange Bedfellows

Single ladies -- can't get enough of men? Then try sleeping in a small hostel room with five of them -- half snoring to blow the roof off a barn.

Many young travelers following the backpackers' trail through the world end up living in London for a year or so -- nurses from Australia, students from Japan. There's a bit of a debate among them as to whether London is the best ever due to all of the entertainment and cultural options, or if its endless rain, dreary gray skies and painful prices make it too blah to bear.

Speaking of which, to some extent you can judge a place by its media. On that score, it's worth noting that the British tabloid press is the worst crap ever -- nothing but endless stories about minor celebrities shagging each others' boyfriends or obscure pop stars getting into barroom scuffles. This lends credence to a line from the *Rough Guide to*

England, which calls the country an irritating "nation of overweight, binge-drinking reality TV addicts."

The hostel is packed with strange bedfellows. Along with the usual backpackers from Germany, France and Australia, there are older travelers from throughout Britain who are staying here on business trips -- people in their 50s and 60s bunking in the dorms with 20-year-olds, then donning their suits to catch a business meeting before returning home on a night train.

Travel tips

On a recent trip, a friend took along nine pairs of old underwear and threw one out each night after wearing it -- America's disposable culture at work. Since I don't have 150 pairs of old underpants, much less the desire to carry them, I've made do with a reusable strategy.

Almost all of my clothing is synthetic for an easy rinse & wear on the road. I have a t-shirt that globe-trotting Jason Bourne would kill for -- it's a nondescript Lincoln green made of 40% polyester, with the rest being cotton for comfort. I can wash it in a sink at night and wear in the a.m. Ditto with my $25 synthetic travel underwear. I have just two pair, with one getting washed each night. Can't say that I'm thrilled with my scratchy beige North Face travel pants though -- they're pretty ugly -- I chose them because they have deep pockets -- harder to lift one's wallet, hopefully.

Beyond that -- thank God for laundry day -- the rinse & wear stuff does get dingy...

A long trip like this is like easing into a hot bath -- you've got to do it slowly. Things will get more foreign from here on as I head for the Continent... even alien by the time I hit India.

That's why I started my immersion into what I call "the Strange" with the familiar countries of Ireland and England. They're not much different than visiting Vermont -- lots of farm animals out in the country and people with funny accents.

I also purposely chose to lead off my trip with the intensely physical act of traveling by bicycle in order to pump masses of endorphins into my head. It's a good way to fight the anxiety of being alone in strange lands for months on end -- I hope.

On the Road, Revisited

Saw Jack Kerouac walk by in Picadilly Circus today. He stepped into a red phone booth and disappeared -- a god of travel who will never die.

Kerouac was the godfather of generations of backpackers who followed in his footsteps. Hitching around in his dungarees with a knapsack and a notebook, Kerouac became the patron saint of today's hostel-dwelling, rail-riding tribe of adventurers.

Don't know if Kerouac ever made it to London, but this city has certainly become one of the capitals of the backpacking world he helped conjure into existence.

I'm always amazed by how many high school and college students have read his book, *On the Road*. The rambling, stream-of-consciousness book celebrated its 50th anniversary this month.

I read *On the Road* three times at a similar age, from 17 to 19, and could barely make a lick of sense of it, with paragraphs that seem to go on for pages and an expressionist style of layering images in free-flowing prose. It's America's version of James Joyce's *Ulysses*, an unreadable book about a single day's events in Dublin.

On the Road has got a lot more laughs, but is still much the same. It's a *roman à clef* of Kerouac's seven years of bumming around America in the 1940s in search of a new 'hip' way of life, inspired by poetry, jazz, drugs, casual sex, and crashing on couches.

The book provides a spiritual sequel to *Huckleberry Finn*, with its impulse to head west into the great unknown of America's underground. It spurred a generation of young Americans to take up the travel lifestyle. God knows how many copies of *On the Road* are floating around Afghanistan today, left there 40 years ago by idealistic young backpackers following the Hippie Trail to India.

Practically everyone has heard of *On the Road*, yet I imagine that few have had the fortitude to wade all the way through its dense, ricocheting prose, which was meant to copy the rhythms of jazz and be-bop. So here's the gist of it -- the *Cliff Sticky Notes* version, if you will.

The book's narrator is Sal Paradise (a stand-in for Kerouac), who worships Dean Moriarty. Dean is the real-life Neal Cassady, whose 1960s sex & drug exploits with Ken Kesey's Merry Pranksters and the hippies were further chronicled in *The Electric Kool-Aid Acid Test* by 'new journalist' Tom Wolfe. Another character is Carlo Marx, a pseudonym for the poet Allen Ginsberg. Famous beatniks, writers and poets are sprinkled throughout the book under other guises.

Sal worships Dean because this "son of a wino" and "sideburned hero of the snowy West" is a modern-day outlaw, living outside the "square" world.

"Dean set a Denver record for stealing cars, gunning for girls coming out of high school in the afternoon, driving them out to the mountains, making them, and coming back to sleep in any available hotel bathtub in town," Kerouac writes.

Dean spends most of the book trying to nail high school girls as he rambles around the country, stealing cars and surviving on petty theft and crappy day jobs. He speaks a form of hipstereze along the lines of "Dig it, daddy-o," that seems corny today.

He and Sal bounce from one sleazy situation to another, trying to break free of the uptight side of America while exploring the hipster underground occupied by cool "spades," jazz musicians and Mexicans. They are the prototypical beatniks, and out of their writings and ramblings comes the Beat Generation, which in turn, played midwife to the Swinging Sixties.

Kerouac and his pals dabbled in bisexuality, or were headlong gay in Ginsberg's case. Yet, much of the book is about their burning lust for making chicks. But the unstated subtext of the book is that Sal is in love with Dean. The result is a psychosexual circus that gives *On the Road* much of its power.

The book also purports to celebrate the nonstop good times of life on the road, but ultimately, it's a sad, unhappy tale with a theme of disillusionment. Like Dorothy, Sal learns that there's "no place like home."

After a few years of rambling, Sal starts to sour on the life of a bum and the fact that he's always letting people down, including the women unlucky enough to live with him. After the book reaches a crescendo with a trip to Mexico City, Sal is deserted by Dean in Mexico. Dean abandons him, even though Sal is sick with dysentery, fever and hallucinations. "When I got better I realized what a rat he was," Sal reflects.

The book peters out from there. A year later, Dean rides the rails from San Francisco to New York to make up with Sal. But Sal has a Duke Ellington concert to go to and no time for his old friend -- the bloom is off the rose.

In the face of this rejection, Dean simply turns around and heads back out West into the great unknown.

The book ends with Sal sitting on an East River pier, looking at the sunset and moping about his old pal, Dean. All that's missing is a rose to sniff.

According to legend, *On the Road* was written in three weeks of nonstop typing on a single roll of paper. But much of the novel was written in advance on scraps of paper during Kerouac's travels. He also spent years of rewriting and self-censoring to keep his nervous publishers happy.

Kerouac claimed that the true ending of *On the Road* was eaten by his cocker spaniel. He also had to tone down the language and use fake names. In 2007, Viking Press published Kerouac's original uncensored version of *On the Road*. The book is also being made into a movie.

There was still a sense of mystery and awe to travel in America when Kerouac was kicking around its glamorless places in the '40s. You could still find yourself sitting next to a Blackfoot Indian -- wrapped in a coat hacked from a blanket -- at a bus stop high up in the gray mist of the Rockies; or talk with an old rancher about how the Platte River Valley was like that of the Nile.

Traveling on a Greyhound bus or hitchhiking, a traveler would encounter cowboys, hobos, truck drivers, migrating southern blacks and cut-bait types. And travel through America's underground had not yet been gentrified with the sort of hostels and guesthouses that backpackers stay in today in distant lands -- Kerouac was more likely to stay in skid row flophouses or on the couch of a distant acquaintance or sexual conquest.

Kerouac wove a romance of life on an endless highway, but the bones and sinews underlying this fresh face were those of two centuries of American drifters: pilgrims, prospectors, canal diggers, wagon trains, Lewis & Clark-style expeditions, cowboys, trappers, traders, Dust Bowl refugees, Depression rail-riders, Gold Rush miners, Mississippi Delta blacks heading for jobs in Chicago or Detroit, Mormans fleeing into the wilderness, displaced Indians, cattle drives, refugees from the Civil War, immigrants in search of the farmland they never had in Europe... America's story is that of argonauts risking death in the wilderness in search of a Dream.

But Kerouac offered a new element to this old tale. Whereas the travelers of America's past were ineluctable squares driven by necessity, the new nomads were hipsters, compelled by the need to be rootless and free of the straight, plastic world. Instead of seeking fertile land to plow, the new travelers came to furrow new visions of the world into their fecund minds.

By the '60s, the reborn mythos of life on the road was expressing itself through pop songs (the *lingua franca* of the day) such as "America," by Simon and Garfunkel (..."it took me four days to hitchhike to Saginaw; we've all come to look for America...") or Bob Dylan's update on Woody Guthrie's railroad-riding ballads. It was cool to be *On the Road*.

But that world was nibbled away by the homogenization of America with chain stores, McDonald's and Red Roof Inns. For Kerouac's godchildren, there's no longer much allure in kicking around America -- things have become too expected. Today's adventurers have to roam farther afield to drink the liquor that intoxicated the hitchhikers of the '60s.

Bitter irony: Kerouac died of liver disease in Orlando, Florida in 1969 -- a place that was soon to become one of the most unhip towns in America. He was 46 years old.

Western Europe

D-Day
Sept. 25, 2007
The White Cliffs of Dover, England

My invasion of France begins in an hour -- off to Calais on the ferry from Dover. From there, I hope to train it down through Germany to the Danube for a bike ride along the river to Vienna. At least, that's the master plan.

Final thoughts on Britain: On a day trip to Portsmouth, I walked the decks of the HMS Victory, the flagship of Lord Horatio Nelson, who won the battle of Trafalgar and saved England from invasion by that devil, Napoleon.

Nelson is a demigod in Britain -- you find his statues and honors everywhere. His battle strategy was simple: "Head straight at them," with cannons blazing.

Nelson was a bit reckless though -- he'd lost an eye and an arm in prior battles and stood right on the quarterdeck during the Battle of Trafalgar off the coast of Spain, where a French sniper shot him with a musket from the 'fighting top' (sharpshooting platform) of an enemy ship. The spot where Nelson fell is marked with a brass plaque, as is the place on the deck below where he died. You can also see the coat he wore and the blood-stained bullet hole through its breast at the Naval Museum in Greenwich.

Reading the Horatio Hornblower novels as a kid and the Captain Aubrey/Dr. Maturin saga of author Patrick O'Brien as an adult has imbued me with an interest in British naval history from the sailing days of 1750-1815. These were the days of oaken frigates and ships of the line, rolling broadsides and two years before the mast. Seeing the old port and its hallowed artifacts puts it all together in a way that no amount of reading old history books can satisfy.

Anyway, I'm off. I'll miss you, England, with your warm beer, busty babes and baked beans for breakfast. But I'll think of those beans every time I see your name inscribed in bold letters in my Lucky Travel Hat. Fare thee well...

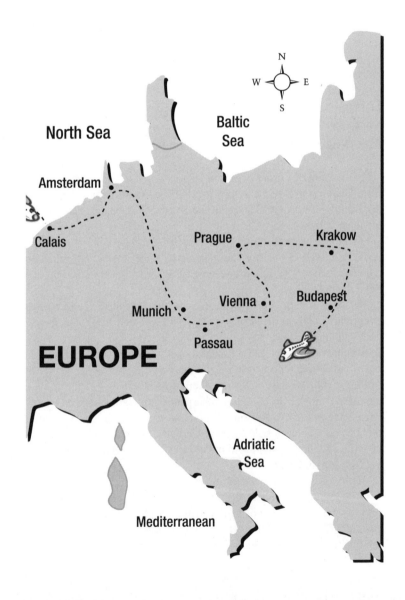

An Old Soldier

It was a sparkling cruise across the Channel under sunny skies, nursing a Newcastle Brown Ale with views of Dover Castle and the White Cliffs. I made this same crossing when I was 19, bumming around Europe. Then it meant sleeping on the soaking deck and hearing the fog horn blow like the bellow of a saltwater god as we made our way through a cloud covering the sea.

Some time later, I met an old soldier who had made the crossing in the D-Day invasion of June 6, 1944. That was nearly 64 years ago. Still as spry as spring at the age of 84, he came over to say hello as I was walking my bike through a farm market back home.

"I wish I could ride a bike," he said. "You save all that money riding a bike. But my joints are all roughed up and I lost my hearing when a cannon went off next to my head at Omaha Beach. You know what you get from the government when you lose your hearing? Not much. And these hearing aids cost $6,000."

Most of us turn our backs on old-timers and their stories. But the old guy was so full of life, I couldn't resist hearing more.

"So you were in the D-Day invasion crossing the Channel?" I asked. "I heard that was quite a fight."

"Oh yes, I was with an outfit of men all thrown together from different units. And we rode around in halftracks with machine guns that we used to spray the hedgerows because the Germans would be hiding behind them. The turrets could swivel all the way around so you could fire those guns in any direction."

"Were you scared? They say the landing was pretty rough."

"Oh sure," he nodded. "The Germans were up on the hills above the beach in pillboxes with little slits in them," he said, drawing a narrow box with his hands. "And they sprayed our men who were landing with their machine guns, cutting them down. And we also had barbed wire and all sorts of obstacles to get through just to get at them.

"I'm lucky to be alive," he added, "but I went on to Paris and then up through Belgium and Holland, all the way to Berlin."

"Sounds like you did alright just staying alive."

"Yes, although I got wounded in the war and got the Purple Heart," he said. "A few years ago, I took my medal down to the coin store and asked if it was gold because it's so shiny. And they said, no, it's fool's gold. Can you believe that? The government didn't even give us medals of gold, and back then, gold was cheaper than it is now. They gave me a tin medal, and here I lost my hearing and the government won't do much of anything."

***

I no sooner made camp in the French port of Calais than it started raining buckets at my campground by the harbor -- a place that's teeming with semi-homeless people. I ran to the shower house to cook some noodles on the alcohol stove Jeannette gave me and returned to find my tent turned ass-over-teakettle upside-down from the wind, with all my stuff, including my sleeping bag, soaked through. Forgot to plant the stakes... Ah me, all you can do is laugh, right? Got my sleeping bag halfway dried out in the shower house and slept like a baby in its damp mush.

Stuck in Lille
Sept. 26, 2007
Lille, France

Early this morning, I pack up my wet gear in the damp mists of dawn and catch the train to Lille, passing through miles of French farmland which served as a battlefield for the American and British invaders in WWII -- the same turf memorialized in *Saving Private Ryan*. Church steeples prick the sky every few miles, marking the site of small villages.

This is much the same route that British Field Marshall Bernard Montgomery took in Operation Market Garden in the fall of 1944. It was an assault by paratroopers and a column of armored vehicles across northern France and Belgium to liberate Holland and capture the bridges on the way.

Their goal was the bridge over the Rhine at Arnhem, which unfortunately, became the "bridge too far." British paratroopers were unable to capture the bridge from the Germans and were pinned down for 10 days of fighting. Meanwhile, British troops heading down "Hell's Highway" 69 were unable to relieve them, due to heavy German attacks at the front of the column -- cutting off the head of the snake, so to speak, much as U.S. forces did on the fleeing column of Iraqis in the 'Highway of Death' out of Kuwait in '91.

In St. Paul's Cathedral in London, you find the American Chapel, dedicated to the 28,000 American servicemen who lost their lives defending Britain from the Nazis. Many died on these farmlands leading to Germany -- somewhere ahead is the forest of the Ardennes where the Battle of the Bulge was fought. That battle took 19,000 lives alone, fighting in the deep snows and subzero temperatures.

In Lille, the locals assure me there is no way to catch a long-distance train to Germany with a bike -- the long-haul trains here don't carry bikes in either France or Belgium -- only the local trains accept bicycles. I march around town in a 50-degree, soaking rain, looking for an internet cafè to gather information --feeling miserable, frustrated, cold and wet the whole day.

Eventually, an option reveals itself and I catch a local train to Amsterdam, reasoning that surely there will be long-distance trains that will accept my bike in the Land of Bicycles.

Passing through the medieval cities of Ghent and Bruges in Belgium, I wonder what will happen to all the folks here when the world's supply of natural gas runs out. These towns are forests of crumbling old brick buildings that look as drafty as wigwams.

Of course, the peak oil crisis begs the question: are these the last days of easy travel around the planet? Today, tourism is the biggest industry on Earth, but once the oil runs out, intercontinental travel could become too expensive to bear. Perhaps people will be forced to travel digitally through their online avatars, save for those who choose to sail or ride bicycles.

Tourist Attraction
Sept. 27, 2007
Amsterdam, Holland

Sitting on the banks of a canal playing my guitar near Anne Frank's house I'm thrilled to find that I'm Amsterdam's newest tourist attraction. Every tour boat that goes by has excited photographers straining to get a picture of the colorful character playin' the blues and blowin' on the harp. Big, big smile on my face. Hey! Don't forget to give me my euro, monsieur...

I made it to Amsterdam near midnight and had a bitch of a time finding a room, getting turned down at every door. I tried sleeping in the train station but the cold-hearted cops kicked me out: "No you must leave -- get out -- the station's closed," the clean-cut Dutch coppers say. No smiles, just a tap on their batons.

The cops don't have a lot of tolerance for riff-raff in Amsterdam because they're already choked to the gills with druggie bums who take advantage of every social welfare perk.

Around 1 a.m. I found a flophouse run by some friendly Chaldeans who had a bare bones room at the excruciating rate of around $100. The alternative would have been sleeping on the streets with the druggers creeping about. Probably not a real problem, but it's hard to sleep on a park bench when you're thinking 'what if?'

The Capital of Sleaze
Sept. 28, 2007
Amsterdam, Holland

I move to a really scroungy hostel (is there any other kind in Amsterdam?) and find dope stores up and down my street along with a bunch of dildo/sex shops. Amsterdam is the sleaze capital of the world.

Was offered a hit off a glass pipe within five minutes of arriving at the Hostel Aroza. I thought it was a crack pipe, but the guy explained that it was "blueberry," meaning I suppose, blueberry-flavored pot. I politely declined, saying I planned to go biking.

Which I did -- far out of town, trailing a long stream of bicycle commuters who fan out along the bike path like the long tail of a kite. We whip past ancient dikes still festooned with windmills. But today, those quaint old windmills have been transformed into gargantuan wind towers -- pretty cool.

Amsterdam is a biking utopia. There are an estimated 600,000 bicycles on the streets here to serve a population of 750,000. There are thousands of bicycles everywhere, both gliding down the avenues and jammed into vast corrals near the railroad station. The riders include little old ladies, men in suits, school kids, punks with green hair, sexy women in the latest styles -- thousands of people riding, all looking strong and slim. It's a blast biking all around town as part of the mob.

***

Shifting gears, that evening I visit Amsterdam's red light district, which is packed with 1,000 nervous men walking in groups from window-to-window -- all of them giggling and trying to get up the courage to go inside the red-lit doorways, where lithe young ladies in thong bikinis beckon.

Some of the prostitutes are drop-dead gorgeous on par with movie stars and have crowds outside ogling them through the windows -- I can only imagine they must be quite pricey. Then there is a selection of obvious she-males and a garden variety of wholesome girl-next-door types.

Much has been reported in the news that the prostitutes are white slaves from East Europe or Russia who've been tricked into a life of sexual bondage. That seems rather unlikely in politically-correct Holland, with its legions of feminist investigators. I'm more inclined to believe reports that the girls are eager entrepreneurs who flock here from all over Europe and Africa to earn tens of thousands of dollars before returning home to attend college or launch new careers with the money they've made on their backs.

The only customer I saw who dared to enter a doorway out of all the hundreds of gawking men was a red-faced teenager who looked like Harry Potter's geeky younger brother -- he must have been 17. He had two slim and energetic brunettes in black bikini lingerie as a welcoming party. Lucky fellow, thought I...

All of the sleazy stuff is a hoot at first, but gets old soon enough. There's nowhere nice to hang out and just read or kick back. Walking the streets is a lonely experience after awhile, but that's all there is to do unless you want to sit around some bar or mope through a museum.

My own vice here is the chocolate waffles. I eat two of these addictive substances before realizing they are setting me back $5 a pop. Ah, the price of debauchery... But boy are they good.

The Pot Thing

I can only imagine that Amsterdam is still talking about my adventures with black 'premo' hashish here years ago at the Captain's Bar while staying at a houseboat hostel at age 19. Back then, I got so high one night on hash and Amstel Pils beer that I crawled across the bar's floor to the filthy bathroom to throw up. I woke up thinking that I was pasted to the ceiling of the john and looking down at the floor.

But that sort of behavior has been off my resume for decades now, so I'm not interested in hitting the 'coffee shops' that draw pot pilgrims from all over the earth.

Only coffee shops can sell weed. These quasi bars have a menu of 10 grades of marijuana which is sold in small batches -- enough to roll a couple of numbers. I'm not against smoking pot, and exhaled a bushel basket of the stuff in my carefree younger daze, but the idea of walking around alone in an introspective mood with a headful of high-powered smoke doesn't sound like a good idea. Anyway, my personal poison is merlot and chardonnay.

When I visited one of these coffeehouses a couple of years ago, I asked for the mildest stuff they had and the Purple Haze reefer nearly put a friend in a catatonic state. I thought she was going to fall off her bar stool and require an ambulance.

At the hostel, I share a couple of puffs with Guilherme, a backpacker from Sao Paulo, Brazil, who's been bumming around Europe for three months; but it's not a priority for me to sit around buzzed in a coffee shop. The stuff they call "mild" here has been refined through hundreds of generations to the point where some smokers have had panic attacks and psychological breakdowns from the extreme THC levels in the herb. At least, that's what a local newspaper claims.

"Hey man, you wanna' have a smokey-tokey with us?" A fellow guitar-toter from Montana has been bugging me to smoke dope with him off and on. He's on a week-long pot vacation, puffing constantly and has a blunt going in the hostel bar.

"Everybody smokes here -- everybody!" Montana man says, shaking his head in amazement.

"Yeah, well it's just not where I'm at this time around, but thanks anyway," I say.

"You gotta' be shittin' me! This is Amsterdam man. Everybody's smokin'."

There's a certain kind of Cheech & Chong person who's dependent on marijuana, even though the experts claim it's not addictive. They're usually doughy, overweight people who look ghastly unhealthy in a junk food diet kind of way. This is Montana man to a T.

I have a difficult time explaining that it's not my trip, man, and he thinks I'm a pretty strange dude for not sharing a "smokey-tokey." Maybe so.

People All Over the World
Sept. 28 2007
Amsterdam, Holland

Amsterdam is a major crossroads for the backpacking crowd. It has the quality of a vortex -- definitely faded in terms of being *au courant*, but still one of the must-visits for travelers heading on to Morocco, Peru, India, Tanzania, Cambodia... There are travelers on every street straining under their packs, heading all over the world. It's a good place to trade notes on faraway locales.

But this town is also a hooker with a steel heart when it comes to expenses, and has become more like a Disneyfied tourist attraction through the years than the old backpacker crossroads I remember from the '70s, where mobs of grimy kids were zoned senseless in Dam Square. I had my first $10 beer last night, rather exorbitant in the "Land of Beer." Also, a small cup of coffee is $6, and it's like *half* a cup of coffee... These are three times what I'd expect to pay back home.

Meal-wise, Amsterdam is as lousy with greasy junk food as Ireland and England. Your best bet is to buy a pre-made lunch at a convenience store.

I'll never knock McDonald's again, by the way. Ironically, the burger giant is often the only place in Europe that you can count on to get a salad. You really crave salads after a steady diet of fish-and-chips, shish kebab, noodles, or the stuff that passes for pizza here.

Hot Wheels

Many times I've wanted to abandon my old junker bike along with its heavy camping gear. It would be nice to cycle straight across Europe, but unfortunately, I don't have enough time for that, so that means taking a train to the route along the Danube. And it's a bitch hauling that bike off and on trains fully loaded and up and down hostel stairways.

But now I'm glad we stayed the course.

Compared to the heavy Dutch 'mule' bikes, Dulcinea looks positively smokin' and I'm quite proud of her. I marvel over the beating this bike has taken with my heavy stuff onboard its chromoly frame.

Sad to think that in a week, we will reach Vienna and it will be time to say adieu.

'Nite, Nite'

Last night, the hostel keeper at the Aroza hauled two more mattresses into the room, so we had seven people sleeping elbow-to-elbow -- including a bunch of giggly Germans who came in at 3 a.m., high on weed and beer. It's kind of fun in a goofy sort of Boy Scout camp kind of way.

Anyway, before he went back downstairs, the hostel keeper said, "Nite, nite, sleep tight," and I realized it was the same thing I used to say to my daughter Chloe when she went to bed. Only he forgot to add the closing line: "Please don't let the bedbug bite."

Fortunately, in this grungy place, I'm tucked into my own sleeping bag, so no worries mate!

Clink-Clink
Sept. 29, 2007
Munich, Germany

The cosmic pancake lands syrup-side up and I find myself in Munich

It was anarchy on the train from Oktoberfest, but eventually the partyers all fell asleep.

at the height of Oktoberfest, the biggest beer-bash in the world.

I snoozed through Germany on a packed sleeper train in one of six couchettes in a car as small as a prison cell. We bleary travelers were greeted at the railway station by the thundering sound of hundreds of young German men streaming off the local trains, singing in full roar and waving black and checkered flags. They were dressed in liederhosen and leather aprons and revved up for the big party. With them were many college-aged girls in 'Heidi' peasant dresses. It was like being in a gay musical about the Hitler Youth.

Most of the action is at 14 circus tents in Wies'n Park, where thousands hoist steins delivered in clutches by bosomy *frauleins*. A high point of any trip to Oktoberfest is barfing from the ferris wheel or Tilt-A-Whirl rides at the nearby carnival.

In town, a worldbeat band is rocking the Odeonplatz -- one of the main squares -- where the beer flows into mugs the size of pitchers. The food here is fantastic -- apple blinis in sweet cream, cherry strudle, bratwurst, spare ribs, fried potatoes in sour cream --I've had it all and more -- oh the food -- followed by rivers of golden beer flowing down my parched and grateful throat, always followed by a "Bitte, mein Herr. Wos is einen pissoir? Danke, danke..." Turns out German is pretty easy to speak -- you just say "Ya-ya" a lot, either kind of nonchalantly or fast and nodding your head -- "Ya-ya -- ya-ya."

This is the fourth time I've been to Munchen as we call it here in sauerkrautland. I check out the world-famous Hofbrauhaus and find the same old hard-boiled German men getting soused to the same old oompah band as was the case decades ago -- it's as if they've been suspended in amber in one of Grimm's fairy tales.

If you've seen one cathedral, you've seen them all, but palaces are all slightly different from one-another -- while still having an eerie sameness -- whether they're in Europe, Asia or some Banana Republic. The same proves true in Munchen.

The Residenz Palace in the center of town once served as the home of Bavaria's royal family, the Wittelsbachs. The palace was ruined by the bombs of World War II, but has been reconstructed enough to reveal the arrogance of power in its gilded cave.

With their velvet-paneled rooms, portraits of pigs wearing silk and satin in golden frames, and forests of tapestries and carvings, palaces remind us of the insane levels of excess people will go to when they gain power over others. Palaces are a good reminder of why revolutions are often necessary. You find the same story written in bricks and mortar in the the capital of every country. Tourists walk their halls, marveling at the excess, never considering the rats in the cradles of the hovels that ringed these lunatic asylums.

The onslaught of Oktoberfest means there's not a single place to stay in town -- even the campgrounds on the edge of Munchen are packed and there are backpackers everywhere, looking for lodgings in vain. So I'm movin' on to Passau on a train later today -- tomorrow I'll start riding the Danube.

The Drunk Train
October 1, 2007
Passau, Germany

Got on the 7:24 train to Passau with 1,000 shit-faced Germans, all bellowing and singing and braying like donkeys. It's standing-room only and anarchy on the train with no conductors, no rules, no one paying the fare. Hundreds of loud, obnoxious, swearing, drunken young men -- still drinking -- with a sullen bunch of their mostly-silent women bearing up. What a switch from the mellow party in town.

"Does it matter where I put my bike on the train?" I ask a conductor. "Do I need a bike pass?" She shrugs, like who gives a shit? and disappears -- the German officials leave the Drunk Train to its mayhem.

American youth have nothing on the German males when it comes to being obnoxious in a group. As far as I can tell, most of these guys have nothing going on upstairs but a headful of farts and sauerkraut. But maybe I'm somehow culpable, considering I'm one-quarter German myself...

I claw my way to a spot for my bike in a train doorway and then have to swing the whole mess out everytime we stop to let people off and on. It's an excruciating two hours, with me wanting to take a swing at one young lout, but deciding I don't want to be a long-term guest of the German government. Or, get the snot beaten out of me by his drunken friends...

Eventually, most of the partyers fall asleep, or turn into *bierleickens* -- literally "beer corpses" -- from going comatose with brew.

Anyway, I reach Passau around 10:30 p.m. and have the usual anxiety of trying to find a place to stay in a strange city late at night.

An elderly innkeeper in a natty blue blazer and running shoes makes me feel more than welcome -- like I'm a visiting princess -- fussing over me and providing the cheapest room in the place -- 30 euros with breakfast. "And here is the bathroom, and here is the shower, and here are a choice of rooms," he says. Very nice chap. Thirty euros is about $50 U.S. -- way more than I want to spend, but this late at night there are no options other than sleeping in a doorway and it's freezing outside. The room smells like an airport smoking lounge, but it's the best place I've stayed at yet.

The Danube

Der Donau
Oct. 2, 2007
Linz, Austria

My heart lifts the next morning when I get my first glimpse of Der Donau (The Danube) beyond the onion dome steeples, winding streets and passageways of old Passau.

Passau was a frontier fortress town created by the Romans. The town flowered under the Germans in medieval times, providing a gateway to Austria with the convergence of three rivers.

Soon I am peddling along a broad, smooth lane by the river -- an old towpath. One couldn't ask for a sweeter trail. Castles and towers dot the high hills above the Danube, which brims with tour boats, ferries and freighters. An occasional propellor-powered paraglider wafts over the river, while to my left, a stream of Porsches, Mercedes, and BMW motorcycles glide by.

You encounter hundreds of cyclists throughout the day, and many outdoor cafès and hotels, all catering to bicyclists who come to ride the famous Danube Trail. Your senses are filled with the aroma of the dank river and the sticky-sweet fermentation of fallen apples.

Lunch is at a pathside cafè along the Danube with sauerbraten, potato pancakes, salad, potato salad and a huge dumpling. Dinner is a calzone with chianti. These Austrians know how to eat, ja?

I resist my natural inclination to be a gear-jamming miles-monkey and resolve to go slow, savoring the ride. I dawdle through the day like a kid on a tricycle -- no worries. Time to stop for a bite of chocolate? Why not... Just 40 miles down the path, I find a campsite beneath an ancient castle tower and call it good.

The next day I roll into Linz, a city which still has a touch of its medieval glory. Adolph Hitler once attended school here and planned to make Linz the capital of his empire. Wonder what the old master-race freak would say if he knew there are lots of well-to-do black African-Austrians living here now, looking quite confident and at home? Funny how things turn out.

Oh, by the way, despite what you may have heard about everyone speaking English in Germany, that's definitely not true -- and even more so here in Austria. Fortunately, my facility for foreign languages has improved with age, and I muddle along with a phrase book and my brand of cartoon German, vich involves talken mitten de nonsensigen endizens, in hopens dat der volks vill understanden me ser gut.

Camp Life
Oct. 3, 2007
Somewhere on the Danube

This being October, it's completely dark by 7 p.m. That means you start scrounging around for a campsite sometime around 5:30 to have time to put up your tent, have dinner and make coffee. It can be a lengthy process, cooking on a Titanium stove that burns a shot of pure alcohol.

Since there's no hope whatsoever of having a fire (not even the campgrounds have them, much less a clandestine campsite), I'm in my tent reading at sundown. I carefully arrange my junk at the lower end of the tent, using my pack to prop up my back for reading by a lithium-powered booklight. But soon enough, I need this thing or that -- more clothing to keep warm or a candy bar or whatever -- and the tiny dome tent looks like wild hogs have rampaged through it, rooting around for truffles. My domain is also permanently damp as a result of being packed up wet the night before.

I toss and turn most of the night. Although I've got the thickest sleeping pad available -- the 'comfort' model that's an inch-and-a-half thick -- it still feels like you're sleeping on hardpan after an hour in the same position. Plus, it's cold; so roll over, snuggle in a fetal position, wake up and roll again, on and on all night.

By 6 a.m. you're fully awake from having gone to sleep so early, but it's still too dark, cold and damp to creep into the haze along the river. So, more reading until you see the sun's first glimmer. (I'm tearing through all five of Martin Cruz Smith's saga of Russian detective Arkady Renko, with the novels bought at used bookstores along the route.) Then it's time to get up shivering in your damp, smelly biking clothes and get the mess packed and on the road.

But I like my little tent -- it feels like home. And I can unzip a side panel and watch vast riverboats sliding by in the night, as long as football fields and lit up like Christmas.

Bandit on the Trail
Oct. 4, 2007
Pohlarn, Austria

When Austrians put a 'camping' symbol on a map, they don't mean to suggest that there will be actual camping available. I stopped at several of these 'campgrounds' only to find that they were long-established residential communities of old trailers on permanent foundations -- they're basically holiday camps without a chance of any traveler actually camping there -- *verboten*!

Yesterday afternoon, I pedalled for miles, only to be turned away. What to do? The sun was going down fast with nowhere to land. So I pedaled out of town a ways and found a pleasant spot on the river for a bandit camp. But first, a picnic... It's good to be back in that happy land where a bottle of wine costs less than a can of Coke or cup of coffee; so it was a pleasant time, sitting by the broad, still river, which shimmered and quaked with the colors of a pearl.

I reflected that for the long-distance traveler, the quality of being 'intrepid' is not something you choose or are born with -- it is simply a matter of necessity -- dealing with every curve ball thrown at you, often with a snap decision.

Speaking of intrepid, an odd sight on the trail today was that of an enormous woman -- perhaps 300 lbs. -- peddling my way with both front and back panniers on her bike. She looked quite strong, more muscle than fat -- huffing and blowing like a steam engine -- but I wondered how her bike managed to carry all that weight without snapping the frame.

Was happy to have roused myself enough the next morning to avoid being run over by a huge tractor mower churning my way through the fog. As usual, my tent was soaking wet, like it had rained all night -- only this was from the heavy dew of the river.

Biking through Europe has made me realize how lucky we are as Americans. Most of these countries have none of the roadside parks or restrooms that we take for granted, and even an old stone hut can be a private tourist attraction that costs $5 to visit.

In much of Europe, there is literally no public property -- even the wastelands belong to some lord or royal family. True, the big cities all have parks the size of airports, but these are usually the former hunting grounds of kings that were seized in violent revolutions (or donated by royals to forestall one). Out in the country, there is little in the way of parks or campgrounds for the common person. It makes me proud of America's public parks and sharing spirit.

On the other hand, the Europeans sure have some sweet bike paths, so call it a draw.

***

The oddest camp was in the clubhouse of a rowing club in Pohlarn, Austria. The club members let me crash on the floor there by the rowing machines -- it's like staying at the Ritz after being out in the rough stuff. And trusting? In the kitchen, there's a drawer full of money they've left to the mercy of a stranger.

At the clubhouse, I learn what Austrians do in their spare time, since it seems to be a rather dull country with no movie theaters, hardly any internet, and not much going on in the towns I've gone through... Opening a refrigerator door, I find it stuffed to the gills with beer and wine -- another room was packed to the ceiling with hundreds of empty bottles. Rowing, biking and booze set the good times in Austria.

***

Beauty has a price, and for me it's paid in loneliness in order to soak up the panoramas of the Danube River Valley. Fewer people speak English as I creep toward East Europe and the Austrians are a bit stand-offish. But after I try my cartoon German on them with my funny pronunciations, they get a twinkle in their eyes and we make a friendly connection.

Speaking of which, folks from Holland through Germany and Austria all have trouble pronouncing my name. "Bub? Bub?" they say. "No, it's Bob," I reply. "Bub? Bub?" Okay -- call me Bubby, if you like, but please, no "Bub." It's Bubby now...

Anyway, I had expected East Europe to be the loneliest part of the trip, so must be a brave little soldier and pedal on, pedal on. Through golden mustard fields, apple orchards and 800-year-old villages.

I do meet a few travelers though. My ride is a measly affair compared to that of an Irishman who is biking a few thousand miles from his home in Connemara to Croatia. "The women are beautiful in Croatia," he says by explanation.

There is also a British couple who've spent the past six months biking thousands of miles to Turkey and back through Romania. They are banking professionals in their early 30s who are thinking of ditching their jobs in order to cycle across America.

These folks live to travel.

"I have no interest in a career other than finding a gig as a waiter long enough to collect enough cash to get back to my travels," says John the Irishman. "I can't imagine doing anything else."

The trail along the Danube is sweet and fast -- all downhill to Vienna.

John lived for several years in the United States and hitchhiked all over the country during the late '90s-early-'00s. He worked as a waiter in Texas and California in between bumming around.

"I was in Michigan," he says when I say where I'm from. "I hitched through the Upper Peninsula on my way out West. It was the scariest place I've ever been. I thought I was going to get killed there."

"You've got to be kidding me," I reply. "No one thinks it's dangerous where I'm from and I live 100 miles to the south."

"No, it's a very dangerous place, believe me," he insists. "I feared for my life."

I find this notion quite whimsical, since I have hitch-hiked through the U.P. (as we call it) a number of times in my college days and have camped in its forests and along Lake Superior. It's about as dangerous as a kindergarten class. There are some terminally rural characters and drunks driving around up there in pickup trucks, to be sure, but they tend to be as soft as nougats inside.

But this isn't the last time I'll meet Europeans who say they are afraid to visit America -- sophisticated travelers who are as afraid of visiting the U.S. as many Americans seem to be when it comes to traveling overseas.

Treasures on the Trail
Oct. 5, 2007
Willendorf, Austria

Have you ever been to Willendorf? It's a tiny village where the 25,000-year-old 'Venus of Willendorf' was found. The Venus is a nude sculpture of a fat cave woman with all of her stuff hanging out quite grotesquely -- considered to be the most beautiful Stone Age sculpture ever found. That's not saying much...

The museum in town offers a pictorial display of other sculptures from that period and they're all fatties -- that was the feminine ideal back in Fred Flintstone's time. The Stoners were into big glacier gobs of fat glomming on the ladies in order to ensure the survival of the species against Neolithic starvation.

The trail also passes the stupendous monastery of the Order of St. Benedict at Melk. There aren't enough words in the English language to describe the decadent opulence of this place and its church. It's like an explosion in a spaghetti factory, with cascades of golden foolerdoodle and religious brick-brac; paintings of cherubs and saints the size of barn doors on the ceiling and baroque gold curlicues squirting all over the place like a madman's wedding cake.

The greatest treasure at the monastery is the Cross of Melk, which is a fingernail-sized piece of the True Cross of Jesus, locked in crystal at the center of a large, elaborate cross of gold and jewels. Also, the shinbones and assorted body parts of saints are fashioned into the centerpieces of crosses and chalices. Imagine your shinbones becoming a tourist attraction and objects of veneration for 1,000 years -- some guys have all the luck.

Then there are the usual corpses of saints under glass in the church, dressed in what looked to be spanking-new brocade of gold and bright colors of silk and satin, although not in the latest styles... They are literally skeletons in party clothes, with -- believe it or not -- smiles on their mummified faces. The Europeans are big on this sort of thing -- I've also seen corpses in Spanish cathedrals. Imagine the Rev. Jerry Falwell under glass in a Baptist church in Virginia. Well why not, Bubby?

It's amazing that the Germanic people went from tree-worshipping barbarians to connoisseurs of such elaborate snickerdoodle in the space of a few hundred years.

I can only imagine that some of these 16th century treasures were made from the gold looted from Aztec and Inca temples, far across the ocean, who in turn, got it from other folks they murdered. The riches are meant to show the exaltation of God, but it feels more like you're in the Temple of Mammon. It didn't feel too spiritual there until three Austrian churchmen started singing a cappella harmonies -- deep with soul -- which had all of the tourists spellbound. We need more singing in the world, and less gold.

In Melk, I see a tour group of around 40 American cyclists who are day-tripping down the Danube from inn-to-inn on upscale bikes with all of their gear carried in sag wagons. It doesn't look like much fun to me -- a packaged adventure.

They turn up their noses at my heavily-laden mountain bike which is strung with camping gear held in place with bungee cords. Admittedly, I look like a traveling circus -- my bike resembles a rolling dragonfly with bulging panniers on either side and my guitar's neck sticking far out over the back tire. To them, I'm a weirdo -- to me they're pussies with daypacks. To each their own.

That evening I make another bandit camp in a gully alongside the river and have a cheerless dinner of an apple and some bread slathered with Nutella, the European version of peanut butter, made of chocolate and hazel nuts. It's my only meal of the day, other than some bready stuff for breakfast. Thank God for Nature Valley Maple Nut bars, the *lembas* of this trip which sustain me like the elven bread that nourished Frodo and Samwise on their trek to Mordor.

Speaking of which, the pounds are melting from my body after near-ly a month on the bike -- it feels like I'm 20 lbs. lighter. Yet I seldom feel hungry -- traveling like this puts you in a state of ecstasy that's literally mortifying.

It's funny how you can be way the hell out in the middle of nowhere and sure as shootin', someone will show up at your clandestine camp-site. Even though I'm several miles from the nearest town, huddled in the woods in a gully by the river, a car passes by on a two-track road near my campsite close to midnight, with another car bumping down the trail in the early hours of the morning.

The Story of Siegfried

This is the land of the *Nibelungenlied* where the epic German poem "The Song of the Nibelungs" took place. The story is retold in Wag-ner's Ring Cycle opera.

Of course, everyone talks about the *Nibelungenlied* (well, not really), but does anyone know the story, other than the fact that the "Ride of the Valkeries" was used as the background music for the helicopter attack in the film, *Apocalypse Now*? Hello?

Here 'tis:

It was here in the wine country along the Danube that the fearless warrior Seigfried reforged the broken magic sword of his father and killed the dragon Fafner. Siegfried bathes in the dragon's blood, mak-ing himself invulnerable except for one tiny spot on his body that is covered by a leaf -- like the fatal weak spot on Achilles' heel. The dragon's blood also turns him into a mind-reader and able to talk with the birds. This new talent reveals that a mentor pretending to be his friend is actually conspiring against him. Off goes the bad guy's head.

Siegfried's quest is one of self-knowledge. Why isn't he afraid of anything, he wonders? Gods, dragons, death... nothing rattles him. Only when he meets a sleeping knight in a ring of fire does he expe-rience fear for the first time in a way that is familiar to every young man: he takes off the knight's armor and finds a beautiful woman, Brünnhilde. He kisses Brünnhilde, waking her from a magic sleep. It's love, baby -- she renounces the world of the gods for Siegfried, and the curtain falls.

At least that's one version -- there are other variations of the myth that are as tangled as the grape vines tendering through Siegfried's vineyards.

This is wine country with necklaces of grapes planted high up on the mountain. Grape pickers in heavy rubber boots pour buckets of green into small trucks bound for the press. It's harvest time and there must be a million tons of grapes in this valley.

No wonder the wine is so cheap.

The Wedding Cake
Oct. 6, 2007
Vienna, Austria

After five days of riding along the Danube, the spires of Vienna rise in the mist far down the river. Soon, I am in the 'wedding cake' of Europe, so named because of the crenelated towers, cathedrals, palaces and heroic statues at every turn.

A funny turn of events led me here. I was following my guidebook closely, trying to figure out the best bridge to take over the Danube to get to the city on the other side. But where were all the churches and spires I had seen in the distance? All I could see were office towers and skyscrapers across the river.

After an hour of futzing around, riding back and forth along the waterfront, I asked a couple which was the correct bridge to take to Vienna? Although they didn't speak English, they knew enough to point me in the direction over my shoulder. All this time, old Vienna had been a couple of blocks behind my back, while the city across the river was simply the new business district.

After riding around town for another hour or so, looking for the alleged 'campingplatz' of downtown Vienna, I say to hell with it and decide to find a hotel. But first, I give my soggy tent away to a nice Arab kid running a pizza stand. "Do you want a tent? I can't use it any more." Indeed he does, and I draw him a damp picture of how it should be set up.

All of my biking and camping stuff is mailed home in three big boxes at a cost of $100. Worth it, considering the panniers cost that much alone, not to mention the expensive biking shorts, vest, gloves, sleeping pad and other stuff. God, I was getting so sick of lugging all that stuff around on my bike. The downside of bicycle camping is that you feel like a dork trucking all that gear around.

Two hundred years ago, Vienna was a Very Big Deal capital of Europe that rivaled Paris and London. Then the Habsburg Empire got handed its ass in World War I and the city lapsed into a backwater. Only now are tourists bringing the town back to life with visitors packed into its streets like a canapè tray of Vienna weiners.

The frosting on the cake in Vienna is its endless plazas, palaces, half-mile-long farm market, and mythic statues of gods fighting titans on horses with flaring nostrils.

Speaking of myths -- the founders of Vienna got the cash to take the city to the next level 800 years ago by ransoming King Richard the Lionhearted back to the English after kidnapping him on his return home from the Crusades.

As a ruler, Richard Coeur De Lion was something of a shit. He spent only six months in England during his 10-year reign from 1189-1199. The rest of the time he was off fighting in the Third Crusade or tending to his possessions in France.

He was shipwrecked off Venice in 1192 on his way back from leading the crusade against the Muslim ruler, Saladin. A warrior who was was said to to a petulant flop at everything but fighting, Richard had conquered Cyprus the year before and nearly took Jerusalem twice.

But the mighty lion was captured on his way home and locked in a tower by Duke Leopold of Austria. He was handed over to the Holy Roman Emperor Henry VI and freed in 1194 after his subjects pledged a huge ransom.

It's a wonder the English contributed a farthing. The ballads of Robin Hood immortalized a king who could have cared less about the English peasants who slaved to save his sorry ass.

Desolation Row
Oct. 6, 2007
Vienna, Austria

When in Vienna, I always attend the opera, and by sheer luck the next day, I happen to stumble upon the world-famous opera house and find that there are tickets available for Verdi's *Otello*. Hmm, should I get one of the last three $220 tickets, or the $5 standing-room-only ticket? I opt for the latter and am jammed in with a bunch of other inappropri-ately-dressed tourists like cattle in the back of the opera house -- but still with as good a view as anyone coughing up $220. I hope (in vain) that I don't stink, since I haven't had time to hit the laundry.

But the jealous Othello makes for a dreary protagonist, and since I'm a bit blue in the gills from a touch of 'King Leopold's Revenge,' I duck out at intermission.

What follows is one of the dullest Friday nights I've ever endured.

The highlight is getting lost and riding my bike around town in the dark.

Turns out Vienna isn't too happenin' at my end of town, anyway. At the bar next door to my hotel there are some skanky old prostitutes in jumbo sizes and heavy makeup who are far past their shelf life. A grandmotherly gypsy in heavy mascara tries waving me inside, since apparently, few of the business travelers in the area are desperate enough to take the plunge. No thanks. The bars hosting these ladies all have red Christmas lights in the windows, which only adds to their desolation.

Blood Ritual

Just before arriving in Vienna, my bike fell heavily on my right calf and I wrestled it upright with some difficulty. About five miles down the road, I looked down to find my leg was smeared with a thick coat of black grease from the chainring, and that a panther's claw of five bloody scratches from the gears were oozing blood through the filth.

I stopped to wipe it clean with a Wash-and-Dry and started to pedal on -- no big deal. Then I remembered the time that Jeannette had flown off her mountain bike in a cow pasture while riding on the high altiplano beneath the Andes mountains in Peru, and how I had treated her cut with alcohol and antiseptic. She'd probably want me to do the same, so I fished out my first aid kit and scrubbed the wound and smeared it with Neosporin. The scar will make a nice souvenir of my ride down the river, along with *Der Donau Radweg* (Danube Cycle Way) written in bold letters on my Lucky Travel Hat.

Prague

The Capital of Cool
October 7, 2007
Prague, Czech Republic

I always feel nervous entering a new city, and for good reason: I never know where the fuck I'm going! Imagine being from East Europe and parachuting somewhere into metro Detroit without a clue and you get the picture.

Such is the case landing in Prague in the Czech Republic, where the train delivers me to a different station than the one indicated in my guidebook, and of course, far off my map. The unfriendly station is littered with trash and weird sticky stains and it's crawling with drunks and junkies, pissing on the walls outside, doping and drinking -- the works.

Here, I consider giving Dulcinea the slip, asking a few of the pot-smoking youth if they'd like a good, dependable American mountain bike. "Hell no, biking is for squares" is the rough translation I perceive.

I strip Dulcinea of gear and leave her leaning under the roof of a kiosk next to the train station, thinking someone will come along... But the bike looks so forlorn and we've been through so much that it seems too ignominious an end for my warhorse. So I saddle up and plunge into Prague's suburban traffic with my pack on my back.

After riding around lost for miles to who knows where, flagging down cops and unsuspecting citizens for directions, I am magically transported to a friendly hostel right in the central city. Woo-hoo!

Yes, Fortune smiles on a Fool -- I've proved it again and again. On the downside, I'm sharing the hostel with a large tour group of very excited teenagers from Denmark -- dozens of them arrived just minutes after I checked in. They are downstairs in the bar right now (which stays open til 5 a.m.), screaming their heads off in giddy glee.

"Ve vant to go to de deesco! Ve vant de beeg deesco mit de dancing, not de dancing at de hotel!" demands a drunken Danish high school princess in a mini-dress that's about one inch from a view of Honolulu. She and seven other kids pile in a cab for downtown.

My first official act here is asking a waitress how to say please (pros-im) and thank you (dekujl) in Czech. Got to keep up those manners.

I also attend Prague's very odd Black Light Theatre. Several balletic actors dance and act out Beatles songs in silent pantomime, with fluorescent flowers, butterflies, lips, furniture, the Yellow Submarine and other stuff lit by black light and floating around against a jet black background. It's cool in a corny sort of way -- and this is one time I wish I had some of that Amsterdam smoke to complete the illusion.

Speaking of which, back in the '90s, Prague was considered the Capital of Cool in Europe -- even cooler than Amsterdam. I'm happy to report that it is still pretty cool with its cobblebrick streets, mammoth castle, clock towers, coffeehouses and cheap beer. There are also travelers from every land swelling the streets... it's Sunday night and the streets are still rockin' at 11 p.m.

***

Good luck smiles again on Bubby -- it turns out my dorm room with eight beds has only two other people in it -- both very quiet. One is a businessman in his 70s. The teenagers are in the rooms next to mine, with a number of them sprawled out on the floor outside my door, giggling in their hormone-induced hypoxia.

But I gotta' hand it to those kids -- although many didn't hit the hay until 5 a.m., most are up by 8 and beat me to breakfast.

The Private Dancers
Oct. 8, 2007
Prague, Czech Republic

There's nothing like a good nudie show to lift a man's spirits, and with two upscale cabarets in the heart of downtown, I decide to attend the 'Prague Ballet.'

I should have been more clued in, passing a roomful of hungry looking women in lingerie who eye me like I'm a box of chocolates. Needless to say, I'm not used to getting adoring glances from beautiful women -- what's up with that?

The dancers are tall, slender -- certainly beautiful -- and look bored out of their minds, gyrating with the frigid poise of models walking down a catwalk. There are none of the lewd moves or tarty humor that gives an American topless bar its fun. In short, it's not a very sexy show, even though the ladies are wearing nothing but nail polish and lipstick. The ice queens pirouette on the stage before melting into the darkness. Still, it passes the time, and I find myself admiring the dancers for their athletic, svelte figures. They look like they spend a great deal of time in aerobics and pilates classes.

Periodically, women in upmarket bras and panties stop by my table and ask if I'd like a private dance. "No thanks, just watching the show," I say, imagining that they want to do an American-style table dance where you get a lesson in gynecology.

A tough-looking Russian drunk glares overhead for several moments, looking like she wants to slug me. "You vant privaht dahnz?" she mumbles.

"No thanks."

"Und vhy nut?"

"Married," I wave my ring finger. "Not interested."

She glares and then glares a little longer. Again, I get this impression she's winding up for a sucker punch.

"Oh, alvays too many married!" she grumbles, weaving off.

It's early in the evening, and there are only a couple of us guys in the bar, with the sharks in lingerie circling. I'm glad when a petite young blonde comes and sits at my table, keeping them at bay. I deduce that she is a Russian -- she insists she is a Czech -- but before long it comes out that she is indeed here from Russia, looking to start a better life. She says her name is something like Natalia or Natasha, but in my mind she is Natalie, like the actress Natalie Wood from the '50s and '60s.

Natalie is a nice girl who comes across more like a kid sister than a stripper. I ask her where she's from, what her hopes and dreams are, etc., none of which I remember from one minute to the next.

"So when are you going to dance?" I ask.

"I can only do private dances," she says. She adds that the women who are dancing on the stage get paid out of the cabaret's $10 cover charge.

She explains that the private dances are held in rooms upstairs for around $100. "I give you private dance, sensual massage, a blow job, and if you want, we can do more for more money, yes?"

It turns out that $150 buys the whole show. At this point, I feel rather naive for sitting in the middle of what is basically Prague's biggest vagina market without having a clue.

Natalie makes her pitch, which is not without appeal, since I am, after all, sitting in a brothel for the first time in my life. But three things run through my mind: For one, I promised my wife that I'd be good on this trip. I remind myself that being faithful is rule number one when you're married. It's a sobering thought that plunges me into a dark mood, like falling into a well.

But there are also practical considerations: I'd have to go out and scrounge around the city streets for an ATM in the dark to withdraw the money, and since I'd want all or nothing, it would mean burning down $150 when I already feel like I'm tossing buckets of cash on a bonfire with little to spare.

Then too, Natalie would be the last girl I'd pick in this cabaret. Like I said, she is quite petite -- less than five feet tall -- and reminds me of a kid sister. My thoughts flash to the California-style blonde bending over a nearby table with buns like ripe honeydew melons. Or a bleached blonde with a hard face, but a body like Angelina Jolie's who is in earnest negotiations with a beefy salesman. Or, most of all, a sophisticated brunette who's a dead ringer for a young Jane Seymour in an impeccable negligee and thong who's been sitting next to me in a cool silence for the past hour. Now there is a prize.

But my window shopping is irrelevant since it would be rude to let my new friend Natalie down after she's gone so far to explain the ropes to me... and it all circles back to being faithful to my wife. So, checkmate.

"Sorry, I'm married," I say, waving my ring finger.

"We can just do the dance and massage if you like," Natalie says hopefully.

Some sort of payment seems required, if only for the conversation, so I pay her what most women seem to crave: a compliment. I tell her she's very nice and good-looking, but no can do. The only part of me I leave at the cabaret is a complaint with the doorman that my beer cost $15 instead of the $5 they promised. He gives a bored shrug, like "shit happens," and I exit stage left.

I heard later from the new guys in my dorm room that the place got pretty wet and wild after midnight. It's a downer to think of sweet little Natalie down there, sucking on penises for a living -- but everyone's on their own trip, so I don't knock what she's doing. Still, I think she'd make a better waitress than a 'lady of the night.'

Hot Dogs for Breakfast
Oct. 9, 2007
Prague, Czech Republic

The Czechs have the English beat when it comes to odd breakfasts. This morning, there was a big platter of steamed hot dogs on the table at the hostel, along with a selection of cold cut meats and cheese, cabbage salad, pasta salad and a gooky looking ham salad.

"This stuff sure looks horrible. How can anyone eat like this?" I say to a fellow American at the hostel. He's a toxicologist from Denver who's ridden his bike all around Europe on numerous trips. Currently, he's heading down the backroads from Prague to Budapest.

"That's what kills most of the people here," he says. "The high fat content in their diet. It's a poison."

Despite a cornucopia of fat on the breakfast bar, I settle for two slices of toast.

It's a glorious sunny day, perfect for marching around looking at more old churches, clock towers and palaces. It's a grind after awhile, but that's what backpackers do all day -- we're itinerant church inspectors.

My meander leads me through the mammoth Prague Castle, high on a hill overlooking the city, where I climb 287 steps round-and-round up the narrow bell tower to the top of its cathedral. There, past a church bell a big as a Volkswagen, I can see hundreds of feet down from above the knife's-edge roof of the cathedral. It gives me shivers to think of those medieval workers perched on these dizzy heights hundreds of years ago, hauling the stone blocks up to build this place.

Much of Prague's charm comes from its most pedestrian quality -- its streets and sidewalks are paved with millions of carved stone blocks. The cobblebrick surface is pleasant to walk on -- like an ongoing foot massage -- and gives the city a feeling that is both organic and ergonomic.

Yet by the end of the day my head is spinning from sensory overload and I have walked myself silly. Fortunately, a call home over an internet phone at the Rock Hard Bar downtown proves to be a fine antidote. That, and the cheap Czech beer, which is of high quality at about $1.50 a pint.

I look in vain for Prague's famed community of expatriates. These are Americans and other nationalities who took up residence in Prague during the '90s when it was a cheap haven for disgruntled wanderers. Haven't turned up any of these characters so far. Perhaps the high prices and falling dollar drove them out.

It's also a grim reality of European life that the average citizen doesn't live in the quaint inner city enjoyed by tourists. More likely, they live in dreary apartment towers far from town -- a long bank of which I glimpse from the roof of the cathedral, outlined like a row of jagged teeth about five miles from the city. Maybe the expats couldn't dig that scene and flew back home to Mama America.

***

Speaking of hot dogs -- last night after leaving the strip club around 10 p.m., I bought a sausage in the center of town from one of the numerous vendors. Got about halfway through this foot-long affair before the discovery of weird, lumpy, fatty things inside prompted stomach-turning feelings of the old heave-ho. A bum with the look of a simpleton was haunting the trash can. "Hey do you want this?" I asked. He sure did -- he wolfed that weenie down in a twinkle. Let the good times roll, sez I...

The face on the wall in Prague.

Imagine
Oct. 10, 2007
Prague, Czech Republic

"I am you, as you are me, as you are we, and we are all together."

-- Writing on the Wall

After Soviet tanks rolled into town to smash the Prague Spring uprising of 1968, the authorities tossed local dissidents a scrap and allowed
them to write protest slogans on a wall down by the Vltava River.
When rock star John Lennon was murdered 30 years ago, someone
painted his portrait on the wall, and it has been known as The John
Lennon Wall ever since.

Today, there is a bas relief sculpture of Lennon's face peering out
from the wall, which is the size of three billboards, located in a quiet
alley, and covered with colorful graffiti and thoughts of peace. Roll
over Jackson Pollock and tell deKooning the news -- this ever-changing canvas created by peaceniks has a glory that no expressionist
painting will ever match.

The John Lennon Wall is a holier place than any church I've visited so far -- a thoughtful, reverential corner of the universe. As fellow Beatle George Harrison might have said, it's a "space beyond ourselves."

You find another kind of art nearby on the 700-year-old Kurlov Most (Charles Bridge). This footbridge is crowded with artists, street musicians and hundreds of people milling about.

Looking down from the stone rails on the bridge are statues of religious figures, blackened with age -- most of them smiling, as if they too are making the scene. My favorites are a pope raising two fingers in benediction, which looks like he's flashing the 'peace' sign. Also, a good-natured cardinal, with a live dove on top of his porkpie hat, paying its compliments in a brilliant stream of white down the side of his black, smiling face.

***

My own artistic efforts involve pondering what to do with the 100-or-so photos of old churches I've shot along the way... the bane of every traveler. Far more interesting are the photos of every meal I've eaten since that memorable bucket of noodles in Piccadilly Circus. I have a theory that if you can remember a meal you ate on a trip, it will bring back all of your other memories from that time. Proust had the same idea in his novel, *Remembrance of Things Past*, where the hero conjured up thousands of pages from sniffing a flower or tasting a croissant -- I forget which.

I pound the streets, imagining that my wife is playing the role of Julie Delpy in our own private *Before Sunrise*. That movie about Prague brilliantly captured a dirty little secret about travel: it's not all that much fun unless you have someone to share the experience with. Without an excited exchange over all of your experiences, it's just bouncing between sights, cafès and grotty public toilets in an endless circle...

So what a godsend the internet has been, because it has allowed me to talk almost daily with Jeannette and even face-to-face sometimes on the Skype 'telly.'

Skype is an internet telephone service which I first encountered in a beach town in Nicaragua earlier this year. For a few cents, you can call anywhere in the world, or communicate for free if it's a computer-to-computer connection. The best moments are those when a vid-cam link is available. It keeps loneliness at bay, being able to see Jeannette's face.

In a way, the internet has been the salvation of this trip, because it transforms the monologue in my head into a sort of conversation over this blog. It's not the real deal, but I have a small sense of sharing the trip with readers back home, and that sure keeps your spirits up.

The Country of the Young

I get a taste of age discrimination: Four of my new roommates in Prague are in their early 20s, and I have to remind them a couple of times to quit calling me "sir."

"We'll try not to wake you up when we come in, sir," says one young guy, who's spent the afternoon playing poker and getting drunk in the room.

"Give me a break with that 'sir' shit, okay?"

"Sorry, I forgot," he says, his face in a flush.

It's an ugly moment, but I feel shoved out of the picture because of my age and it makes me angry. Don't I deserve a break? I'm bicycling across Europe and backpacking around the world, solo. Doesn't that count for something? I doubt that any of the kids in this hostel will be bumming around the world when they're my age -- they'll be leaning back in their LazyBoys, mainlining reruns of whatever passes for *The Surreal Life* 30 years from now. I don't deserve this "sir" stuff.

But let's face it, after a certain point, you can no longer enter the Country of the Young. For instance:

These guys sit up playing cards and drinking heavily of vodka and rum each night until 10 or 11 -- about the time I'm going beddy-bye. Then they head out to the bars until 4 a.m. to drink and party some more. I haven't been into that scene since I was 23 (or maybe it was 33 or 43, come to think of it).

I was sitting on the hostel stairs the next morning, having coffee at 5:30 a.m. and waiting for the bus; and one of the guys came in from alley-catting around and said, "I thought you had to get up at 5 today?" I replied that I had just gotten up and it was 5:30 in the morning. He was shocked -- so blasted that he didn't even know it was morning. His buddies were still out getting wasted at the strip club.

Those were the days, my friends -- but like the writer Thomas Wolfe said, you can't go home again.

Farewell Dulcinea
Oct. 11, 2007
Prague, Czech Republic

I remember being aghast early this summer when my nephew Brian asked to borrow my old 'cottage' mountain bike to ride 40 miles around Crystal Lake back home in Northern Michigan. I thought back then that the old junker would never make it around the lake in one piece, but Brian made the trip just fine, and now, so have we -- about 700 miles along the west coast of Ireland, across England and down the Danube.

It's been a sad farewell coming. The Celts believed that everything of note in their lives had a spirit -- every boulder, tree, pot, sword, sheep -- each thing had a personal name and was considered to be alive and interacting with the community. The American Indians believed this too, with their concept of the manitou -- the spirits filling everything from rocks to rattlesnakes. We moderns have lost this sense of being, although I'm well aware that there are powerful spirits dwelling within my guitars, and in some of the favorite old cars I've owned.

And of course, there is a spirit in this old bike that has been brought back to life by this trip. If anything, Dulcinea seems to have grown stronger during the course of the ride, taking on a life of her own. We've been across the ocean and over two seas, on board 12 trains and through the streets of Dublin, London, Amsterdam, Vienna, and now Prague. We've ridden through some of Europe's finest storybook scenery, up the west coast of Ireland, across England and down the Danube. It feels like I'm dumping a good friend.

On the other hand, I'm donating the bike to the hostel in Prague, so the guests or whoever wants her can keep riding. And it occurs to me that Dulcinea has achieved what passes for a bicycle's sense of glory. Rather than rusting away in my cottage garage in a feeble state of disrepair, the bike has had one last good ride and is going to keep on rolling -- on the bumpy streets of old Europe.

I was going to leave a little note with the bike, telling its story, but have decided to let its history remain an enigma. Someone will look at the decal on the bike: McLain Cycle -- Traverse City, Michigan -- and wonder how the hell it got to Prague. Take care, old friend.

Poland

I 'Heart' Krakow
Oct. 12, 2007
Krakow, Poland

Got into Krakow in southern Poland late in the afternoon, and after marching around for an hour with my backpack and guitar looking for a place to crash, I found a bed at Count Dracula's hotel.

It's amazing how the Europeans spare no expense to make the hallways of these old beater pensiones as creepy as possible. You enter through a 10-foot-tall door that's thick with 30 coats of lead-based paint going back 200 years or so -- c-r-e-a-k -- then up a cavernous stairway, so dark and gloomy that even a bat would get the shivers. Broken windows and crumbling masonry? You bet, pasted here and there with old peeling posters. Another ancient door with an old skeleton key bars the way, and so on to your room.

The room was suitable for a vagabond bum like *moi*, though, and where else can you watch *Lost* on TV in the original Polish? Funny, but the same male narrator does all the voice-overs for American TV shows, and even for actress Charlize Theron in a film, *The Astronaut's Wife*.

The Drunks

I'm beginning to notice that some Europeans have a bit of a drinking problem. Or, more like it, a monster of a drinking problem. Yesterday, I took the bus to Krakow from Prague for a change of pace (10 hours to go 300 miles). At the station, three young guys were already drunk at 6 a.m. They kept on drinking on the bus throughout the day until one of them started blubbering in his beer that afternoon, cryin' like a little baby for his momma.

"Momma! Momma! Oh Momma!" he sobbed, collapsing in his seat

with his arms around his head, his face as red as a spanking. He was about 20 years old -- full of pain at such an early age.

Then, when it came time to make a transfer, I looked back and saw that all three of them were passed out on the floor with their arms and legs wrapped up together, like the aftermath of a gay orgy on quaaludes. The bus driver went back and started slapping them and shaking them and then slapping and slapping some more. Nothing. Were they dead? Finally, he got them on their feet and dragged them to the door. Hard to believe, but no one barfed.

"These are not typical Polish boys," a woman passenger assured me. "They are probably city boys from the border with Ukraine."

I'm willing to believe it because everyone in Poland seems very nice and certainly more presentable than your's truly in his scruffy travel togs.

But back to that drinking thing -- you often see the Europeans drinking at breakfast in the cafès and all day long. It's nice to sit in a shopping mall and have a big beer in the food court -- something you'd never experience in America -- but the culture of alcohol seems a bit out of control here. Plus, there are many volunteers in the Lung Cancer Army here -- everybody smokes...

***

But the women of Poland are the most beautiful I've seen in all of Europe. They have angelic faces of a clear-eyed purity, like they just got done playing the harp after bathing in milk. Adorable.

At a bus station on the way to Krakow there was a woman of startling beauty with the look of a supermodel, dressed in a micro miniskirt and black lace hose, which set off her fabulous legs. As tall as a giraffe with rich honey hair flowing far down her back, she was so ridiculously beautiful that the men standing on the platform couldn't help giggling self-consciously, like, "Did you see that!?!'" She picked up on the juvenile gawks & glances and stamped around the station very prettily, looking for her ride. I bet he caught hell when he showed up late.

The Dragon of Krakow
Oct. 12, 2007
Krakow, Poland

Years ago, a dragon lived in a cave within the big hill under the palace in Krakow. He used to come out at night to eat people, with virgins being a favorite treat.

One day, he set his sights on the king's daughter, who was of course a virgin and the prettiest girl in all the land. The king got irritated at this and decided it was time for the dragon to go. So he packed a sheep's carcass full of sulfur, lit a fuse, and tossed it down the dragon's throat.

Boom! No more dragon -- he was blown to smithereens. But you can still see his bones hanging from the door of a church next to the palace and visit his cave. Legend has it if the bones ever fall from their chains, it will be the end of the world. Must say, they don't look very secure...

The Invaders
Oct. 13, 2007
Krakow, Poland

Word has it that less than 20 years ago, the citizens of communist East Europe were still standing in line, waiting for shipments of potatoes and beets at truck depots. Maybe that was just Cold War propaganda, but it's true that the museums here can't seem to say enough bad things about the bad old days of life under communism.

Today, all that has changed. I walk out of the grungy, grimy train station in Krakow and through a tunnel into a huge three-story mall. It has your typical mall babes walking around in the latest styles and many of the same stores found in the U.S. If it weren't for the great Polish food and generous beer steins in the food court, you'd swear you were in Dayton, Ohio, or someplace similar. That's globalization for you.

After two weeks of barnstorming around Central and East Europe, I find the streets of Vienna, Prague and Krakow filled with invaders -- foreign tourists from all around the world. In Prague, I heard more American voices downtown than those of the Czechs. East Europe is the new 'in' place to visit, owing to the (slightly) cheaper prices than France, Britain or Germany.

If anyone needs a break, it's the Poles. The blini-flat plains of Poland made it an ideal platform for invading armies over the centuries -- the Mongols, Tartars, Crusaders, Turks, Vikings, Swedes, Habsburgs, Napoleon, Austro-Hungarian Empire, Nazis and Communists -- all have taken their bite out of this place. It's a wonder there's one brick lying on top of another after all the ransacking that went on here.

But in fact, there are enough palaces, churches, grand plazas and mad statues of sword-swinging heroes in this part of the world to pound the most resolute walker into the pavement.

As was the case in Ireland, I see many people seeking their heritage here, but these are Jews, eager to wander the old Jewish quarters of Prague, Krakow and Hungary. Their's is a bittersweet journey due to the events of the Holocaust, not so long ago.

In Krakow, for instance, the Old Jewish Quarter is filled with the city's finest restaurants and nightspots. At the High Synagogue, I see photos of the happy families who lived here in the 1930s. But the Jews who once lived in this neighborhood are long gone -- 65,000 of them were murdered by the Nazis. Some 3.5 million Jews lived in Poland in the 1930s, but today there are only 200,000.

Krakow was barely a blip on the tourist map until Stephen Spielberg filmed *Schindler's List* here in 1992. That, and the fact that Pope John Paul II served as a cardinal here for 14 years and is considered a saint by the locals. That double-team combo of tragedy and religious celebrity made Krakow the top tourist destination in Poland.

Times have changed: My tour guide in Krakow was born in Russia and grew up thinking communism was the A-OK wave of the future.

"I moved to Lithuania after the Soviet Union fell apart, and now, you see, I am tour guide here in Krakow," Yuri says.

"Do you like it here?"

"It's not so bad, but someday I will move again -- maybe back to Russia."

It's a surprise to me that any expat would want to return to Russia.

"When I was in school, we used to have a special propaganda class that said bad things about the Soviet Union and communism," I tell him, thinking back to my 'current events' class in the seventh grade in the thick of the Cold War. We had study sessions each week, reading from special booklets about how the communists took over Romania, Yugoslavia, Czechoslovakia, Poland, Rumania, East Germany, Hungary... It didn't mean much to us kids, since those places were unimaginably foreign and far away.

"We had class like that too, saying bad things about America," Yuri says. "I was a member of the Young Pioneers and we thought communism was the best system in the world. I still think it's a good thing."

I decide to sidestep a discussion on the dubious merits of Marxism-Leninism, not wanting to be a buzz-killer. If Yuri thinks communism is cool, who am I to step on his opinion?

The Young Pioneers were a kind of Boy Scout group established by Russia's Communist Party -- the first step in grooming the leaders of tomorrow. As we walk around Krakow, we share the bent ideas we learned about each others' countries when we were children. Those were the days of nuclear terror and Mutually-Assured Destruction.

We were 12-year-old enemies then -- friends now.

The Death Camp
Oct. 14, 2007
Auschwitz, Poland

A tour of the Auschwitz concentration camp unfolds like a bad dream. At first, the camp's row-upon-row of brick buildings looks a bit like a college campus -- it seems rather pleasant. But like a nightmare, its horrors are unveiled as you drift deeper and deeper into a tale of insane levels of cruelty beyond imagination.

Located 35 miles southwest of Krakow, the camp is now a national museum and a big tourist destination -- one million people visit Auschwitz each year -- the same number as were exterminated here -- although some believe the number was more like four million.

We've all seen dramatizations of the gas chambers on film, but it's quite another thing to walk through an actual chamber with its gabble of ghostly voices -- a dark bunker of rough cement with a low ceiling -- you look up to see the holes where the SS poured in the Cyclone B insecticide gas that killed people by causing them to suffocate. The chamber I was in was smaller than my newspaper offices back home -- around 1,700 square feet -- yet here, 900 naked Soviet prisoners of war were packed like minced meat for a trial run that led to even bigger chambers being built nearby. These chambers were filled with up to 1,000 people -- 90 percent of whom were Jews.

The camp grows increasingly horrifying -- a room 100 feet long by 30 feet wide is filled with a haystack of women's hair -- some of it still pathetically tied in long braids. The hair was used to make felt cloth and socks... Then there are 40,000 pairs of shoes in another room... A mountain of suitcases that the SS methodically picked through for hidden valuables... A room full of hairbrushes... A pyramid of eyeglasses.

The place that gives me the biggest chill is the clinic where gynecological experiments and surgeries were conducted without anesthetic on 15-year-old girls in an attempt to find an easy method of mass sterilization. The Nazis wanted to find a way to control the racial destiny of conquered nations. There are also hints of the maniac Dr. Josef Mengele, who practiced his evil genetic experiments on children here -- all of the kids were killed after the experiments, if they survived them.

The Death Block reveals its punishment cells -- this dismal building includes starvation cells, torture chambers and cramped 'standing' cells the size of broom closets that were meant to be packed with four men. The Death Wall is at the end of a courtyard where naked men were lined up and shot.

"Did you know anyone who died in Auschwitz?" I ask our guide.

"One of the members of my family died at this wall," she replies, her face tightening. "He was one of four people in my family who died in this camp."

To see these dungeons and the photos of the guards and their dogs lording it over frightened, unsuspecting people is shocking beyond words. It made me feel sick, numb.

Nearby, the 400-acre Birkenau camp presents a bleak plain filled with scores of icy wooden barracks and two huge gas chambers that could kill 60,000 people a day.

At the "place of selection." a wooden platform where the trains emptied after weeks of travel, all mothers with children under the age of 14 were sent straight to the gas chamber. So were the elderly, the handicapped, and pregnant women. Some of the children were burned alive. Only 20 percent of the arrivals were selected to live temporarily for slave labor and slow starvation. The average woman slave weighed 50 lbs., the average man, 90.

The slave workers who occupied these barracks weren't meant to live long. They slept 10 to a bunk, three bunks high, with those on top being the strongest, who secured the warmest spots. Those on the bottom bunk were covered with the shit and piss of those lying higher up.

"Everyone in the camp was covered with the effects of diarrhea which comes from slow starvation," our guide says. The slaves were literally covered with shit and crawling with lice and insects, with no chance to wash.

"Why didn't anyone do anything about Auschwitz while all this was going on?" a woman asks on the bus back to town.

"It's human nature to ignore the problems of others," our guide says. "Look, you toured the camps, but now you will go back to Krakow, have a nice dinner, talk about it a bit and then think about your own problems. But there are people starving right now in Africa, and in Darfur it's like Auschwitz, and what do you do?"

Good point.

About the only good thing I see at Auschwitz is a small wooden gallows on the site of the former Gestapo building. The gallows was used to hang the camp's first commandant when they caught him after the war. It was used just one time, for that one man.

Of the 8,000 Nazis who worked at Auschwitz during the war, only 800 were caught and brought to trial.

Hungary

Welcome to Sunny Hungary
Oct. 14, 2007
Budapest, Hungary

The mountains of eastern Hungary take shape far across the plains in the dawn -- purple-hazy and dreamy in the rising sun. For the first time on this trip, I feel I've arrived at someplace truly foreign. For me, Budapest is the boundary between being an ordinary tourist and taking the next step as a traveler heading around the world.

Sorry, Slovakia, I look at my itinerary and realize there isn't enough time to make a stop. Next time for sure, Bratislava. I see glimpses of you passing in the dark from the overnight train. Wasn't able to get a sleeper car, but fortunately, I secure a dirty narrow bench in second class -- keeping one eye open all night for the infamous train thieves who hop on and off after picking you clean. Not that it was possible to sleep much -- I am frequently awakened by conductors and border guards from Poland, Slovakia and Hungary.

Bang, bang, bang -- "Your pazzport, pleez."

I can well imagine these guards don't want anyone sneakin' into Slovakia! Thus the need for "Pazzport, please..." The newly-prosperous countries of East Europe have problems trying to keep out desperate Ukrainians, Chechens, Georgians and such. They don't want any of these lowlifes scruffing up Slovakia... it's the same story as the Europeans trying to keep out the Muslims and the Americans tied in knots over migrant workers from Mexico.

(Ironically, a couple of months later, Slovakia, Poland, Hungary and several other nations ditch their passport requirements at the border as part of their inclusion in the European Union. This, while the United States has started requiring passports for the first time ever to get in and out of Mexico and Canada.)

It's much warmer here in Budapest, the Land of Goulash, which gets sunshine almost every day of the year. This town on the Danube reminds me of Chicago for reasons I can't put my finger on -- maybe it's because the air feels the same as that of the Windy City. Kind of dirty.

I have another currency to figure out after Czech crowns and Polish zlotys, receiving 17,000 Hungarian forints for $100 U.S. Hmmm, that means 8,500 forints is $50 dollars and 1,700 is $10... you have to get used to figuring the exchange rates on the fly from one country to the next.

In Hot Water...
Oct. 15, 2007
Budapest, Hungary

An old woman in a kerchief chases me around the train station, begging me to stay at her hostel, but I've already decided to reserve a place through the room booking office on the premises. She looks so sad that I feel crushed walking across town to the Marco Polo Hostel. Why didn't I give the old lady a break? Why am I such a rotten rat?

I've learned to take nothing for granted in the hostels. Several times I thought my snoozing roommates were guys, only to discover the next day that they were women. A surprise today, however, is learning that my 14-bed dorm has a co-ed shower, with zero privacy other than the shower curtain. It's one of those kinda' different European things, like corn on pizza.

It's a nice place though, with no screaming teenagers from Denmark to drive you nuts. My dorm is a long room with bunkbeds and a tall cabinet for your stuff at the end of each bed.

Didn't need a shower today because I went to the famous Turkish baths of Budapest. 'Twas a rather odd affair -- they give you a little white cotton apron -- open at the back -- and you walk around bare-ass from thermal pool to pool. The idea is that when you sit on a bench in the sauna or steam room, you turn the apron around and sit on it, and so forth. The old switcheroo.

The main room is an ancient, atmospheric grotto beneath a domed, octagon roof of stone. A dim blue light filters down from colored octagonal windows in the dome, and it feels like you are sashaying in the 16th century, kickin' back with your Magyar buds in the lukewarm pool. Around the pool are smaller pools of varying degrees, the hottest being about 110 F.

The steamroom is smokin' hot, with the steam imbued with eucalyptus -- very nice, but it must be at least 125 F. The dry sauna is something like 150.

The price of the baths includes a full-body nude massage from one of several burly old masseurs; and they will also wash your hair for you. Regrets, I decide to save this pleasure for another lifetime.

The baths are open two days per week each for men and women, and one day for both sexes. Can only imagine the old switcheroo gets kind of interesting on the day when both ladies and men bathe together.

Night Clubbin'
Oct. 16, 2007
Budapest, Hungary

As luck would have it, the Marco Polo Hostel is located above downtown Budapest's most happenin' live music club, the strangely named After Music Club.

Most Europeans prefer giant disco clubs to live music, but after hearing an excruciating disco version of "Africa" by the soft rock band Toto, I crave live music like a horse dreams of oats.

It's a small place and the band tonight is Soulbreak System, which is just two guys up on the stage. The singer is a Hungarian, about 40, and dressed all in black with black tennies and silver chains. Backing him is a guy on kickass keyboards with a drum machine and chest-pounding bass -- nice and loud, the way I like it. The guy sings a blend of emo and goth, very passionate: *"EEEEeeeowww boolamalooogaaaaa!"*

The coolest bars in East Europe are all located underground, with domed, brick ceilings. You feel like you're back in the Dark Ages and it is indeed very cool, my friends... So cool I only wish I'd worn my sunglasses and black beret.

Like with your average Dawn Patrol show (my band), only the best of his very best friends and family members bother to show up. Three guys are videotaping the show and the small crowd is observing with the utmost seriousness, like this is deeply cool stuff we're hearing. I repress a smile, but can't help the twinkle in my eyes, not because I think it's flakey, but because it's great to be here in a local nightclub, hearing a guy pour his heart out in the Magyar language.

Magyar is one of those languages like Finnish or Basque which has no parallel anywhere else in the world. No roots, no connections -- it's not Slavic -- it's just good ole' Magyar. I am able to make myself a bit understood with my college Russian, however, and many people in the 'tourist bubble' here speak English.

***

That night a little guy from India showed up at our hostel dorm room about midnight. He started snoring like he was strangling cats at jet engine volume, and I could tell by the heavy sighs in the dorm that he woke all nine of us up and kept us awake for hours. He looked quite puzzled by our black looks in the morning. The only guy he didn't wake up was the other snorer... And so it goes for the good life here in Budapest.

Egypt

Culture Shock in Cairo
Oct. 17, 2007
Cairo, Egypt

The boot-heel of Italy slips into the sea and I kiss Europe goodbye at 32,000 feet. Soon, the beaches of North Africa appear, and then the long, flat desert of the eastern Sahara; and then the Pyramids themselves, far below on the red sands. Beyond the desert, I cross the Nile and land in a city of nearly 20 million people.

Was a bit flipped out at first -- it's always a bit of a shock whenever you're in a supercity of more than 10 million, I say. But Cairo is at its best today, owing to a torrential downpour this morning -- the cabbie says it only rains three or four times per year, so all of the plants and flowers have popped.

Nonetheless, this is the filthiest city I've ever seen, with grime heavily caked on all the stores and sidewalks, garbage in the streets, and dust blowing up your nose and down your lungs. I'm cheered however, to think that this gradual immersion into grunge will prepare me for even gamier places farther on.

Most of the women on the streets wear the hijab, a scarf which covers the hair and neck, and some wear the full head-to-toe black chador with only an eye slit. These women are called "letterboxes" by some Western travelers because they look like walking post boxes.

Rambling through the filthy streets, I find tumultuous markets and exotic food and hear the muezzin call to prayers for the first time. I find a bustling restaurant, Qom, which seems to be the Denny's of Cairo, and am cheered to have a hearty pizza and a cappuccino for less than $4. After being raped in the wallet in Europe, I can sure get into these lower prices. And who knew that Egypt had such good pizza?

Tomorrow, I plan to just walk the streets for miles through the city with a headful of awe and wonder.

As an American, I had some slight reservations about going to Muslim countries on my trip, but decided to hell with paranoia -- after all, you can't very well travel around the world and avoid Islam at every turn. I'm here as a lone traveler to soak up my own impressions -- not what my government and our twisted media try to sell me. Still, it's a bit of a strain making small talk with the cab driver while my first glimpse of the Muslim world unfolds on the drive into the heart of Cairo. I'm a foreigner here, and I feel it. I feel very small, and alone.

Kickin' in Al Qahira
Oct. 18, 2007
Cairo, Egypt

I'm as inconspicuous as an ostrich, walking around Cairo. I march around for a few hours and am the only Westerner in sight. Where are all the tourists? This is supposed to be one of the biggest tourist attractions on earth, and has been for 5,000 years.

After a visit to the Egyptian Museum, I discover that they are all in tour groups traveling in buses that zip straight back to their hotels. They haven't the luxury of walking the streets and staying on a trash-ridden lane full of plumbing supply shops like the digs of my hotel. I track them to their lair in the Hilton, walking through the lobby and a metal detector to get to the Nile. That's my brush with the tourist world -- they are pretty well insulated against Cairo, except for what they see on the bus.

No one gives me a hard time walking around though, and lots of young people say hi and "Welcome to Egypt." One young guy tags along with me for a mile or so because he wants to practice his English.

"Be careful of the dodgy people who might try to take advantage of you," he warns. "Not everyone is nice, like me."

Yeah, yeah.

But I cringe is when I see a movie theatre playing *The Kingdom*, starring Jamie Foxx as part of a team of scared-silly American FBI agents who shoot it out with some uppity Arabs in Saudi Arabia. Some young men gesture angrily at the movie poster, and I tip-toe on by, unnoticed behind them... I hate that kind of macho shit that feeds xenophobia in America -- and hatred of us overseas.

It's a shock to see people dressed like out of the Bible. I round a corner this morning and here is a young man in a full length robe with the cap of a devotee, accompanied by his girlfriend in a head-to-toe black bedsheet with only her eyes showing through a narrow slit. It's like a scene from the bar in the *Star Wars* movie... The women in black take care to make up their eyes with extravagant care -- it's the only way they can show off their charms.

Later, I learn that especially beautiful women choose to wear the all-black shroud -- even adding gloves -- because they are considered simply too good-looking to be seen in public. Imagine that attitude in America or Europe.

But many women in traditional dress are gathered in front of the store windows full of Western clothes on manikins which are bereft of shawls -- obviously, these are infidel manikins. Also, there are many sexy lingerie shops (what kind of kink goes on under those robes?) and just a jillion shoe stores. This makes sense, since shoes are the only apparel that's allowed to peak out from under their dowdy robes.

The women take care to wear hijabs decorated with bangles and bright colors, but these scarves don't do anything for their looks. Yet there are many young sweethearts showing affection and hugging each other down by the Nile, so Egypt doesn't seem to be prone to all of the nasty hardcore Muslim stuff, like you hear about in Saudi or Afghanistan.

In fact, I walk by a mosque and hear the call to prayers which is issued from a loudspeaker five times a day -- including around 4:30 a.m. Although I don't speak Arabic, I can easily translate the message: "Get your ass to pray-ers, all you sinners and de-vout be-liev-ers!!! It's time to say your p-r-a-y-e-r-s!!!!" I don't see anyone diving towards Mecca in the park next to the mosque, however. Being no fan of organized religion, especially one where people have to be reminded five times a day to say their prayers, I find this ambivalence quite cheering.

I wonder how long this women's cover-up thing will last because the TV here is packed with a great many American shows with Arabic subtitles -- including the likes of *Desperate Housewives*. There are also plenty of sexy hip-hop music videos on the tube. And many of the Western women tourists have a habit of showing off their generous bazzooms in halter tops, which must surely be a scandal here. Perhaps it's no wonder the Muslim radicals are so freaked out about our encroaching culture. Give it 20 years and I'll bet the veil and hijab will be goners.

As for the guys, they are uniformly skinny and dressed in Western t-shirts and jeans. Most look bored out of their skulls, working at menial jobs. My modest hotel must have a staff of 40, with most of the employees moping around without much to do.

Then there's the Tourist Police -- guys in white uniforms and black berets -- many sleeping in their cars on the job -- looking as bored as can be or zoned-out in the 90-degree heat. Funny, but for some reason, all of the metal detectors and guys with submachine guns in the tourist zones aren't making me feel all that safe.

A Friendly Smile

In America, we're taught by the mass media to be scared silly of the impoverished, virtually powerless Muslims. Walking through neighborhoods that few tourists will ever see, I wonder if anyone will hassle an obvious gringo, not to mention an American.

Far from it. Countless people stop to say hello, or "Welcome to

Egypt," with broad smiles. I feel safe just walking around with a smile and a "Hi, how are ya?" as my umbrella.

Many people ask if I'm an "Ozzie," meaning "Aussie," or Australian, those heroic world travelers you find everywhere on earth, especially the scruffy spots where prices are cheap.

"Are you an Ozzie? An Ozzie, yes?"

"No, I'm from northern Michigan in the United States of America," I say, which gets a puzzled response. It turns out that there are few American tourists wandering the streets here, if any, so the people don't seem to know what the "United States" is. "It's America," I say, and they nod. The folks on the street know about America.

What is dangerous here, however, is the murderous traffic. Cairo's streets are mired in a fierce gridlock with hundreds of Fiats and buses fighting to get through the intersections, leaning on a symphony of horns. You just walk straight into the oncoming traffic and weave through the cars. No one seems to be getting run over, however, and the only one I see scooting a bit more than the rest is yours truly.

The Egyptian Museum is an unexpected treat. I expect thousands of dusty old relics, of which there are plenty -- but the entire second floor is given over to the treasures of the boy king, Tutankhamun. The artifacts include golden war chariots, a fleet of model ships to carry Tut through the afterlife, his three golden coffins, and a mask of gold which was placed over the linen wrappings of his embalmed head.

Tut ruled Egypt for about three years, starting in his teens. Some believe he was murdered -- a common occupational hazard for pharaohs, kings and such all through the ages.

The death mask was made as lifelike as possible so that his soul -- *ba* -- would be able to recognize him in the afterlife and help him to become resurrected. Can only imagine that Tut must be rather freaked by now, because all of his servants and goodies are in the museum, yet they left his mummy at his tomb in Luxor, a couple hundred miles south of here. The guy's been in the afterlife for 3,300 years and all of his bling has been blown.

Dingy Dog
Oct. 19, 2007
Cairo, Egypt

Cairo is a whirl of color at night -- tens of thousands of people walk the streets, having a good time. This is a 24-hour city: Men smoke hookah bubble pipes of tobacco flavored with apple and bananas - kids

Making the scene in old Islamic Cairo.

dream at the huge display of dolls in store windows. People dine out on falafel and shish kebab at packed restaurants...

"It's funny, but at this time of night in America, everyone is home watching TV and no one would be out on the streets like this," I say to Esam Abd Elsalam, the leader who will be guiding a group of 11 of us backpackers through Egypt.

"Yes, I found the same thing to be true the time I went to Europe for a visit to Denmark," Esam responds. "No one was out on the streets at night and it felt very lonely and scary. You would never have such a frightening situation in Egypt -- the people all come out at night to visit."

Esam is a guide with Intrepid Travel, a backpacker group that specializes in cultural immersion. You ride on the rickety local buses and cabs, eat in local restaurants where most tourists would never dream of going -- and stay in budget hotels and guest houses favored by the locals.

Esam seems to know everyone in Egypt -- all of the police chiefs, mayors, cops and merchants along the route. Everyone high-fives him wherever he goes. A diving expert from a small town on the Red Sea, Esam is blessed with a welcoming smile and an open face -- good properties to have for putting up with whiny tourists -- bitching about their missing towels and such.

Our party is a snapshot of the backpacking circuit -- people who seem at home almost anywhere on earth:

Jason and Helen are nurses from Massachusetts. Jason is my roommate and has a wry, dry sense of humor and a wandering spirit. Little do I know it, but Jason and Helen will turn out to be among the very few Americans I'll meet from here on through Asia.

Olan (nicknamed Habibi, Arab slang for "baby" or "darling") and Imari are Londoners with ethnic origins in Pakistan and Sri Lanka respectively. They are software specialists in their 20s who have taken time off to travel around the world. So far, they've been all over South America, and are planning to head for Kenya and Tanzania after Egypt. Then, on to Pakistan and other horizons.

Charlotte is a Londoner with a veddy proper British accent, and the ethnic heritage of southern India. She's planning to go skiing in Romania after wrapping up Egypt. Like the other backpackers in our group, Charlotte thinks nothing of skipping from London to south India or Australia.

I find kindred spirits in Steve and Andrea of Melbourne, Australia. Steve is a chef at a posh club that caters to government officials and businessmen, while Andrea is preparing to become a lawyer. Andrea is a tall, green-eyed goddess in the looks department, earning Steve many offers to trade her for "one million camels" (or more) from appreciative Egyptian men.

Steve and Andrea are practically in a state of mourning over the fact that their nine-month trip is half over.

"I can't stand to think about going back, we've been having such a good time," Andrea says. "It's seems like we've just gotten started and now we're halfway done."

"What will you do when you get back?"

"I'm starting a new job at a law firm," she says, adding that she's worked her way through law school as a waitress, which is how she met Steve.

"Well, I can't say that I blame you for not looking forward to that," I say, imagining the notorious hours that lawyers have to work. What a turnaround from nine months of backpacking around the world.

Andrea and Steve have already toured east Europe, motored around France, and are fresh from Morocco, where they spent several days in the Sahara on a camel trek. Like many other backpackers, they've traced a crazy-quilt route across the planet. I can only imagine they've spent a boatload of cash to make the trip, especially considering the Australian dollar is worth only a little over half of a euro. But it turns out that Steve has made a killing in real estate with the sale of a house

-- apparently, the real estate bubble of the early '00s has been percolating even Down Under.

"Where was your favorite stop so far?"

"Turkey," they answer with a single voice.

"We loved it," Steve says. "Especially Cappadocia. It's a place with all of these caves carved into the side of the hills where the people live. Our hotel room was a cave with a beautiful view."

They rave about Turkey's fabulous bus system, with comfy palaces on wheels plying all corners of the country. Their description of the mammoth, multi-level bus station in Istanbul makes it sound like one of the Wonders of the World.

Turkey is a sweet spot for many Australians because it is where the Battle of Gallipoli was fought in December, 1915, which claimed the lives of more than 7,500 of their countrymen. Mostly forgotten by the rest of the world, this battle of World War One was the first major military action for both Australia and New Zealand, which took part in the allied invasion of Turkey. Unfortunately, the incompetence and arrogance of British military leaders resulted in the massacre of the troops from Down Under. The Australians and Kiwis were pinned down on an indefensible beachhead and shot like dogs on a leash. Today, many Australians visit the beach at Anzac near Gallipoli and cry their eyes out over events of nearly 100 years ago.

The anti-war song, "And the Band Played Waltzing Matilda," is about a hopelessly crippled soldier returning from Gallipoli, thankful that no one is there to greet him at the dock in Australia because he is mangled beyond recognition and couldn't stand the shame of being recognized.

Up the Vent Hose

We take the dank Cairo subway and a junker bus to the pyramids at Giza. These are the biggest in Egypt, with the tallest at 450 feet, built for King Cheops as his final resting place.

"It took 20 years to build, and rather than slaves, it was local farmers who built this pyramid in the off season," a local guide says.

"Why would they do that? Didn't that make them slaves?" someone asks.

"No, they were told that if they built the pyramid, they would be able to join King Cheops in the afterlife. For them, it was an honor to build the pyramid, and a chance to live forever."

A long line of tourists crawl into the heart of the second largest pyramid through a 3.5-foot high tunnel -- it's an extremely hot and airless sluice with people gasping for breath all the way. It's a wonder some of the fatsos don't have heart attacks... they probably do, but that sort of thing gets hushed up, just like all the rip-tide drownings at the resorts of Mexico. Oh well, it is a tomb, after all. It's like crawling up the vent hose of a working dryer.

Then we were squeezed like jello through a frosting funnel into another temple, the walls of which serve as a frame for photos of the Sphinx. Riddle me this: why subject yourself to this bit of nastiness when you can see the critter plain as day just outside the temple?

How the Sphinx Lost Its Nose:

The face of the Sphinx is a mess, with its nose chipped away. Yet our guide says its all bunk that the Sphinx was used for target practice by French artillerymen during Napoleon's invasion of Egypt. This was just British propaganda.

What really happened was this: After Alexander the Great conquered Egypt, the country fell into a long period of decline under successive invaders. The Sphinx was neglected and was slowly buried up to its neck in the desert sands.

Gradually, the locals forgot the old gods and drifted into paganism and idolatry. The Sphinx was a frightening presence in the desert outside Cairo and some of the nomads and locals started worshipping it as a god.

This irked the hell out of a Coptic Christian monk. To prove to its worshippers that the Sphinx was not a god, he took a hammer to its nose and defaced the statue. Rather than rousing herself to bite his head off, the Sphinx just sat there and took it.

And that's why the Sphinx needs a makeover today, because another religious busybody couldn't resist taking a stab at someone else's beliefs.

But is this what really happened? Only the Sphinx knows for sure, and she's not talking.

***

I appreciate the pyramids -- 'mighty' is the word that comes to mind, but when all is said and done, they are just a pile of rocks in the desert. Of more interest is walking the backstreets of Egypt at night, seeing the local people out having fun, going to restaurants, talking with their friends -- there's even a wedding party with a loud band playing drums and chanting. Forgetting the dirt and the noise and the oncoming traffic and just trying to fit into the scene -- saying hi: "salaam" -- and thank you: "shukram."

I've become a dingy dog o' the desert -- my only other t-shirt is white cotton and it's as gray as the Cairo smog, earning me weird looks and wrinkled noses from the women in our group. I look for an "I Partied at the Pyramids" t-shirt or something on that order in vain.

By the way -- don't ever get bit by a camel -- those ridden by the touts at the pyramids seem to have wicked tempers and nasty horrible tongues with long, yellow-brown teeth to match...

Getting My Fix:

I duck down a narrow alley just off a pungent fruit market, being careful not to slip on the street-paste of rotting, mashed produce. Here, beyond a battered doorway is where the junkies go, looking for their connection. Their internet connection, that is, and this alley has the good stuff, even if the computers look old enough to have been excavated from a pharaoh's tomb.

This internet cafè has computers which look like tomb artifacts from 1985 and run just as slow as Egyptian dial-up can manage. A dirty vanilla light suffuses the cafè, making even the air seem dingy, and there's the sour stink of sweat in the air with 20 of us webheads packed shoulder-to-shoulder in a narrow room not much wider than a hallway. But it also boasts webcams and Skype, the computer phone service that is the Mr. Goodbar of Backpackerland. Within minutes I'm talking face-to-face with my wife on the other side of the Earth and waving at the kids in her daycare -- from a souk in Cairo! Sure beats sending postcards...

The Kingdom of Nubia
Oct. 21, 2007
Aswan, Egypt

Going downhill in the dark on a camel can be a tricky business, I have found. It's smooth-going on the straight-a-way, especially with the even-tempered sweetie I'm riding. But these boney beasts are all wobbly angles on the downhills, resulting in violent lurches in all directions and my tendency to pitch forward in the saddle.

True, if you fell, it would be on a mattress of sand, but it seems like a long way down. Plus, I'm getting the 'cowboy splits'.

An overnight train carries us 500 miles down the Nile. Morning brings a green, biblical land of date palms, sugar cane, sorghum and donkeys in the fields, with all of the farmers in flowing robes. I'm in the ancient land of Nubia -- also once known as the Kingdom of Kush, where the black Egyptians live.

We take a boat to Elephantine Island across the Nile from Aswan. Once, this isle of waving date palms and mud brick homes was the capital of Nubia and a major trading post for thousands of years. Here, the Egyptians traded for ivory, elephants and other goods from sub-Saharan Africa. My camel hoofs it into the blood of the dying sun toward an ancient monastery silhouetted against the red sands like a vision from *1,001 Arabian Nights.* Allah akbar!

At dark, our camels pull into a village where we are welcomed to a Nubian family's home. It has a big open-air interior courtyard like a hacienda with a sand floor. A matt is rolled down and we sit, eating Bedouin-style with our fingers from dishes of deep-fried fish, chicken, eggplant and veggie stews, chickpea soup and rice. The fish are fried to a black, inedible crisp, drenched in oil. Then a band of locals bursts through the door for a drum-beating singalong. That's the beauty of the group of backpackers I'm with -- it's all about walking the dirt streets and hanging with the locals -- for a price, of course.

Have to admit though, that the 'edge' is off the trip now that I'm with a group and don't have to worry about where I'll stay each night in the Land of the Strange. But I guess I can take a break from being stressed out. Will certainly have that in spades in India, so it's said...

Ugly Vibes

Have decided to avoid the tourist bazaars, because most interactions -- which should be lots of fun, considering you're in a big, colorful market -- are in fact an ugly experience.

"Here sir. Look here, look here, look here!" a hyperactive merchant gesticulates frantically, hoping to divert your attention from something truly interesting.

"Yeah, thanks, but I'm not interested in plaster bust of Pharaoh. I'm just looking."

"No, no, no. Look here my friend. What do you want? A t-shirt? Look, I have many, many shirts." Every shirt in the shop comes flying off the shelves. "What do you want? A camel? Here is a camel, right here on the shirt."

"Whoa! Yeah, I see the shirts -- don't do that -- no need to pull them all out. That's not what I'm looking for, but thanks."

"Why you don't like it? It's a camel."

"It's just not a good design."

"What? It's a t-shirt. It's a camel. You buy it. What price? Name your price."

"No, I just don't like it."

"No, I give you less price. How much do you want to pay? How much?"

You start moonwalking backwards towards the door... muttering that you've got shit for brains, thinking you could enjoy a quiet look around. Even making eye contact is a wrong move inn the market.

There's always a tremendous hassle from salesmen trying to sell you stuff you have no interest in. And the problem with shopping outside the Western world is that showing the slightest bit of interest -- what we call browsing -- means that serious negotiations have begun in the mind of the desperate merchant.

The Egyptian government is currently airing commercials, instructing the merchants not to hassle Western tourists, explaining that they're more likely to buy if they can browse in peace. Thus, many shops have "No Hassle" signs outside their doors. But poor Ahmed and Muhammad can only hold still for so long -- they're like Mexican jumping beans -- and centuries of Arab sales technique kneejerk into gear like an instinctual response, resulting in a perfect storm of hassle, signs or not.

But if you decide to buy, watch out, because every transaction seems to have some element of rip-off. As in the merchant or taxi driver swapping out lesser bills and saying you didn't pay enough, or begging for a 'tip' for selling something at an agreed-upon price, or never, ever having the change. It debases the people selling the stuff and has a habit of turning the buyer into a prick or a patsy, both of which leave bad feelings.

I've learned to insist on seeing my change first and having it in my hand before I pay -- boy, do the merchants hate that too, because it implies that they're dishonest (which they are, for the most part). The funny thing is, I always pay a higher rate than I know I can get because I don't mind spreading the cash around. Anyway, put the bazaar in my 'pet peeve' column.

Resolution: when I go to the souk, it will be with a sense of humor -- a rare and precious commodity in such a place.

Abu Simbel
Oct. 22, 2007
The Sudan Border

Today we got up at 3 a.m. and took a convoy of more than 30 buses to the spectacular Abu Simbel temple, only 30 miles from the Sudan border. The convoy is for safety while crossing the endless dustbin of the desert, which is as devoid of life as Mars.

But what are we being protected from? Jihadists? Sand fleas? Jinja-weed raiders out of Sudan? We pass military checkpoints under the guns of men sitting in towers overlooking the road.

This temple at Abu Simbel was built by Ramses II as a warning to the tribes of Sub-Saharan Africa. Anyone showing up here with an army bent on conquest would get an instant reminder from the colossal statues overlooking the Nile that Egypt is a mighty land -- a place filled with giants ready to smash your puny army like a pack of bugs.

They will cut off your balls, cut off your hands, put out your eyes, and make you slaves.

Engineers from around the world spent 10 years, from 1961-'71, moving this temple block-by-block to higher ground to save it from submersion by the construction of the Aswan Dam. The walls inside are covered with thousands of *bas relief* carvings and paintings of pharaohs, gods, wars, and Queen Nefertiti with her ladies and lovers.

The dam was necessary to control the annual flooding of the Nile which wreaked havoc throughout Egypt for thousands of years. The Brits built an earthen dam when they occupied Egypt, but it was soon rendered obsolete and inadequate.

It's around 95 degrees Fahrenheit here, but not unpleasant. Tomorrow, we set sail down the Nile.

A great lesson is starting to unfold on this trip: the knowledge that I am mostly ignorant of the people of the world -- who they are and what they dream. For instance, I assumed that the Egyptian women would be eager to ditch their Islamic slave clothes and head scarfs at some point, only to find out that more of them are adopting the hijab these days, rather than rejecting it. A generation ago, most Egyptian women didn't wear the hijab or the letterbox drapes, but economic despair has turned many in the country to Islam for the comfort that religion provides in tough times.

I also learn why a woman always walks behind a man in Islamic countries. It's not to degrade her -- it's to protect her modesty, because if she were first in line, the man behind her would ogle her body.

Personally, I sort of like that ogling thing, and it's hard to imagine that much male fantasizing would even be possible here with the gals all draped in bedspreads... but different strokes for different folks.

Like most Westerners, I arrogantly put my values on other people and imagine things about them that are far off the mark. It dawns on me that by the time this trip is over, I will have the blessing of knowing that I am one of the most ignorant persons on earth.

Behold! King Ramses... minus his nose -- perhaps the result of some jealous pharaoh who came after him.

The Nile

Sailing the Nile
Oct. 24, 2007
The Nile, Egypt

With a black Nubian captain in a flowing robe at the tiller of our boat and afro-pop music playing from a boombox at his feet -- not to mention the constant halo of flies around my head -- it finally feels like I'm in Africa as we sail down the Nile. It has the quality of a dream -- slightly unreal.

In contrast to the filthy cities, the riverbank is lush, green and as pleasant as Hawaii. Huge riverboats full of tourists can be found jostling with wooden rowboats of fishermen and their nets. Along the banks, farmers ride donkeys and chip at the fields with hoes, just as they've done for thousands of years.

We spend two days and nights sailing on a felucca, a riverboat about 35 feet long and 12 feet wide, with a triangular lateen sail. We sail with the current, but north against the wind, so Mustafa tacks the whole way, going zig-zag from one shore to the next, about a mile across the river.

The Nile runs for thousands of miles out of black Africa into the 'two kingdoms' of old Egypt. Upper and Lower Egypt ran for more than 600 miles along the river, but the combined kingdom was only a few miles wide. And no wonder, because when we land to make camp one night, the few scraggly small bushes and date palms end about 100 feet from the shore. Beyond them is a stark desert of rocks and sand which runs for more than 3,000 miles to the Atlantic without a single tree or plant, except for the rare oasis.

The deck of the felucca is covered with mats under a canvas shade, and the 12 of us lounge about the whole day, reading, playing games, and watching the river roll by.

No doubt, Queen Nefertiti and King Ramses enjoyed much the same trip, thousands of years ago. I like to speculate that the ancient Egyptians weren't much different than us -- they had their parties, their concerts and promenades around town. Their women fussed with their hair, their jewelry and gowns, making you late for dinner...

***

Even here, far out on the Nile, you can hear the "call to prayer" blasting from a loudspeaker from miles away at 4:30 in the morning -- helpful for alerting the farmers to jump out of bed and face Mecca on their prayer carpets.

In the towns along the river everyone is wearing traditional dress, with all the men in light cotton robes. I'm envious, because my nylon pants are hot as hell in the 90 degree heat and my t-shirt is a masterpiece of grunge. I only have two t-shirts with me, and some of the women on the trip are starting to comment... oh dear.

How nice it would be to don one of those cool bedsheets to keep off the sun and the flies.

***

At night, we camp on the boat drawn up to the shore, snoozing under woolen blankets provided by the crew. We chip a latrine in the hard-pan of the desert and surround it with a makeshift tent. It gets skunky soon enough, aided by all the stomach bugs we've acquired.

My tinny guitar comes in handy -- I play the 'warm-up' show around the campfire and am invited to sit in with the Nubian drum band in a big dance party for five boats.

With everyone dancing around the fire and husky African voices

To the Valley of the Kings: Jason and the donkey.

singing a variation of "She'll Be Comin' Round the Mountain When She Comes - Ah, ya, ya, ya!" I pick out an afro-pop lead and have a once-in-a-lifetime performance thrill. Must make a note though to learn more Bob Marley tunes -- I only know a couple and that's what the Africans want to hear.

I make a stab at "Buffalo soldier -- dreadlock rasta..." but something gets lost in translation and the crew gives me sour, quizzical looks, like I just called someone a sisterfucker or something (a huge insult over thisaway). Maybe the Nubians aren't too keen on the rastas in this land just north of Ethiopia. Fortunately, they're aware that I'm an idiot tourist and I'm soon back in their good graces.

***

Oh yeah, forgot to mention -- virtually everyone on our boat has come down with either diarrhea or the pukes from the different bugs in the food and water here.

Two members of our group are curled up in fetal positions, still suffering the after-effects of being too adventurous with the Egyptian food back in Cairo and Aswan. Even the best meat markets here hang their mutton, beef and chicken out in the scorching sun where it's covered all day long with a carpet of flies... yum.

My bowels were running like the mighty Nile itself the morning we set sail -- only a good deal muddier. Fortunately, my roommate Jason gave me some Imodium, which worked like a charm. Otherwise I would have literally been blowing the pants off my legs and forced to jump in the Nile so as not to embarrass myself. Believe me, when it hits, you can't stop it. It's a runaway train of diarrhea barreling down your colon with no brakes.

Speaking of which, I got to swim in the Nile twice at afternoon stops, trying not to swallow any of its water. A shit soup of bacteria, no doubt, but the Nile had a very clean feeling and left me feeling fresh and strong -- most of the others didn't take the plunge -- their loss! I mean, how many chances do you get to swim in the Nile?

Donkey Love
Oct. 25, 2007
Luxor, Egypt

I do believe that riding a donkey has become my new favorite way of traveling. We mounted up just past dawn and made our way up the high cliffs overlooking the Valley of Kings across the river from Luxor.

Thought I might be too big for my little white sweetheart, but with my feet nearly touching the ground, she carried me uphill around 600 feet for a fine look over sheer cliffs alongside the trail. It's hot enough to bake a rattlesnake on these rocks.

Steve is not so lucky. The cinch on his saddle was loose and he flipped over into the dirt while mounting his beast. He just missed cracking his head on a rock and took a painful bang on the ribs.

Jason was wondering why his donkey demanded to stay directly behind another critter the whole way up the trail. We soon found out when Jason's donkey grew a monstrous ebony erection that was something like 18-24 inches long, waving gaily back and forth like a metronome as we wandered up the trail.

The hopeful donkey's *amour* was just ahead, and he would not budge an inch from her charms.

Needless to say, it amused the whole group and I got a fine picture which Jason agreed could make a nice postcard with a "Having a Good Time -- Wish You Were Here" message.

There's more, but I'll spare you...

***

Down, down, down we went, walking deep into a cleft in the mountains to the heart of the pharaohs' tombs in the Valley of the Kings -- a natural oven that feels radioactive under an intolerable sun.

Luxor was once the ancient city of Thebes, capital of both Upper and Lower Egypt, and 25 kings chose to be buried here in the valley across the river because the mountain above it looks like a natural pyramid. The ancient Egyptians felt that the gods themselves had shaped the crest of the mountain into a pyramid form to show the pharaohs where to place their tombs.

When a new pharaoh took office, work began immediately on his tomb and ended as soon as he kicked the bucket. Thus, some pharaohs have little tombs, because they ruled for only a few years, while others have tombs that go on for hundreds of feet and have hundreds of rooms, such as that of Ramses III -- very impressive digs.

Poor King Tut has a tomb the size of a shoebox by comparison to the others because his reign lasted just three years. His tomb was so insignificant that graverobbers and archeologists walked over its door for thousands of years, never realizing it was at the center of several much larger tombs. Nonetheless, his was the only tomb that escaped being plundered until it was discovered in 1922 by archeologist Howard Carter.

All of these tombs and temples are decorated with thousands of *bas relief* sculptures and incredible paintings of giant Pharaoh, smiting the puny Hittites on his war chariot, or accepting a gift of their chopped-off hands and such. These guys were on the ultimate power trip. Often, when a new pharaoh took over, he sent his goons to the older temples to deface the pictures of his predecessors. Thus, the faces of many sculptures and paintings look like they've been attacked with hundreds of ice picks.

Go Down Egypt
Oct. 26, 2007
Luxor, Egypt

It was all downhill for the Egyptians after Alexander the Great invaded the country in 300 B.C. No more pharaohs - no more grand temples and glory. The new rulers, including Cleopatra, were Greeks. Then came the Romans for 600 years, the Coptic Christians, the Muslims, French, Turks, British...

Esam claims that the Egyptians weren't allowed to join any of the occupying armies until the mid-1800s; they had no weapons and were unable to mount a successful revolt. It wasn't until 1952 that their revolution against King Farouk succeeded and they got their country back.

But for all that time -- more than 2,200 years -- their temples continued to be desecrated and worn away. Such was the fate of the vast Temple of Karnak, which is the largest columnar temple in the world, with 134 columns shaped like papyrus flowers at the top.

Once, this vast building had an 82-foot-high sandstone roof. But the roof was pulled down to build the town of Luxor. And when the temple dikes were destroyed, the Nile filled it many times over to a depth of seven feet, deepening the wreckage. Like most Egyptian temples, it had no protection at all for over 2,000 years.

So, much of Egypt's splendor has been lost, and while the temples you see today are indescribably glorious, still, this country is just a shadow of what it was 'back in the day.'

And of the 250 pharaohs who ruled Egypt over the course of 3,000 years, we have information on only 50.

And so it goes.

The Sinai

Lock & Load
Oct. 27, 2007
The Sinai Peninsula, Egypt

As was the case in Aswan, we roll out of Luxor in a giant convoy of buses, bound for the Red Sea. For the next 100 miles, traffic is blocked at every intersection along the route by local militiamen armed with shotguns, stopping local vehicles to let us pass by at high speed. The convoy is coming!

It turns out that no tourist is allowed to travel out of Luxor or Aswan except by convoy or a guarded train. The terrorist thing... Egypt, after all, was the incubator for the ideas Osama bin Laden hatched when he declared jihad on the Western world.

I regard the upper floor windows in the towns we pass through, speculating that it would be easy to take a shot from such a perch at the buses passing by. But I suppose that if some Islamic militant wanted to waste us, it would be a cinch to plant a roadside bomb instead.

But the idea of the convoy is much older than 21st century terrorism -- it goes back thousands of years to a time when Arabs traveled in caravans through the desert to protect themselves from raiders, ghosts, demons and evil genies.

Then too, not everyone is nice as lamb pie in Egypt: 63 tourists and locals were massacred by radical militants 10 years ago here in Luxor, blowing the tourism scene to smithereens and putting thousands of tourist-dependent Egyptians on desolation's row.

Six members of the terrorist Islamic Group (Al-Gamaa al-Islami-yya) attacked the Temple of Hatshepsut in the Valley of the Queens in the early morning of November 17, 1997. Using automatic weapons and knives, they spent 45 minutes systematically murdering 36 Swiss, 10 Japanese, a family of six Britons, and four Germans, among others. Three Egyptian police officers and a tour guide were also killed.

After fleeing in a hijacked bus and crashing through a police check-point, the killers fled into the desert hills where they apparently killed themselves. Their bodies were found in a cave.

People wondered how the young killers could be so cold-blooded and why they would target such a disparate group: one of the British victims was a five-year-old girl and four of the Japanese couples were on their honeymoons. The killers had apparently trained at Osama bin Laden's camps in Afghanistan and their goal was to destroy Egypt's tourist trade in retaliation for government suppression of a movement called the Islamic Group.

Shock waves shook Egypt to the floor of its tombs after the massacre and thousands were arrested. The tourist police were beefed up and new precautions were established, such as convoys to temples. Today, that sort of craziness is unlikely to happen - knock on wood - because the locals would presumably inform on anyone planning anything cal-culated to blow their livelihood to kingdom come again.

Today, no one can travel anywhere in Egypt without passing through numerous military checkpoints under the gaze of soldiers with auto-matic weapons. And every hotel, museum and store of any size has a metal detector you must pass through (although no one ever checks when you set them off -- they ring constantly, barely meriting a glance from the guards). The Egyptians are prisoners in their own land, held captive by fears of religious fanatics.

A few days later, on the Sinai Peninsula, we are allowed to travel in a solo bus because the stark desert and numerous checkpoints offer protection. Yet, even here, by request of the U.S. and British embassies, the citizens of our countries are supposed to have a police escort. I'm glad that Esam talks the local police chief out of the escort because any lurking terrorist who might want to hit us with an RPG would be able to instantly identify us as a choice target by the police presence.

But this sort of thing is not one of my fears, because no American tourist has been killed in Egypt in 40 years.

Far scarier is the thought of a head-on collision in the insane traffic, or gushing a bucketload in your pants in public as a result of persistent diarrhea. Now that is a scary thought, my friends...

The Red Sea
Oct. 28, 2007
Hurghada, Egypt

It's a good thing Moses was able to part the Red Sea for his people because he spared them a 2.5-hour ferry ride in a barf bucket.

Within five minutes of leaving the port of Hurghada, a young Arab man in the seat behind me is puking his guts out to the hearty laughs of his three friends, who practically roll on the floor with glee. At this point, the boat is hardly rocking. But within half an hour, they aren't laughing any more.. they too are heaving, with their faces a lovely shade of green.

Soon, we're bucking like a mule with a bee up its bum and dozens of people are vomiting into the sea-sickness bags provided. "Hey everyone, we're on the Vomit Comet!" I yell to my mates, who smile... for awhile.

This is the only boat I've ever been on that has seatbelts, and people are literally flying up in the air out of their seats. Fortunately, the crew passed out hits of Dramo as we were getting on, and I wisely took one. When someone offers you something free in Egypt and doesn't ask for any money, you know it's pretty damned serious.

Hurghada, by the way, is the Puerto Vallarta of the Red Sea. I had never heard of it before, but it has miles of restaurants and shops and at least 30 huge hotels catering to the divers who come from all over the world. There's even the ubiquitous Hard Rock Hurghada Cafè, although this seems a rather unlikely spot to find any 'rock' other than in the desert.

In the bustling tourist district I dine at the best seafood restaurant of my life -- a palace piled high with sumptuous fruits of the sea. Dinner is a tomato stew of spiced meat and shrimp baked in an iron pot along with fried giant prawns and filet of sea bass. Elsewhere, there were platters of fish nearly three feet long. Egyptian cuisine certainly is an overlooked commodity.

Hurghada caters to Russians, who are here by the thousands. There is a new prosperity in Russia and its people are flooding the beaches of the Mideast. The Russian women dress delectably trashy, with big bouffant '70s hairdos, six-inch heels, tiny polyester miniskirts and a generous view of the bosom, which tends to be ample. The Russian babes prompt catty comments from the women in our group, but a diplomatic silence on the part of us men.

***

"Bop? Bop? No, it's Bob. Bub? Bub? Okay, Bub, but I prefer Bubby." The Egyptians have as much trouble with my name as the Euros did...

Our band of backpackers spends two days at a resort of rustic palm huts on the Red Sea, snorkeling by day and sitting on carpets and pillows at night under an open-air bar/restaurant, smoking the hubbly-bubbly, drinking Stella beers and playing games. Ahhh... I'm living a dream from the Arabian Nights -- but unfortunately, no harem to round out the illusion.

That evening, I make a shy stab at entertaining with my guitar, and mindful that one must be a performer first and a musician second, I compose a tune called the "Vomit Comet" which goes over well. Alas, the words are lost to the ages.

The Red Sea offers spectacular diving on its reefs, and a group of us snorkel out to view the jeweled fish darting amid the coral. Unfortunately, Charlotte swallows some water from her poorly-fitting snorkel and stands up in a panic. She steps on a sea urchin -- a black pin cushion of spines, six inches long. It's an excruciating walk for her back to shore, where the spines are dissolved using a solution of vinegar, hot water and lemon through several hours of tears. Absent those items, it's said that warm urine works wonders -- just pee right on the wound.

Across the water, the red mountains of Saudi Arabia march above the sands just a few miles away. And down the gulf are the lights of Jordan and its neighbor Israel. It's a perfect beach paradise, but alas, too romantic for a single man, and I feel lonesome for my blond beauty, Jeannette.

Forbidden Love

Speaking of romance, a good price for a bride among the nomadic Bedouins on the Sinai is 10 camels, although many of them have switched to offering jewelry as a dowry.

"When you are born into a Bedouin tribe, your father or uncle picks your bride while you are still a child, and that's it -- there's no disputing the choice," Esam says.

"I had a friend who was a Bedouin from a well-to-do family and he went away to study in Europe, where he fell in love with a Danish girl," he adds. "They planned to get married, but then his father said he had to come home to marry his cousin. So that's what he did."

"What would happen if he disobeyed his father?" I ask, thinking of the tragic Danish beauty, jilted by her desert prince.

"That would be it for him -- the family would never see him again."

There are no Romeo and Juliets in this desert. Disobeying your father's choice is a mortal insult that could get you thrown out of the tribe to wander the desert alone, with all other tribes warned not to help you or even speak to you. The price of forbidden love here is death...

Of course, nowadays, I suppose you'd just hitchhike to Cairo and get on with your life.

Red Sea Blues

Wrote this song sitting on the beach of the Red Sea with the stars just coming out and a red harvest moon coming over the mountains of Saudi Arabia, strummin' on the old guitar. It's a simple song, but says it all.

G C D
When the moon comes over the old Red Sea,
You know I'll be thinking of you.
You can ride your camel through all my dreams,
any old desert will do.

You have golden hair and a golden smile,
and gold is my memory of you.
And I'd trade all the seashells on a Red Sea mile,
just for a moment with you.

CHORUS

C Bm D G
Would you be willing to fly away,
on a magic carpet with me?

You'll be my genie and I'll be your slave,
in a little palm hut by the sea.

Well I saw the twinkle of stars in your eyes,
the cool desert wind in your hair.
And the sand in your toes as we walked a mile
On the shores of the Red Sea, so fair.

When the moon comes over the old Red Sea
I sit on the shore all alone,
Thinking of you, sitting here with me,
Wandering so far from my home.

On Holy Ground
Oct. 30, 2007
The Sinai Peninsula

"And the Lord came down upon mount Si'nai, on the top of the mount. And the Lord called Moses up to the top of the mount; and Moses went up.

And the Lord said unto Moses, Go down, charge the people, lest they break through unto the Lord to gaze, and many of them perish."

-- Exodus 20 & 21

The last 750 steps of the Stairs of Repentance run straight up the crags of Mt. Sinai, but once at the top, you find yourself at one of the holiest spots on earth -- the place where God delivered the 10 Commandments to Moses.

"Isn't this fantastic?" I gush to my fellow backpackers, feeling agog at being in such a holy place. "We're at the same spot where God spoke to Moses!"

They give me quizzical looks, like what's this guy smoking? For them it's just a long, exhausting hike and a pretty view of the mountains tumbling off into the desert.

It's a 4.2 mile hike up the mountain which is the second highest in Egypt at more than 6,000 feet. Camels led by Bedouins wend their way up the mountain trail, bearing tourists who are unable to make the hike.

There was no trail here when Moses made the climb thousands of years ago. Just stark peaks rising from the desert, signifying glory to God in such a desolate wasteland. You can imagine him clawing his way up through the loose rock on his hands and knees, searching for a way up through the cliffs. He must have been bleeding from head to foot and covered with flies by the time he reached the summit. But here, in a state of exhaustion and ecstasy, he spent 40 days and nights communing with God. At least, that's the claim of the book of Exodus.

But, when Moses brought the stone tablets of the Commandments down from the mountain, he found that his people had grown bored and fearful in his absence and had melted their gold to make a golden calf to worship. In a rage, Moses hurled the Commandments at the calf, breaking both the tablets and the idol in his wrath.

Beneath Mt. Sinai is the Monastery of St. Catherine, which was built around the Burning Bush of the Bible. At 1,400 years of age, this is the oldest Christian monastery in the world, hidden deep in the desert of the Sinai Peninsula.

In the Book of Exodus, God spoke to Moses from this bush, ordering him to return to Egypt to confront Pharaoh and demand the release of the chosen people from slavery.

But the monastery is anything but holy today -- it's one of Egypt's biggest tourist attractions, packed with hundreds of people from every land -- Africans in tribal dress, tour groups from India, France and Germany, and most of all, Russians, who come by the thousands to the beach resorts of the Sinai. They're all elbowing each other and shoving in the narrow passageways -- straining to pluck a twig from the willowy Burning Bush. It would be plucked to pieces were it not perched on a wall 10 feet above the grasping crowd. To add insult to injury, we are told that this bush may not be the original, but a stand-in while God's bush is off who-knows-where.

***

One of the recurring themes around the world is the exaltation of religion in every land.

In Europe, the focal point of every city was its cathedral, some of which took hundreds of years to build. Most of them were packed to the rafters with golden relics and paintings of saints and angels the size of barn doors. The emphasis on gold and jewels seems rather hypocritical, considering the hundreds of millions of people who died in pursuit of this glittering gunk.

Then there's Egypt, which is one vast monument to the religions of its past, crammed with temples and tombs covered with thousands of sculptures and paintings of the weird old gods. It's hard to believe that rational people were crazy enough to worship beings with the heads of falcons, jackals, snakes, beetles and an ibis, among others.

But these gods were meant to symbolize our connection to the natural world -- half animal, half human. They represented ideals to be worshipped; and so, even today, a statue of Anubis, the jackal-headed god of the dead and protector of tombs, sits outside the Luxor Police Department... along with an ominous gun-metal green paddy wagon of steel-riveted sheet metal -- that, and some bored cops with submachine guns.

Then there's the Muslim world of today, amazing to an American traveler. Imagine if there were loudspeakers on top of every church in America, and every morning at 4:30 a.m. they began blaring a message five times a day: "Hey everybody -- get up! It's time to say your prayers! It's time to say your p-r-a-y-e-r-s!!!" This, followed by readings from the Bible.

People would flip, yet that's the reality of the daily "call to prayer" of Islam, with readings from the Koran. And in less secular countries than Egypt, failing to toe the line can get you busted by the religious police, with a month in jail, or worse.

But back to the Sinai. On the beach by the Red Sea, I can see the shores of Saudi Arabia across the gulf. Down the way are the lights of Aqaba, Jordan, just east of Eilat, Israel.

These countries all coexist peacefully, but not because they are at the heart of holy ground and three great religions: Christianity, Islam and Judaism. It's because tearing each other limb-from-limb these days would mean nuclear annihilation from Israel's atomic weapons.

Strange, isn't it, that religion teaches brotherly love, yet is the fountainhead of so much hatred in the world. Perhaps Moses set the mold here at Mt. Sinai when in his own frenzy of intolerance, he threw the 10 Commandments at someone else's object of worship.

The Price of Pee
Oct. 31, 2007
Cairo, Egypt

The average Egyptian makes between $60 and $70 per month.

If you wish to buy a donkey in Egypt, it will set you back $100 -- a lot of money for a farmer, but an absolute necessity to carry his goods to market.

A camel costs much more -- about $800, though you can get one cheaper if you make the long trip to Sudan, south of Egypt, and make a deal with the Nubians. Cheaper still if you ride it 40 days back home through the desert.

But, if you desire a racing camel, it will run you $20,000 or more.

Conservatives back home will be pleased to know that there is no free ride for the poor in the Old World. For instance, you are charged a fee to pee everywhere from Ireland to Egypt. It cost me $3 to use the bathroom in the Munich train station, but happily only about 20 cents per visit here in Egypt.

In all, I've probably spent more than $100 on visits to grotty, nasty bathrooms during my trip so far and have the dubious honor of knowing the location of most of the stinkiest public pissers in most of Europe's greatest cities.

And you simply can't sneak a pee here -- there's always an attendant outside the door, loudly demanding the fee with an outstretched hand, even if the john is a filthy, broken wreck that hasn't been cleaned since Methuselah was a kid. Even the 'free' bathrooms in hotels and bus stops require 'baksheesh,' which I've come to understand is a measure of respect for the attendant -- whether he's doing his job or not.

***

Speaking of money, it's a beggar's banquet for me here in Egypt, where a cup of yechy Nescafè instant coffee is about $1, and slightly more for the sludgey, syrupy Turkish coffee served in espresso cups. A big dinner runs about $6, last night being rice with potatoes, zucchini and lentil casseroles, 'kofta' spiced sausages, a delicious lamb shish kebab and shanks of lamb, bread, drinks and salad.

Lunch today is a delicious baked pasta with minced meat and tomato sauce and a Pepsi, all for $1. Am I obsessing about food too much in this blog? Forgive me, it's a backpacker thing.

At the start of this trip, I gave myself a budget of $66 per day -- I often spent more in the cities of Europe, but am now spending less than half that amount, and expect it will be so for the rest of the trip.

Garbage City

Garbage City is a village of several thousand people who sift through the Cairo dump and recycle the cast-offs of millions.

We drove through the quarter with our windows rolled up tight against its ripe aroma and saw hundreds of haystack-sized bags of garbage in one state of sorting or another. At a gift cooperative, the residents make handmade paper, clothing, handbags and artwork from recycled materials.

"God, it stinks here," says Sara, one of our party.

"Yes, that is why we keep the windows rolled up, even when it is so hot outside," Esam says. "Don't open your mouth when you get out of the car."

Sara gives him a quizzical look.

"The flies," he says. "They will get in your mouth."

Damn right. There's a perfect blizzard of flies to wade through when we exit the mini-bus, all buzzing with the manic energy that insects take on when the temperatures rise above 90 degrees.

"You might think these are poor people, but that is not true," Esam says of the hundreds of people combing through shipments of trash. "They are actually fairly well-off, compared to most people living in Cairo. They make a good living recycling the trash."

If you call this living, I think to myself, flailing at my halo.

***

At the vast Muhammad Ali Mosque in the heart of Cairo I take off my shoes and marvel at the intricacies of Islam (well, sort of). Despite all the paranoia pumped out of the U.S. media, even infidels are welcome to walk around Islamic mosques, assuming there are no prayers in progress.

Unlike Christian cathedrals, there are no paintings of saints, angels or Allah in the mosques because Muhammad gave the thumbs-down to images 1,200 years ago to differentiate his religion from the idolators who were rife in the deserts and towns of Arabia. So the mosque is decorated with various curlicues and geometric patterns. This is a bit of a shame because one can only imagine the Koran would be filled with marvelous scenes worthy of illustration.

"Do you know the meaning of Ramadan, the month of fasting from sunrise to sunset?" Esam asks. "It's to remind people of the plight of the poor, and what it's like to go to bed each night hungry. At the end of Ramadan, everybody makes a gift to the poor."

"It's a custom we would do well to adopt in America," I say, although I'm not sure the poor are venerated any more in the Muslim lands than they are back home, where they tend to be reviled, if anything.

***

The dust of centuries settles on you, walking through old Islamic Cairo and tramping down the long alleys of a vast market that many tourists never see. This quarter of Cairo is filled with enchanting scenes of ancient gates and 500-year-old buildings, castle walls and mosques -- people waving censors of incense, chickens waiting for their heads to get cut off, women shopping for their bridal garb... it's a place out of the visions of Aladdin or Ali Baba -- you imagine yourself in the same scene here 1,000 years ago.

Then comes a vast tourist market, perhaps half a mile long and a quarter mile wide, with every wonder of jewelry, musical instruments, leather goods, metal lanterns, headdresses, Eyes of Horus, t-shirts --

fabulous tourist junk, perfect for a sucker like me. I order one of each item in the market -- well, not really -- but I do pick out an expensive belly dance outfit for Jeannette to go with a silver ring, various ankhs, scarves and other tourist doodads... Simply must find a way to ship all this stuff home tomorrow before I head East.

On that score, I get a bit of a shock the next morning. After going to great lengths to find an outlet for the DHL shipping company in Cairo and undergoing all the hassle of inspecting and wrapping a 10-pound bag of presents to mail home, I am presented with the bill: $360 U.S.!

Fuggeddabouddit... I do some creative repackaging of my gear and stuff the equivalent of a grocery sack full of goodies into my already full pack.

A final image of Cairo: on my last early morning walk I learn that an attempt is made to clean the filthy streets here, spotting a cadre of old ladies with switch brooms attacking the sidewalks. But it's mostly just sweeping the dust, grime and gook from one spot to another.

Speaking of which, I'm off to another strange place...
Salaam alukah!

The Garden of Eden

In the Garden of Eden
Nov. 1, 2007
Kingdom of Bahrain

"And the Lord God planted a garden eastward in E'den; and there he put the man whom he had formed.

And out of the ground made the Lord God to grow every tree that is pleasant to the sight, and good for food; the tree of life also in the midst of the garden and the tree of knowledge of good and evil."

-- Genesis 8-9

My trip around the world takes an unexpected turn to the land of Adam and Eve. The Kingdom of Bahrain is a small island which biblical scholars claim was the historical site of the Garden of Eden.

The original inhabitants wouldn't recognize the place from Adam these days. Located south of Kuwait in the Persian Gulf, just off the coast of Saudi Arabia, this desert isle bubbles with oil money. Somewhere, Satan is smiling.

Flying in from Cairo, I get a taste of how it must feel for a Muslim traveling through the States. I wonder if I'll be a victim of racial profiling -- the only Yank in the airport. Will they suspect me of being a terrorist CIA agent? Just spoofing, but I do stick out like a purple giraffe and catch a number of folks checking me out -- shy ladies peering through their veils, little kids and wealthy looking sheik types darting suspicious glances my way. With my long braided hair and guitar, I must look as odd to them as they to me.

I fly in at close to midnight without a clue as to where I will stay on my overnight layover in an Arab country. No worries, sahib -- Gulf Air puts me up free of charge in a swanky suite downtown, with transportation, a dinner buffet and breakfast to boot. All free. This is a backpackers's dream -- the Big Rock Candy Mountain, without the cigarette trees and whisky creek, of course.

But first I skedaddle downtown as fast as my heels can fly to check out Arab Central. Many of the men are walking around in full-blown sheik outfits with coiled rope headbands over their robes. There aren't many women in sight, but there were plenty at the airport in head-to-toe black chadors of fine silk. Very rich looking, these gals, and some have beautiful eyes. Funny, but a woman wrapped in a bedsheet can look quite beautiful if she only has her eyes to work with... What would they be like on a date?

And what a hoot! Downtown, you walk past every depressing fast food joint known to man: Burger King, McDonald's, Popeye's Chicken, Subway, Papa John's Pizza, Pizza Hut, Baskin Robbins, Hardee's, KFC -- each one with guys dressed like Prince Saud sitting in the window enjoying their deep-fried chicken planks, or whatever. There's the usual Hard Rock and several discos defiling the Land of the Prophet.

At 5 a.m. the next morning I see several young princes stumbling out of a hotel disco next door, calling out drunken salutations and looking shit-faced. "Hey, Ahmed my friend! Whazzup?!? Boy, bring my Beemer."

Bahrain, you see, oozes money as a consequence of all the Texas tea and sheik's pee beneath its sands. On the palm tree-lined causeway into town, huge TV screens serve as billboards. And although not as stunning as the skyscrapers of Dubai, the architecture of this town runs a close second, with buildings that sweep like the wings of a bird of paradise along the Persian Gulf. This lively architecture gives me a wistful thought that America is falling behind the Arab world, the Russians, the Chinese... our best was the Twin Towers -- not all that inspiring to begin with, looking like elongated shoe boxes -- and they of course, are gone, thanks to some of Bahrain's neighbors.

The wealth isn't shared with everyone though. On the way back to the airport, I meet Thomas, a mechanic of Chinese descent from the Philippines, who's en route to work on heavy trucks in the city of Jeddah in Saudi Arabia.

Thomas is here for the money, such as it is. He works six days a week for $500 per month on a three-year contract to support his family back home in Manilla. He sees his family once every three years for 30 days.

"Why don't you just get a job in the Philippines? Wouldn't you save money on traveling?" I ask.

"No -- the Saudis pay my expenses and for the plane," Thomas says. "In the Philippines I can only make $350 a month for the same job. It's not enough money to give my children a good life and an education.

"It's not so bad here, though," he adds. "I watch DVDs and talk to my wife on the internet. I like watching movies. But you should not go to Jeddah," he nods at my guitar. "They are very conservative there, and they wouldn't like that."

I can well imagine the cranky Islamists of Saudi Arabia wouldn't want a rock & roll rebel like me prowling around Jeddah, poisoning the minds of the youth with my subversive protest songs and wild acoustic guitar playing. Fortunately, I have no plans to go. Plus, it's nut-busting hot there. I can only imagine it's a prison inmate's life for Thomas, spending three years at a stretch in such a constrictive hellhole.

***

One last thing about Bahrain. When God kicked Adam and Eve out of Eden, he must have laid a curse on this place for all time, making the local internet connection as slow as the creature which crawls the earth without any legs. And we're not talking about that dastardly serpent here -- we mean the snail.

The Family Feud

Just a stone's throw from Bahrain is Saudi Arabia, while across the gulf lies Iraq, both of which are key players in a family feud that started more than 1,400 years ago...

Imagine an infant born in 569 in old Arabia. Since his father had died a few months earlier, he was given to a Bedouin foster mother to be raised as a nomad in the desert. She died when he was six. Passed from one poor relative to another, young Muhammad began to earn his own living at the age of eight as a shepherd. By age 10, he journeyed in a camel caravan to Syria with his uncle. It was the start of his career as a merchant. He soon became known for his honesty, charisma and kindness.

At the time, Arabia was a desert land of pagans and idolators. No one knows much about Muhammad's religious beliefs until he was about 35 years old, but it's said that he never worshipped idols. He was reportedly kind to orphans, the poor, and widows in need. Like his grandfather, he spent the entire month of Ramadan in a cave in the Mountain of Light, fasting, praying and meditating on the problems of life in Arabia. He shared what little food he had with people passing by.

At the age of 40, about five years into his yearly retreat, the Archangel Gabriel visited Muhammad and said that God (Allah) had chosen him to be his messenger to all mankind. Over the next 23 years, Muhammad received messages from God through Gabriel which he wrote down in a holy book called the Qur'an.

Allah told Muhammad to call his religion Islam, which means "submission to the will of God." The new religion would have two themes: harmony between the material world and the soul; and that all believers would be equals without any regard for class, race or country.

He started preaching secretly at first to friends and members of his own tribe, and then openly in cities such as Mecca. But even pagans don't like others stepping on their beliefs, and Muhammad's followers were considered a threat to the status quo. Soon, the followers of the Prophet were tortured and persecuted -- stretched on burning sands in shackles and branded with blazing irons. Muhammad advised his followers to flee Mecca and he moved his act to the city of Medina. But this only made the sheiks of Mecca angrier.

Among his many adventures, Muhammad had a vision that he was lifted to heaven for a visit with Allah. He and Gabriel toured heaven and hell, visiting the prophets Abraham, Moses and Jesus. He returned from this ascension with a divine gift: a prayer called the "salaat" which offers communion between the human race and God.

Through all this, Muhammad and his growing band of followers were terrorized by the rulers of Mecca. Over the course of 10 years, there were many battles throughout Arabia. Unlike the religions of Jesus or Buddha, the birth of Islam was marked by the flash of scimitars, charging camels, rivers of blood and the siege of sandstone castles. Eventually, Muhammad and his followers triumphed, conquering Mecca, unifying Arabia, and converting many pagans, Christians and Jews to Islam with a like-it-or-lump-it offer that few could refuse.

Here's what the Prophet Muhammad said he believed in, delivered in a famous sermon to 140,000 of his followers in his *hajj*, or pilgrimage to Mecca:

"Belief in One God without images or symbols; equality of all the Believers without distinction of race or class, the superiority of individuals being based solely on piety; sanctity of life, property and honor; abolition of interest, and of vendettas and private justice; better treatment of women; obligatory inheritance and distribution of the property of deceased persons among near relatives of both sexes; and removal of the possibility of the cumulation of wealth in the hands of the few."

Muhammad left the earth in 632 at the age of 63, happy in the knowledge that he had created a progressive, enlightened religion that worshipped one God. In those medieval times, mixing religion with government produced a well-organized society out of the chaos of tribal Arabia.

But things quickly fell apart after Muhammad's death. A group of Muslims who called themselves Sunnis believed that Muhammad's rightful successor was his best friend, Abu Bakr, who was elected to the post by Muslim leaders. Another group, who called themselves the Shia, believed that the leadership of Islam belonged to the Prophet's descendents, beginning with his cousin and son-in-law Ali.

Those religious differences grew through 1,400 years of doctrinaire squabbles.

That's why today, the Sunnis and Shiites of Iraq kidnap and terrorize each other with death squads. It's why they use electric drills on their captives and carve religious slogans on their bodies before dumping them into the streets to be found by their horrified families. It's what all the beheadings and car bombings and riots over cartoons are about: because 1,400 years ago, people couldn't agree on whether Muhammad's best friend should take over the family business or whether his son-in-law should get the job.

Some religion, huh?

This rundown on the life of the Prophet Muhammad is adapted from a piece by Muhammad Hamidullah, writing in Paris, 1969.

He made the following points about Muhammad, Buddha, Jesus and Moses, who tried to reform the world only to see their good work perverted by their followers:

"Two points are to note," wrote Hamidullah. "Firstly, these reformers claimed in general to be the bearers each of a divine mission, and they left behind them sacred books incorporating codes of life for the guidance of their peoples. Secondly, there followed fratricidal wars, and massacres and genocides became the order of the day, causing more or less a complete loss of these divine messages."

Bombay

The Shores of India
Nov. 3, 2007
Bombay, India

India, at last. That legendary land which is the quintessence of all things exotic and foreign, like an unexpected green god who turns up at the dinner table with eight arms and glittering ruby eyes -- Shiva, with his necklace of skulls -- performing the dance that created the universe.

It's a place reputed to be almost supernatural in its strangeness. All my life I've dreamed of coming here, believing that you can't really call yourself a traveler until you have this jewel in your crown. When I first started traveling as a young man, this was the ultimate destination -- the end of the long trail through the world.

My first sight of India is that of a towering cloud bank over the coast, rising eight miles high or so in brilliant white with a wide cloud top that gives the appearance of a flat roof over a vast temple. Then, from my jet window, I see a rainbow plunging into green canyons and mountains that run far out of sight. These certainly seem to be auspicious signs...

Then, rearing up from the green comes a forest of hundreds of rotting high rise apartments -- streaked diarrhea brown and smoggy gray -- with the earth rushing up to reveal people scrambling by the thousands on the streets below and a landslide of slums tumbling for miles past the airport. This is Bombay, baby -- or Mumbai, if you like -- one of the biggest cities in the world.

20 million? 40 million? Know one seems to know how many people live in Bombay, aka Mumbai.

The Baby in the Street
Nov. 3, 2007
Bombay, India

The first thing I see as my taxi rounds the corner from the airport is a baby crawling just a foot from the curb of a five-lane highway where thousands of three-wheeled tuk-tuks and old beater Fiat taxis stampede in a mad rush.

The baby's family is chatting on the sidewalk; their ramshackle home, built of old junk, spills to the edge of the curb like a tipped-over trash can. No one is paying the baby a lick of attention as we speed by, but it looks happy enough, crawling around in the grime.

I practically jump out of my skin on the hour-long ride into town. The sensory overload of sight, sounds and smells seems almost too much to bear. The route looks like it's been through an aerial bombardment, with people lounging without a care in the filth and trash lining the tin roofs of their homes and along the crumbling sidewalks.

But these are some of the better homes, because soon there are warrens of slums with kids running naked through dirt lanes, and then the homeless street people, propped up against weary old walls with all their possessions spread out on the sidewalk. There looks to be thousands of these folks, bedding down for the night on the sticky, black sidewalks. I see toddlers playing in the street who can't be more than four years old, jumping around amid the reckless traffic that rips past in a river of rolling metal.

And there are no traffic rules here, by the way -- we run red lights and blast through intersections in a game of 'chicken' that's standard operating procedure here. As in Cairo, lane dividers and traffic lights are meaningless.

Being a rookie here, I've opted not to stay at an $8 per night guesthouse out in the urban boondocks because I think the lower end of Bombay might be a bit overwhelming. Instead, I'm roosting at a three-star hotel, tucked into a side street in the Fort district.

Yet even here, there are people sleeping on the street just outside the door. Here in the gathering darkness is a young mother, as thin as a beggar's chicken with the look of a kicked dog in her eyes. At her feet are her two daughters, a baby and a three-year-old, sleeping on rags and a mat of cardboard. It pierces my heart, knowing that they are the same age as my granddaughters.

Determined to eat as little meat as possible (on the advice of some Indian travelers), I find an all-veg restaurant and have a meal of curried veggies and ginger-garlic rice for about $2.50 -- the price of a cup of coffee back home.

Outside, I give a coin to an old man in rags and he offers me a blessing. I perceive that he is some kind of monk or guru. He scrutinizes the coin and makes a bow with clasped hands and beams with a pure inner fire, his eyes lighting up with an incandescent spirit. For a moment I bathe in his brilliant inner light.

"Thanks," I mumble. "Have a good one." Turning, I walk off into the darkness.

Land of the Helpful Harrys
Nov. 4, 2007
Bombay, India

There's nothing like getting lost on the streets of old Bombay at night to make a chap feel electrifyingly alive -- especially when it a pounding downpour unloads just when you're at the point of despair.

I walk the streets from dawn to way past dark, joining the throng of millions. How many people, no one seems to know. Officially, Bombay has a population of 15 million, but one restaurateur tells me there are an additional 25 million undocumented residents for a total of 40 million.

For decades, the poor farmers of India have been fleeing to the cities to escape the chains of debt that bind generations of families. Currently, there's a suicide epidemic among the farmers in India who despair of drought and debt -- tens of thousands have killed themselves by drinking pesticide. It's said to be a horrible death -- rips your guts out. Others simply drop everything and flee with their families to live on the streets of Bombay, Calcutta or Delhi.

Built on what is literally a landfill, this town has been passed around for centuries, starting with Hindu fishermen who fished a small archipelago of islands 1,000 years ago, then their Muslim conquerors who ceded the port to the Portuguese. The Portuguese named it Bom Bahia or "Good Bay," and then gave it to the British as part of the dowry of Catherine of Braganza, who married Charles II in 1662. Today, it has been renamed Mumbai after an age-old tribal goddess named Mombadevi.

My exploration of Bombay includes making the night scene at Chowpatty Beach for a mango *lahsi*, India's popular yogurt drink. There must be at least 10,000 people gathered on the beach in the dark, bathed in the sherbet pink and orange light radiating from the huts of a dozen food vendors. I saw the so-so Gate of India, a much-touted arch on the waterfront built to honor the visit of King George V in 1911. It was here on the Apollo Bunder dock that tens of thousands of British soldiers and merchants arrived to plunder India over the centuries. I also poked around Elephanta Island, checking out the temples, and marched around the labyrinth of the Crawford Market.

It's a bit spooky getting lost after dark in the tangle of streets between Chowpatty Beach and my hotel in an alley behind Bombay Hospital. I feel lost in a bee hive or an ant hill, teeming with endless unwinding coils of people. Surely, Edgar Allan Poe would have appreciated the horror of being buried alive in all of these people, I think, wandering past a train station which buzzes with humanity. The nuclear sun going down behind the station casts thousands of commuters in a searing backlight, rendering their bodies indistinct in shades of brown and red, like a vision of souls percolating in hell. The buzz, the hive, the endless faces and limbs and the skitter of bodies in the dark, seem almost overwhelming to a small-town boy like me.

I manage to find what must be the only lonely stretch of road in the entire city -- it's completely dark and a seems like a great place to get jumped. It takes me hours of wandering a labyrinth of streets, alleys and paths before finding my hotel in the rain. I feel as if I'm swimming through a river of people flitting past one-another in the darkness. I try to wave down the stream of taxis passing by in the rain, but no one stops.

The trip across the city includes walking past many homeless people making their dinners on the street, who give me a cheery hello. Some of these folks are covered head to foot in dirt, but they manage to look pretty happy, just sitting on the sidewalk, making a new life in the big city.

I should sleep with them on the street, if only to exercise my half-assed credentials as a journalist. Jack London did as much during his *Down And Out* days of living in the ghettos of the East End in London. But I don't get it together to make it happen. Also, I suspect that I'd have to stay awake the entire night, since the word would soon be telegraphed that a wealthy Westerner was camping out. There's a thin line between being an adventurer and a fool.

For the most part, I'm the only Westerner on these crowded streets. I take few photos because I'm intimidated by the human tide coming at me from all directions and am mindful that I may be a target for pickpockets in these crowded streets. Plus, it's hard to take photos when everyone's looking at you -- hundreds of eyes sweep over me, wondering, perhaps, why the tall Anglo is walking far off the tourist track.

By the way, my sincere apologies to Cairo for calling it filthy. That immaculate jewel of Egypt is spic and span compared to Bombay. There are no trash cans anywhere here, not even in Colaba, the "classy" tourist part of town. Even Elephanta Island, one of Bombay's premier tourist attractions, is strewn with trash as a result of the prevailing attitude: people just toss litter wherever they happen to be standing, creating a patina of grimy trash, excrement, urine and sticky gunk, cooking in the dense smog and 90-degree heat.

The Indians are meticulous about their hygiene and clothing, but don't seem to give a damn about what happens beyond the confines of their own bodies (India's intellectuals have puzzled over the fact that there is no civic spirit of public cleanliness here, according to journalist Suketu Mehta in his book, *Maximum City*). Besides, it would be pointless to have trash cans, because millions of homeless people would just tip them over to grub for scraps. As a result, everyone just throws their trash into the street.

The next morning, you might see some little old lady out cleaning up the mess with a willow broom -- perhaps the only thing that keeps India from disappearing beneath an ocean of trash.

I'm starting to look past the filth, however; Egypt was a good warmup and I don't feel as flipped out as I expected. I've heard stories of backpackers being paralyzed with temporary agoraphobia by India's overwhelming freakout -- they stay locked in their hotel rooms, afraid to hit the streets. Maybe I'm tougher than I thought, I think with some satisfaction. After awhile, you just block it out -- I'm sure the Indians don't even see the trash they're wading through.

***

A couple of times I put my ugly face on to say, "What are yew lookin' at?" when some punk stares at me too long. Said this to some kid sniffing a vaporous substance like gas or glue at a cricket match and he responded with some hostile stoned babble, with a crowd of his teenage mates looking on in amusement. After awhile, it occurs to me that it might be a cool idea to get back in the fold of the 'tourist bubble' where I'm not such an oddity.

But having spent my college days living in Detroit's inner city, I'm somewhat immune to the more intimidating side of Bombay. It's a big dump, but not what I'd call scary.

Safety is a concern for any traveler, especially if you're alone in a country where you don't speak the language. If you get into trouble, you're sure to be considered a pain in the ass by the local constables. Basically, you're on your own.

Common sense and a healthy streak of skepticism are the traveler's best defense against assault and a plethora of con games.

For instance, my friend Jim Hanson made the mistake of getting buzzed on wine and walking around the streets of Rome late at night some years ago as a 19-year-old backpacker. Someone hit him over the head from behind with a wine bottle and left him bleeding in the gutter. Jim woke up in a pool of blood with his pack, passport and all of his money stolen. He had a terrible time getting home to the States.

In Nicaragua of this year, I talked to a college-aged American backpacker who made the mistake of opening his pack in the notorious

Managua bus station to find some change to tip a cab driver. "All of a sudden, everyone in the station swarmed me and stole everything in my pack," he said. "I couldn't do anything to stop them. I had most of my money in my pack and they got it all, along with all of my other stuff."

Fortunately, he had friends in-country who were able to bail him out.

I too have been a victim of my own carelessness. While returning from a day of hiking around the Moorish fortress of Sintra in Portugal in the early '90s, I got on a crowded subway car in Lisbon. The car was packed, but I was still too busy rhapsodizing over the beauty of the favorite haunt of the poet Lord Byron to take much notice of my surroundings.

Wedged in like a cigarette in a full pack on the subway car, I suddenly felt hands restraining my arms, with other hands going through my pockets. "Hey, someone's trying to rip me off!" I yelled, but none of the miserable subway riders took action, even though I'm sure they could easily translate my distress into Portuguese. For them it was just another 'shit happens' moment on the Lisbon tube.

Not knowing what to do, I got off at the next station and cradled my head in my hands on a bench. Oh fucking hell! -- surely Lord Byron would have said the same thing -- my passport and train ticket were gone, although I still had my money belt and all of my cash under my pants. What would I do? I knew it was horrendously difficult to replace a passport overseas and there was no way of crossing any border without it.

A few minutes later, a kid in his early teens sauntered around the corner of the underground station and handed me my passport. "Obrigado, obrigado," I mumbled. Five minutes after that, he returned and gave me my train ticket -- the teenage gang of pickpockets had decided that my ticket and passport were of no use to them and took pity on a lone traveler. For their kindness, I pulled a bill from hiding and gave them the equivalent of $15 U.S.

On another occasion, while bumming around Europe in my teens, I was attempting (unsuccessfully) to catch the ferry from Palermo, Sicily to Tunisia in North Africa when I met a beautiful young gypsy girl at the ticket office.

"Can you help me?" she said. "I'm here all alone with nowhere to stay until my father and uncle arrive on the boat tomorrow. Could you stay with me on the beach tonight? I'm afraid to be by myself."

She was a dark-eyed beauty with long, sleek hair, about 15 years old, and I thought with horror of this vulnerable girl cowering on the beach alone that night. Palermo was a sinister place, full of sleazy young *mafioso* types lounging on every street corner. Stone greaseballs who gave me the evil eye and a curling lip at every turn. But I had already bought a train ticket on my way back to Italy and wasn't anxious to hang around Palermo. Owing to my long hair and ratty torn jeans, the ferry officials had denied me passage to Tunisia unless I paid a $50 deposit, and I didn't have the money to spare. I barely had enough left to make it across the continent to the airport in Luxembourg. With my heart breaking with regret, I begged off and caught the train.

I always wondered whatever happened to that poor girl at the ferry terminal, torturing myself that I hadn't been her Sir Galahad and imagining that she got raped on the beach. It wasn't until many years later that I realized that it had all been a setup. Of course it had -- no family from her culture would have let such a treasure wander around Palermo on her own. More likely, she was the bait for a naive young American backpacker, with the reward being a good shit-kicking and a robbery down on the beach that night.

Since then, I've come to realize that anytime a stranger asks me for help in a foreign land with some tale of desperation, it's probably a con game. Would I ask a Japanese or French tourist for help if I were in a jam back home? Of course not -- I'd seek help from my friends and family. The same logic applies overseas.

Another strategy for safety that I learned from my days as a student in Detroit is looking over my shoulder every 100 feet when I'm in a risky neighborhood. Turning around and taking a good look identifies anyone who may be following you and puts them on notice that you've got their number. Or, lets you know it's time to run...

It's a habit I put to use while wandering the streets of Bombay late at night; but I'm cheered to find that no one seems the least bit interested in giving me a hard time.

***

I read two depressing bestsellers on Bombay to prepare for the trip: *Shantaram* by Gregory David Roberts and *Maximum City*. Both authors went on and on about how this city is crawling with gangsters, pimps, whores, murderers, bombers, religious fanatics (ie. Hindu nuts who will gladly set you on fire with a can of gasoline if you're a Muslim), and hit men who hire out for $5 or less. But both authors also swore they love this place, saying there's nothing so grand as lively old Bombay.

Personally, I think there's nothing more butt-ugly than crummy old Bombay, but that honor, I've heard, goes to Delhi, up north of here.

And far from gangsters, I've found that this is the land of the Helpful

Harry.

I was walking down the street yesterday when some guy came up to me and said, "Excuse me sir -- there's a wasp in your ear."

"Wasp?"

"Yes, wasp, I help."

Oh my God -- I've heard of bugs crawling in your ear and this is the buggy tropics. Is it possible there's a tiny wasp in my ear? But it turns out this guy was saying there's "wax in your ear" and wanted to dig it out with a metal sliver. He actually stuck the thing in my ear.

What the fuck! "Get the hell away from me!" I yelled, fleeing down the street. But I soon perceived that earwax removers are an honorable profession in India, and other people were having the procedure done on the sidewalk. He was just being a Helpful Harry.

"Do you want a giant balloon, sir?" a vendor asks, waving what appears to be a bouquet of eight-foot-long condoms. No thanks. "Would you like a spirograph to make little circles on paper, sir?" No. "Would you like a dress, sir?" No. "Drink?" No. "Jewelry?" No. "Postcard?" No. "Are you sure you don't want a postcard, sir?" No. "Very nice postcard?" No, no. "A mat to lie on sir?" No.

You can't go 100 feet in the tourist part of town without Helpful Harry appearing by your side. Just now, I was looking at the sign outside the internet cafè and a Helpful Harry appeared. "That is internet cafè, sir," he said, pointing.

"Yeah, thanks -- I got that."

Matters of Style
Nov. 4, 2007
Bombay, India

The women of India are like wildflowers, each one dressed in colors to make a garden blush.

Canary and tangerine salwar suits; saris in coral, turquoise and royal purple, the fabric ribboned with silver and gold or spangled with sequins. Colors of sapphire, topaz and electric red... Most of the women here are dripping with intricate gold jewelry and many wear a tikka powder spot of bright color on their foreheads which marks them as Hindus.

And their hair is one of the wonders of this country, falling thick and lustrous in raven black tresses, always looking freshly washed.

***

Speaking of style, what's the well-dressed traveler wearing these days? For starters, I have the cheapest looking nylon belt imaginable, with a chintzy plastic buckle, like one of those you get free with cheap cargo pants. But folded inside this improbable money belt is $1,000 in $100 and $50 bills.

Concealed under my shirt is my passport pouch with backup cash, an ATM card and a credit card.

My wallet is rigged to a chain that loops around my belt. It's thick as a dictionary with Indian currency, and plunged into a deep front pocket.

I also have a "fake" wallet full of expired credit cards and small bills from places like Cuba, Nicaragua, Mexico and Canada, meant to be carried in dangerous neighborhoods where robbery is a possibility. This is a trick I learned a few years ago from some backpackers who were robbed in northern Mexico. So far, there hasn't been any need for it.

A back-up credit card is duct-taped into my camera bag. If I get ripped off of everything, all is not lost: my credit card numbers are written in code on a Hotmail account. And photos of my passport and visas are also parked in my email. I feel like a walking armored car.

***

Speaking of security, if you're ever in India, don't pet the monkeys. I saw a huge monkey -- about three feet tall with wicked bared fangs -- attack a young woman from New York on Elephanta Island. I grabbed a rotten stick to give it a whack, but someone yelled to her to put her Coke down and it took off. It turns out these vicious brutes will jump you if they see you carrying any kind of food. Some French travelers got the same treatment. As for the girl, she was scared white as a ghost.

Hide those bananas, folks!

***

On the dining scene, the Leopold Cafè in Colaba is a must-do for everyone from backpackers to cruise ship daytrippers. This is the restaurant where author Gregory David Roberts' druggy hero hangs his hat in *Shantarum*. It's a big room that opens onto the street, packed with customers and waiters on the run. My lunch is a volcanic red veg curry with noodles, garlic naan flatbread and a mango *lahsi* (a growing addiction). Leopold's is "the" place to be in Bombay almost by default because there's not much else to choose from on Colaba Causeway in this supposedly hip part of town.

The travel magazines go on and on about what a swinging place Bombay is, but I don't see it. It's just some writer embellishing a story; I'd expect to have a more lively time in Toledo, Ohio.

Yeah, sure, there are probably some hotel disco bars in the tourist zone far uptown where the "beautiful people" of Bombay's upper class hang out with package tourists. But that's not really a "scene" like you'd find in New York's East Village or Chicago's Wrigleyville.

Hullo My Fren'...

A parting shot: in Bombay you discover that you've got friends everywhere you go in India. Walk down any street and you'll hear these words, repeated in a mournful monotone: "Hullo. Hullo my fren'... Come see my shop, my fren'... Jus' loook, no buy. Jus' loook, my fren'..."

Indian hustlers all believe that tourists are automatic shopping robots. They're right of course, but one can only buy so many statues of Shiva or ankle bracelets. My only consolation is knowing that it's far worse in the "tourist triangle" of Rajasthan in northern India, which is said to be a perfect hell of hassle.

South India

Kochi Kowboy
Dec. 5, 2007
Kochi, India

Egad, my head is frying like an egg in the 95-plus degree heat of Kochi -- a town also known as Cochin -- here in southern India.

Surya, the Lord of the Day rises in the east with his chariot borne on flaming steeds with agate hooves... and the sun god roasts me alive on the frying pan sidewalks of this town.

Most tourists visit northern India to see the Taj Mahal and such, but I've opted for the slower pace of the south. My itinerary will take me 1,500 miles in a circuit around the tip of India, wrapping up in the ultimate beach party hangout of Goa.

Desperate for something to cover my broiling head, I pick out a ladies white plastic sun bonnet that seems to fit and manages to look like a jaunty cowboy hat.

Still the best way to travel in India.

"Only Mad Dogs and Englishmen Go Out In the Noonday Sun." Some of us oldies recall that as the title of a Joe Cocker album from the early '70s. Actually, it's a line from author Rudyard Kipling to describe India's cruel sun, back in the days of the British Raj (rule) when the English were ripping off India from the Maharajas.

During their campaigns from the 1740s on, the Brits lost some battles because they insisted on wearing heavy wool uniforms and fell victim to heatstroke and dysentery in the Indian summer, when temperatures can reach 120 degrees.

"At best a none-too-healthy creature, the British soldier could not campaign in temperatures of over 100 degrees," writes Lawrence James in *Raj: The Making and Unmaking of British India*.

In the campaign of 1857-'59, the British lost 8,000 soldiers to sunstroke and disease, with another 3,000 sent home as invalids. As in the U.S. Civil War, more soldiers died from heat and infection than enemy bullets. Doctors at the time argued in vain that many lives could have been saved if the Brits had allowed their men to wear light cotton uniforms instead of red serge tunics with leather collars. Not to mention brass helmets that literally cooked their skulls.

***

I need a new hat because all my gear was lost on last night's 1,000-mile flight from Bombay, along with that of 100 other passengers. Losing luggage is apparently SOP for India Airlines. I hope it turns up tomorrow, because aside from many gifts, my pack contains my malaria pills, and as everyone knows, Kochi is the Mosquito Capital of India.

Advice for travelers in India -- always set out for the airport at least four hours early -- if the traffic doesn't get you, the insane bureaucracy and long lines passing through at least four metal detectors will. Everything in India seems to require a triple-handling approach to keep people employed. At least our plane was on time -- it was only three hours late.

Southern India is vibrantly green and much more relaxed than the filth and anarchy of Bombay. The countryside opens up in a lush green of palm trees, rice fields and grazing cows, raising your spirits. Misty blue mountains rise like Hindu gods in the distant haze.

Kerala is the wealthiest state in India, per capita. Some say it's because of reforms the state's communist government put into effect decades ago.

There don't seem to be any people living on the streets of Kochi, but there are beggars. Just now, I gave 10 rupees to a leper with no fingers on either hand. He was sitting on the sidewalk at a busy intersection, roasting in the sun, with the white stubs of his palms cupped for my coin.

Begging is the social safety net of India, and every good citizen has a religious obligation to give to the poor. Wealthy tourists should pony up. The 10 rupees are only 25 cents to me -- enough to fill a rice bowl.

Here come those mosquitoes! Got to scoot...

The Cutting Edge

I had to dash out of the dank internet cafe in downtown Ernakulam (the business district in Kochi) because the airless booth was buzzing with some big brute mozzies, and this being southern India, it's also malaria country, and dengue fever country, and Japanese encephalitis country... probably nothing to worry about, unless you're a chickenshit like me.

This is also the gateway city to the southernmost state of Kerala, which boasts the gorgeous beaches of southwestern India and the Kerala Backwaters, both of which have been discovered in a big way by the travel magazines this year.

Kerala has become the new must-do destination for backpackers -- one of the last unmolested refuges under the sun; the kind of obscure, beautiful place that freebooters are constantly on the lookout for, as in Alex Garland's novel, *The Beach*. So, welcome to the cutting edge.

But the tourist invasion is still tepid on the bubbling hot streets of Kochi. There's a stray Westerner here and there, but for the most part, this town is just another anonymous city in India that most Westerners have never heard of.

It's here in Ernakulam that I discover the ISN phone lines that seem to be available in every snack shop and convenience store in the country. You walk in, pick up a cheap, dirty, flimsy phone that's encrusted with the grime of 10,000 hands, dial the country code of 001 for America and make your call.

I talk to Jeannette almost every night (for her it's morning, nearly 12 hours difference), with a fee of around $2 for 10 minutes conversation. It's like we're not even apart.

Younger travelers would no doubt wonder, what's the big deal? But it seems a miracle that you can make a call from any small village in India for such a pittance. Only a few years back, you would have been soaked for half your wallet -- if you could find a phone to begin with -- and somehow get an overseas connection.

When I first met Jeannette, I phoned her from the only international call center in all of Madrid during a trip in 1992 and it cost me $25 to speak to her for four minutes. Today, you can stroll into any one-goat, two-chicken town in central India and make a call halfway around the world for pennies.

Being able to communicate with home has made backpacking infinitely less stressful. The thought of it puts me in awe of the feat of my friend, Jim Moore, who hitch-hiked around South America for nine months in the early '80s when there was no internet and few opportunities to use a telephone.

Jim, who plays lead guitar in our band, is one of the most daring backpackers I've ever met. Just out of college and with little money in his pockets, he hitch-hiked and cadged rides through Venezuela, Brazil, Uruguay, Paraguay, Argentina, Patagonia, Bolivia and Peru.

His trip included hitch-hiking the then-new Trans-Amazon Highway, which was a narrow, red-dirt road running for 3,000 miles through the Brazilian jungle. "There were times when I didn't know if I was going to make it out of there," he recalls. "You could stand by the side of the road all day and only see a single truck go by, and they don't have many hitch-hikers in Brazil, so they don't know what to make of you."

Truckers who did give him a lift made frequent stops at roadside brothels, where grandmas would cook Jim dinner and kids would frolic in the kitchen while the drivers had their way with mama. And often, whole villages would turn out to gaze awe-struck at Jim, whose appearance was as strange as an alien visitor. His travels also took him on hikes of several days down obscure sections of the Inca Trail in Bolivia, sleeping in a hammock in the jungle, far off the tourist track. Perhaps there aren't many American backpackers in the Third World, but those who indulge tend to go the extra mile...

Heat & Dust
Nov. 6, 2007
Ernakulam, India

I survived the 40-mile round-trip to the airport to pick up my lost junk. Someone has gone through my unlocked bag and lifted my "fake" wallet -- the work of the notorious Bombay mafia, no doubt. (Months later, someone will try using my expired credit cards to make purchases in Italy and Brazil -- proof of the international spread of organized crime and identity theft.)

The driving technique in India involves blasting the horn the entire way to the airport and back. In fact, many vehicles have bumper stickers saying "Horn Please," because the drivers want to know which direction the traffic is coming from so they can avoid veering into the honkers.

Every trip here involves whiplashing through a maelstrom of junky old buses, tuk-tuks, bicycles, motorcycles with whole families on-board, pedestrians, and other taxis, while veering into oncoming traffic at breakneck speed every so often just for kicks. Potholes the size of bathtubs, roller-coaster pavement and rotting concrete along the route? You bet. Glad we had plastic Jesus on the dashboard for protection. Sometimes it's Ganesh, the elephant-headed god of good luck. "Remover of obstacles."

At any rate, I think my toes will be permanently curled from fright by the time I get home. That and a headache from the Beeeeeeeeeeeep! Beeeeeep! *BEEEEEEEP!* and smog.

***

After a tough day of tramping around in the heat and dust, dodging Helpful Harrys and beggars, I return to my hotel, which retains the tradition of the British Raj, with someone to help you with everything short of wiping your bum. There's the laundry boy, the room boy, an elevator operator, several doormen in turbans and a staff of 10 waiters. Most of these guys look so bored I haven't the heart to tell them I can carry my own guitar or push the elevator button by myself.

It's also quite strange to have someone serve your dinner -- spooning

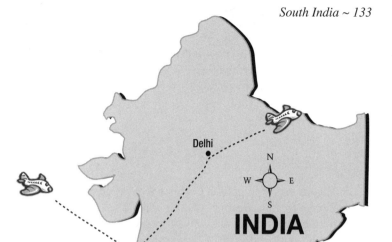

up more rice and shrimp on your dish whenever you've eaten a tad. I feel like Little Lord Fauntleroy -- but again, it would be unkind to deny these folks their existence.

***

Speaking of food, McDonald's, Subway, and other fast food restaurants here serve only veggie burgers or chicken. This is because Lord Krishna, king of the Hindu gods, is a cowherd -- literally a cowboy god -- and Shiva, god of destruction, has a pet bull who happens to be a demon. To the gods, cattle are a cut above the human race.

So obviously, cows are sacred to the 800,000 or so Hindus in this country. When McDonald's came to India, they were informed that fanatical Hindus would bomb their restaurants if they served beef. Members of the Shiv Sena party even forced Micky Dee's to drop beef flavoring from the french fries served in India.

Thus, you can see holy cows and Brahma bulls wandering around town or lounging by the highway, free of the fear of ending up in a bloody pool on someone's plate -- Cow Kings of the World, man...

Sleepin' On the Job
Nov. 7, 2007
Ernakulam, India

The Hindus have 333 million gods -- one for every occasion -- and many of them are reincarnations of other gods. Thus, Krishna is something like the eighth incarnation of Vishnu, and other gods are reincarnations of Krishna, and so on. Got it?

One can only imagine that the gods are sleeping on the job, however, because India (or Hindustan -- 'land of the Hindus') -- is a dreadfully bollixed up place. There's a good reason for this, however, because the gods are engaged in a perpetual soap opera of backstabbing, mistaken identities, double-dealing, fooling around with someone else's old lady, and in general, manifesting all the foibles of the human race.

This is the basis of mythology -- to illustrate the human condition through the goofs of the gods. I've given up trying to sort out who goes where, filing the whole Hindu god thing in the Horseshit folder (with the exception of my personal favorite, Ganesh). However, if there was a handy card pack featuring the best of the bunch, that would be cool... Trade 'em like baseball cards.

***

I hook up with a new group of backpackers who've signed on for two weeks of bumming around southern India. We're a bit crestfallen to learn that we are only three.

Our leader is Vinit Nair, 28, who has lived in both Kerala and up north in dusty Rajasthan. Compact as a fireplug, Vinit is an open-faced soul with a lively expression and raccoon eyebrows who has the gift of being instantly likable.

Vinit is eager to hear details of my ride across Europe because he dreams of making a similar trip to promote some ill-defined cause -- a common affliction for idealistic people in their 20s.

"I want to ride a bicycle across India. Do you think this is possible?" he asks.

I shudder to think of anyone attempting a bike tour on the narrow roads of India -- many of which are basically one lane with bad shoulders, shared by two oncoming vehicles. Not to mention the thousands of miles such a trip would entail. It would be a suicide mission.

"I think it would be very dangerous," I say. "The roads are much narrower here than in Europe or America and the drivers are very bad compared to what we're used to. You'd risk getting hit by a car."

"Yes, but perhaps I would ride the small roads," Vinit says, undeterred.

I'm tempted to warn against the possibility of life in a wheelchair, but this would be a gross laying-on of bad karma, and besides, people in their 20s tend to be deaf to advice from their elders.

And really, who likes getting advice? People need to learn on their own. Maturity is the process of disillusionment that erodes your dreams through the years. Wisdom is the result of falling flat on your face enough times to pound idealism out of your head.

Our party is rounded out by Florence, a 37-year-old French investment banker who lives in Germany, and Ann, a 64-year-old retired hospitality specialist from Leeds, England. It's not going to be much of a party without any Australians along, but I resolve to make the best of it and try to poke my personality (such as it is) out of its turtle shell a bit more.

Florence has a proud Gallic bearing, which is enlivened by a passion for telling it like it is on subjects which set her off, even though she's a romantic at heart. Over dinner, she reveals that she's at loose ends with her career in Germany, where she's stuck working with an all-male group of sophomoric salesmen.

"All the salesmen at the bank want to talk about is how big their penises are and who they'd like to have sex with," she says. "Everything is a big joke to them -- they can never have a normal conversation, and you get tired of hearing the same thing every day. I have a good job in Germany, but I don't know if I'll go back."

"That must get to be very tiresome," I say.

"Yes, that is why I am taking these trips. From here, I go to Nepal for two weeks and then Vietnam and Australia. And then, I don't know -- maybe I will find someplace new to live."

For her part, Ann is delicately inquisitive, with a twinkle to her eyes and a Brit's sense of decorum. High on life, she didn't begin her journeys until she was in her 50s, going it alone on the train across Siberia. Since then, she's traveled around Africa, back through Russia, and to other Third World countries.

We make for an odd bunch, but with our passion for travel, Florence, Ann and I manage to have a good time comparing notes on destinations. By the end of the trip I have a great deal of respect for them -- they are brave -- they are adventurers.

Central Casting

"What about castes? Are people still members of castes here" I ask over lunch.

Officially, we don't have the caste system in India anymore, but still it exists," says Vinit. "I myself am from the warrior caste."

"Would you ever marry anyone outside your caste?"

"I don't think my parents would allow it," Vinit says with a smile.

I'd all but forgotten India's caste system -- a pecking order that you're born into with no way out: the brahmans are the top-dog priest caste, ruling the head or intellect; the warriors are the strong guys, ruling the chest; the merchant caste rules the stomach and guts; an artisan and agricultural caste symbolizes life from the knees down; and then come the untouchables who are somewhere underfoot -- not even considered to be in a proper caste and getting all the dirty jobs like cleaning toilets -- forbidden from even looking up at their superiors.

Perhaps the untouchables would benefit by reading a bit of the French philosopher Albert Camus, who wrote that -- if nothing else in life -- we all have the power to say "no" and resist oppression.

In particular he said: "What is a rebel? A man who says no."

If I've gotten the caste system wrong, it doesn't much matter, because like the Hindu gods, there are so many manifestations of the caste system here that even the Indians don't seem to have a handle on it. India is a fluid place -- ever-changing, yet always staying the same.

"Castes have been replaced by a 'class' system in India," Vinit says. He notes that while the brahmans and such were busy preening themselves and acting 'too good' to stoop with the changing times, many untouchables settled into positions such as movie stars, musicians and entrepreneurs. "They are the new top dogs of India -- the people you see on television."

But for those who still believe, the caste system remains a religio-psychological prison. If you lead an upright life, you will ascend to a higher caste in your next life. But, if you live an impure, evil life, you could be reincarnated to a lower caste -- or worse -- an animal.

I had trouble going to sleep last night, thinking of how horrible it would be to be reincarnated as an octopus. Can only imagine that Hitler is a sea urchin or a worm right now. I resolve to try living a more upright life to forestall this horrible fate.

Pardon My Ignorance
Nov. 9, 2007
Ernakulam, India

No sooner had I gotten done expounding on things I know nothing about than I was humbled by my ignorance of the Hindu gods.

That night, I heard a talk by a Hindu teacher who explained that the 333 million gods are all manifestations of a single supreme being, Bhagavan, who exists as a shapeless force in the universe.

This godhead is composed of a trinity of gods: Brahma (the Beginning and the Creator) Vishnu (Existence and the Preserver) and Shiva (the End and Destroyer).

Thus, the many gods of the Hindus represent all the hopes, desires, dreams, energy and power of one all-encompassing god, operating in the past, present and future.

Worshipping the gods channels all of the power of human imagination to a supreme being, willing divine intervention into existence.

It's no different than Christians praying for a new Cadillac by invoking a saint or a biblical passage, or new-agers using the 'power of positive thinking' through "The Secret."

If God is the sum of 333 million elements and energies inhabiting the universe, who am I to argue? As a confirmed deist, I'm surprised to find that the Hindu view of religion isn't that far off from my own beliefs -- it's a more sophisticated way of interpreting monotheism.

And once again, the teacher's words make me realize how easy it is to be ignorant and arrogant when you're outside someone else's culture, looking in with a blindfold over your eyes.

The Bad Hand

"Why are those Indian people laughing at us at the next table?"

It's because our party is eating with our left hands -- even tearing pieces of bread and putting it into our mouths... Yuck!

"But what is wrong eating with the left hand?" Florence asks.

Vinit delicately explains that the left hand is the "bad" hand, and blushes when I add, "the bathroom hand."

In Africa and Asia, people use the left hand to scrub the lower deck with a splash of water. The squat toilets here have two footpads, a hole, and a bucket of water -- no TP.

Most people eat with their fingers in India, which involves rolling a gooey ball of rice, dripping with curry sauce and chunks of fish, chicken or eggplant, and popping it into your mouth, *always* with the right hand, of course.

Eating with the bathroom hand is a *faux pas* on par with... well, fill in the blank, won't you? So I learn to tear pieces of bread with my right pointer finger and thumb, and overcome squeamish feelings of dipping my fingers in sauced-up rice.

The Festival of Light
Nov. 10, 2007
Udhagamandalam, India

It's simply luvly here in Udhagamandalam, also known as Ootaca-mund, or simply Ooty by the British, who established this town 7,000 feet up in the cool Blue Mountains back in the days of the Empire. You get here by way of a narrow road that loops up the mountain in a series of hairpin switchbacks that reveal green jungle vistas to the far horizon.

Today, Ooty is a tourist town catering to upscale Indians, packed with hundreds of excited middle-class families. But back in the day of the British Raj, Ooty was a hill station, meaning the refreshing cool place the army and administration would retreat to during the sizzling summer. Thus, "Little England" includes a colonial-era golf course, garden and artificial lake, and I'm staying in a quaint old hotel out of a Kipling novel that also welcomes officers of the Indian Army.

This is also the heart of tea country, and much of the world's sup-ply is grown on thousands of acres terracing the mountains. Picking the leaves is menial "womens' work." You see clusters of women in an ocean of green rolling far down the mountain. Their hands are as tough as iron from picking tea 10 hours a day.

We arrive in time to celebrate Diwali, the Festival of Light, which honors the return of the god Rama from exile. A national holiday on par with Christmas, Diwali involves blowing off so many fireworks it's like war has broken out with Pakistan. And, boy, they explode some big suckers here. Most of these "crackers" are on par with a long string of M-80s or cherry bombs -- bite-sized chunks of dynamite which are illegal back in the States.

Vinit is positively ecstatic over blowing off crackers, something I haven't gotten a charge out of since I was 10 years old, back when we used to pack pumpkins with explosives at my family's home in rural Michigan.

"Don't you love crackers?!" he exclaims with glee, eager to blow off more mini-bombs at any opportunity. He's purchased a bagful for us to explode over the next few days.

In vain I search for my inner 10-year-old, trying recapture the old thrill for things that go "boom!" that gives Vinit so much pleasure. But I have to admit, that kid is long gone...

Secret Agent Man

"What scenes he saw! What adventures he went through! But who would believe, even if he ventured to detail them?"

-- Sir Richard Burton

Sir Richard Burton passed through here in 1847, riding up the long, winding hairpin road in the Nilgiri foothills to stay at a convalescent home in Ootacamund. Burton had contracted cholera in Karachi (or claimed that he did), earning time off from his military duties.

A secret agent, Burton was perhaps the most daring adventurer of all time and a key figure in the "Great Game" of wresting control of Central Asia for the British. Familiar with 29 languages and many dialects, he collected intelligence in disguise -- masquerading at times as a poor trinket peddler, a wandering *dervish* holy man, or a nomadic gypsy laborer. He often infiltrated native markets, brothels and mosques to catch the word on the street, which was invariably expressed in hatred for the British.

Possessed with a mania for sex and a passion for both marijuana and opium, Burton had numerous affairs and quasi-marriages with native women, not to mention frequent visits to brothels. Six-feet-tall, with gypsy eyes and dark good looks, he managed to look both fearsome and compelling. Also notorious: it's said that when he proposed to a beautiful young Persian noblewoman, her relatives had her killed to keep her from his hands. An "honor" killing.

Burton is said to have been the first Westerner to make a pilgrimage to Mecca at a time when discovery meant certain death by decapitation or stoning. Biographer Edward Rice notes, however, that at least 12 Europeans made the trip to Mecca before Burton, but primarily in the role of unwilling Christian slaves. Having converted to Islam, Burton disguised himself as an Afghan peddler and entered the holy city of the Muslims during the annual pilgrimage.

Other feats include his translations of *1,001 Arabian Nights* and the *Kama Sutra*, both of which retained their raw sexual power under Burton's pen, shocking readers of the Victorian era. Casting the template for Indiana Jones, Burton was also a noted ethnologist, detailing the lifestyles of many tribal peoples and their religious beliefs.

After his *hadj* to Mecca, Burton risked execution again by entering the forbidden city of Harrar in Somalia, a land where his face was wickedly scarred with the plunge of a warrior's spear. The blade went in one cheek and out the other, cleaving his palate and knocking out several teeth. But this did nothing to dissuade Burton; after his recovery, he plunged into the African wilderness, seeking the source of the Nile.

But long before those adventurers, Burton was a sick man on a Maharatta "man-eater" nag, making his way up to the cool sanctuary of Ooty, across the jungle from the port of Calicut on the Indian Ocean.

Fresh from trying to abduct a pretty nun in Goa, Burton found the English women of Ootacamund to be lovely, but distant -- more inclined to dabble at flirtation and mindgames than what he had in mind. He looked down on English men and women alike as being ignorant of the pleasures of love-making, which he had learned from a succession of Muslim *nautch* (dancing) women he lived with while serving in the army.

Without any horse racing, gambling or hunting action to keep him occupied, the restless adventurer soon bored of Ooty and its tepid British *memsahibs*, leaving Dullsville as soon as he recovered his health. But he did squeak a book out of his stay: *Goa, and the Blue Mountains; or, Six Months of Sick Leave*, published in 1850, which remains a good read for those visiting India today.

How Ganesh Got His Head
Nov. 11, 2007
The Blue Mountains, India

How did Ganesh, the god of good luck and "remover of obstacles" get his elephant head? Glad you asked.

One day, Parvati, goddess of power, decided to bathe in the pool of a jungle glade. She didn't want her jewelry and clothing stolen while she skinny-dipped, so she scooped up a handful of clay and made herself a new son.

"Son," she said, "keep guard over my things and don't let anyone come down this path, no matter what."

"Yes, ma'am," her son replied.

But soon, Lord Shiva, the destroyer of evil, came along and demanded that the watchman get out of the way. No.

"But I am Parvati's husband," Shiva explained.

"Sorry, can't let you pass."

Shiva gets angry easily, so he swept out his sword and sliced off the upstart's head.

When Parvati finished bathing and saw her headless son, she demanded that Shiva repair the boy. So, Shiva took his bow and said he would use the head of the first creature that his arrow struck.

That critter was the elephant, of course, and the new assemblage has been known as the god of good luck ever since.

By the way, if you are ever desirous to worship Shiva and Parvati, simply stop by one of the many lingam temples which dot India. You can identify them because they are buildings that look like a stubby penis, with the circle of a vagina comprising the base, symbolizing the connection between man and woman.

Welcome to the Hotel Ooty Pooty

I've said some cruel things about India -- all true, by the way -- but now it is time to say something nice.

After nearly two weeks here, I'm starting not to see the trash. It disappears from your attention after awhile, and I'm sure the Indians don't see it at all.

Also, here and there you find public parks which are impeccably clean. Ditto for the hotels and restaurants, so there is some sort of 'clean' ethic at work. It might even be catching on, because there are signs around the various towns, pleading with people not to litter, and also appeals for "No Plastic."

There's also a booming middle class, which is why the roads are so crazy -- many people are buying new cars and SUVs and the ridiculous single-lane roads just can't handle them all. All of these new drivers are sucking up what's left of the world's oil supply, wreaking havoc at the gas pump back in the States.

There are wild elephants by the road in the jungles of the Blue Mountains, along with water buffalo, monkeys and deer. And each town has its contingent of goats and sacred cows, munching trash in the streets.

I'm currently at a jungle retreat, rubbing elbows with IT professionals from Bangalore, the 'Silicon Valley' of India. All are well-to-do people, weekending in the jungle.

Had a lot of fun playing the old g'itar for the folks here, including that great Eagles hit, "Welcome to the Hotel Ooty-Pooty..." The small crowd also seems to like my cover of the calypso classic "Yellow Bird," and "That's Life" by Frank Sinatra.

Here in the jungle, one's time is spent watching elephants take baths while monkeys prance, locking eyes with water buffalo, and marveling over the women and kids washing dishes in the river. It's not hard to imagine Mowgli, Sher Khan and all the wolves and monkeys of *The Jungle Book* here. In the distance, you can almost see the faces of Hindu gods peering from the azure mist of the mountains.

I've been to other supernatural places: in Lake Michigan there is an island which the Chippewa believe is alive with the spirits they call manitous; and you can feel their presence there, beyond the veil of our reality. And on the coast of Lake Superior, I've heard the crack of the thunderbird's wings and the stir of Misshepezhu, the sea panther of the deep in a way that seems to go beyond what is explainable. The Japanese also have these feelings with Shinto -- a religion which worships nature -- finding *kami* spirits in waterfalls, mountains, trees and the sun. These locales serve as vortices to the spirit world.

That same feeling is strong in India -- like that strange, sinister cave where the Englishwoman fell prey to hallucinations in E. M. Forster's *A Passage to India*. At times you feel that wandering down the wrong path might lead you to places far off the map of this world -- and that there are supernatural beings clambering just beyond your vision.

The Story of Murthy the Elephant
Nov. 11, 2007
Mudumalai Wildlife Sanctuary, India

Once there was a naughty elephant named Murthy who lived in the jungle beneath the Blue Mountains of southern India. There are several versions of the killer known as Murthy (or Loki as he is sometimes called), but this is the story they tell at the Mudumalai Wildlife Sanctuary, south of Mysore.

Murthy was a crop-raider -- a rogue elephant who would eat all the crops in a poor farmer's garden, destroying the family's home as well. Some farmers tried to stop Murthy by throwing firecrackers or beating on pots. But Murthy wasn't afraid, and he proved it by killing at least 14 people in the forests of Tamil Nadu and Kerala in the course of three years in the mid-1980s -- trampling them into the bloody dust of their fields. Some say he killed as many as three dozen farmers.

Enough, said the government: Murthy must die. Game wardens in Kerala shot him several times in the legs, hoping to capture him. But Murthy escaped and went on to kill another farmer.

But a veterinarian named V. Krishnamurthy, DVM offered to take

Murthy alive with the help of tame elephants who were specially-trained to capture their wild cousins.

And so it was that five elephants and a party of rangers went on a safari in July, 1988. They set a trap for Murthy and shot him with tranquilizer darts, which were new to India at the time. Then, the elephant police surrounded him and moved in, leaving him no chance to escape.

Murthy was escorted in chains by the five elephants for 56 kilometers to the Mudumalai Wildlife Sanctuary with his legs still bleeding and infected from his month-old bullet wounds. The trip took three days, winding through villages and along jungle roads.

"Jostling against the other elephants, he was gored and dragged to some extent. No one denies it. The alternative might have been more homicide," states one account, defending against charges of abuse by animal rights advocates.

At the sanctuary, an elephant tender claims that Murthy was placed in a stout wooden cage for four-and-a-half years. The close confinement was intended to heal his wounds and get him used to captivity. (And possibly because kindness to animals is a vague concept in the developing world.) In all that time, he never laid down to sleep even once -- he slept on his feet. He was very restless for the first two years, but gradually, he became gentle.

At the end of his confinement, Murthy became a good elephant (or perhaps, quite insane), not trampling people like before. He learned to be ridden by a tender, and enjoyed a bath in the river each morning and afternoon. But just in case the old naughty elephant ever returned, his tusks were cut down to nubs.

And today, the family members of those who were killed by Murthy sometimes make the long journey to the park to see the old crop raider. They look at Murthy in awe, and then they turn around and go home.

The Wisdom of Sir Laugh-a-Lot
Nov. 12, 2007
In the Blue Mountains, India

Back in Ireland, I made a friend named Sir Laugh-a-Lot, a crusty old knight who had been through many adventures.

Whenever the going got tough, I'd say, "What do you think of the pickle we're in today, Sir Laugh-a-Lot?" And he would reply with a lusty laugh: "Ha, ha, ha, ha, ha!"

But sometimes, if things were going really bad and he was in a sour mood, Sir Laugh-a-Lot would say, "Just remember, you asked for this, asshole."

Either way, it made me feel good.

Yet with the trip half over, and halfway around the world, I got a touch of the blues the past couple of days. I've only been gone a little over two months, but it seems like years, piling on each day's adventure. This is a very strange land, and I'm homesick for snuggling with my wife and simple things like wearing bluejeans and my leather jacket, sipping red wine and playing good guitars. Oh yeah, and seeing all of you guys back home too...

Fortunately, Sir Laugh-a-Lot showed up today during my funk and reminded me that had I made a sacred vow when this trip started to enjoy myself, come hell or high water.

"Ye must uphold yer promise, Bubby," he said, not unkindly. "Don't let the buggers get cha down..."

So, even when I have a sleepless night of projectile-vomiting and greet the dawn feeling 20 lbs. lighter and a dizzy shade of sea green (like last night), I am grateful that my trusty friend has reminded me to buck up.

So thank you, Sir Laugh-a-Lot, for your wise words, and for holding up the toilet seat at 2 in the morning while I was puking like Niagra Falls...

The United States of Dangerland

On our way through the Blue Mountains, my fellow travelers and I get into a philosophical discussion of America.

Florence is of the opinion that most people in America own guns and it's a very dangerous country.

"Not everyone owns a gun in America," I respond. "In fact, most of the people I know don't own one. In my town we never worry about gun violence."

"Oh, I find that hard to believe," Florence says. "Do you own a gun?"

"No, I had one, but sold it at a garage sale last year. My father gave me a .20 gauge shotgun when I was 12, but I never got into hunting, so it was stowed away in a closet for years. The stock was broken, and it was held together with electrical tape. It was a ridiculous gun, so I decided to get rid of it.

"But I don't have the fear of guns that you have in Europe, and I might decide to own one again someday," I add, failing to mention that I've never bought a handgun because it seems pointless to lay out $400 for something you don't plan to ever use.

Although I have liberal beliefs, they run along the same lines as the liberals who occupied the heights of Bunker Hill in 1775, or the union-member Americans who liberated Europe in the 1940s. I thought it was quite sensible of the Black Panthers to pose for newspaper photos brandishing their shotguns in the late '60s, vowing to protect their neighborhoods from the brutality of white cops. This is the branch of the "don't tread on me" liberals.

"Under the Second Amendment of our constitution, it would be impossible for a dictator like Adolf Hitler to ever come to power in America," I say. "He'd be unable to control people because so many of us have guns. Sooner or later, someone would shoot him down. And that's why the ownership of guns can actually be a good thing."

The group is spellbound by Professor Downes' dissertation, since defending the idea of owning a gun is a complete novelty to Europeans and Indians. But I remember to qualify my lecture:

"Of course, the downside is that we've got a lot of crazy people running around America with guns who are impossible to control," I add lamely, thinking of the many campus and schoolhouse shootings that plague my country.

"Yes, that is the thing. That's what we don't like," Florence responds.

I'm not sure that Florence or the others are convinced of the value of an armed society, but it's not my job to sell my country's ideas.

Florence also scoffs when I tell her there are virtually no prostitutes where I come from. "Oh pffft!" she exclaims, waving a hand in disbelief.

Hookers are only a distant rumor in my town, which has a regional population of around 80,000, At best, we've got a few meth addicts from downstate who show up to service the hunters during deer season, or some gals who are experimenting with online booty calls. In fact, it's been 17 years since a prostitute has been arrested in Traverse City -- an incident involving an Oriental massage parlor.

But the cities of Europe are jam full of prostitutes. When you roll into the train station in Brussels, you can see them standing in their red-lit windows near the tracks, even in the cold, gray light of a Monday morning. So Florence believes the same must be true of America.

How can I explain? Good-looking women have better things to do in America than playing at being whores -- they get married to doctors and lawyers instead.

Down the Hatch
Nov. 13, 2007
Mysore, India

For adventurous diners, India is a garden of gastronomical delights, especially if you're a vegetarian.

But for fraidy-cat squeamish types like me, it can be a bit hair-raising, sitting down to dinner of ghastly mush.

Last night, we dined with an Indian family at their home in Mysore. Overall, it was a good experience:

-- a salad of chopped red onions mixed with sour yogurt (awful).

-- a main dish of saffron rice and mutton (good).

-- an eggplant stewed in spices which looked like something from the bottom of a swamp (but was quite good).

-- a deep-fried donut hole in syrup and a fruit custard for dessert (both quite good).

I've avoided meat and only eat one real meal a day, filling in with cashews, bananas and a continental breakfast. Some things I've found appealing, however, are:

-- tikka chicken, which is boneless chicken chunks, coated in red chili pepper and bbq'd.

-- ginger-garlic fried rice.

-- garlic naan -- a flat bread.

-- and the South Indian breakfast, idly kava. An idly is a doughy rice pancake, while a kava is a donut made of a flour of rice and lentils. You dip them in coconut curry or a veggie dip.

There are also fresh-squeezed, pulpy juices made from many exotic fruits here -- mango is my addiction -- but I must say, visions of pizza, burgers and antipasta salads are starting to dance in my head.

I've made my own contribution, introducing India to the Mexican habit of placing a lime in my Kingfisher beer to the amazement of various bartenders.

After dinner, I learn how India reduces its landfill problem and provides for the disposal of waste: Organic trash is placed at a site away from the houses in the neighborhood, where dogs, cows, birds and goats munch through the bones and garbage. A dust bin is out front of the house for the disposal of paper, plastic and solids. Each day, trash collectors come in a three-wheeled tuk-tuk to clean out the dust bin, much of which is recycled.

***

Somewhere along the line, I also share a bit of slang with Vinit, who warns me away from the rigors of Turkish coffee - a shot glass of espresso sludge with a grit that edges your teeth.

"Mmm.. that's the real mud," I say in appreciation.

"Mud? What do you mean, this is mud?" Vinit asks.

"I mean this is dirty. It's got that dirty mud taste."

"Dirty? The coffee is dirty?"

"Yes. In America, if someone gives you a good cup of coffee, you must always say, 'That's the real mud -- that's dirty.'"

I have no idea if anyone actually says this in America, but it sounds good.

Love & Romance, Indian-Style
Nov. 13, 2007
Mysore, India

Saw the latest Bollywood blockbuster, *Saawariya*, last night, and have to grudgingly admit it was pretty good, despite being bathed in the syrup of romance.

The film is based on a story by Fyodor Doestoyevsky called "White Nights." It's about a struggling musician who falls in love with a beautiful young woman. But to her, he's "just a friend," and although they have lots of laughs over the course of a few nights together, her heart belongs to a brave soldier who's away on the front lines. Yet after knocking himself silly and pouring his heart out, the musician wins her love... then, oops -- the soldier comes back into the picture and she flies back to his big strong arms. In the final scene, the musician is left twirling his umbrella, his heart broken while she strolls off with Mr. Right.

Even though the film was entirely in the Hindi language, I understood this tale of unrequited love easily enough -- like most men, I've 'been there' -- and was quite impressed that the likable musician got dumped at the end and didn't win the girl. It was an honest ending.

Bollywood, based in Bombay, is the biggest film center in the world, cranking out than 600 movies each year. Most films seem to be sugary sweet musicals, with big dance numbers that are the Indo version of the Electric Slide. As in *Saawariya*, the male star tends to be sickeningly cute to the point of being girlish and the female lead is always simply adorable, batting her long lashes. Many films seem to be variations of *Romeo and Juliet*, backed by hundreds of singing, dancing actors... but the films are so chaste that not even kissing is allowed onscreen.

***

But although Bollywood drips with romantic goo, the reality of love in India is much more clinical and weighed in gold. This is still a country where 85% of marriages are arranged by the parents.

At dinner last night with a local guide's family, our host proudly told us of his daughter's recent wedding and how the match was made.

"I had heard that a rich man's son was looking for a wife, so I sent word that I have a beautiful daughter who was available," he began his tale.

"The young man's parents arranged for a meeting, and on the chosen day, my daughter got all dressed up and traveled to meet them. She was very nervous because they are quite well-to-do, but that is how things are done here," he continued. "They spent the day with her and gave their approval for the marriage. Then, they sent their son to meet us. Of course, we found that he was a fine young man who would make a good husband for our daughter."

Here's where the romance comes in. Once both parents approved of the match, the young couple got to meet -- FACE TO FACE! -- at the dinner table for a talk with all of the parents sitting in. Word has it they even got an hour alone to talk a little more freely.

Then, with a flourish of his hand, the young man announced, "I'll take her," and the deal was done.

Ah, but first the bride's father had to provide eight lakhs of rupees as a wedding dowry to the groom's rich parents. A lakh represents 100,000 -- so he had to come up with 800,000 rupees in money and gold jewelry. This is about $20,000, U.S. -- a lot of money in India, especially for a tour guide. The equivalent in the U.S. would be like a blue collar family having to come up with a quarter of a million dollars.

No problem -- the father simply called all of his relatives and told them that his daughter had a golden opportunity to marry a rich man's son. Could they contribute? Money poured in from all over India as well as from relatives in California and New York.

The wedding included 4,500 guests -- not unusual in India where even middlin' folks invite 2,000 or so. The newlyweds went to live at his mamma and daddy's house, as all Indian couples do, to get to know the perfect stranger they'll be spending the rest of their lives with.

As for the dowry, the groom's parents keep the cash, and the bride keeps the gold jewelry "just in case" things don't work out. A married woman who doesn't wear heaps of gold jewelry is laughed at on the streets of India.

***

But what of the wedding night, you say? No worries -- many Hindu temples include carvings of the sexual positions of the *Kama Sutra* (literally, "sex techniques") to serve as instruction for those who are new to the marriage bed. Another ancient Indian text is the *Ananga Ranga*, a sex manual written for men to keep the spice in the marriage bed.

"This is so young people will know how to have good love-making when they get married, because otherwise, there is no way for them to know," Vinit says during a visit to an elaborately carved temple near Mysore. Every imaginable sex act is carved into stone on the temple walls for the Indian version of sex education: blow jobs, three-ways, upside down, doggy-style, cunnilingus, the works.

Imagine this graphic sex guide on the walls of your church back home. But the thing is, the Hindus don't have our Calvinist/Puritan tradition of considering sex to be "dirty." They consider sex to be a gift from God and want to make sure their kids are doing it right.

On the other hand, the people of India are incredible prudes: both dating and premarital sex are unheard of, and even kissing is taboo in their movies and on TV. How this squares with the kinky temple carvings, I haven't a clue. Perhaps only Western tourists are looking at the old temple porn today.

The Green Land
Nov. 13, 2007
The Night Train to Chennai, India

I start to understand why many Westerners are at first horrified by India and then slowly fall in love with this "land of contrasts" (a cliche that every travel writer who visits India is forced to resort to at some point).

Imagine a rainbow all in shades of green: electric green, sea green, misty green, neon green, sunstruck green, lightning green, Lincoln, emerald, golden green -- green so full of energy it makes your body swell with -- well, what else? Envy. This green rainbow is what southern India looks like today, passing by for five hours on the train. Men and women stoop over in the rice fields and there are endless lazy palms beckoning you to r-e-l-a-x and bow to the distant hazy mountains.

This land is the sister to Sri Lanka, the island once known as Ceylon, and long before that as Serendip. It floats just off the coast of southern India, and is inhabited by the same Tamil people who live here on the mainland. The island provided us with the word, serendipity: a charm-

Florence, Ann, and the Little Angels of Mamallapuram.

ing coincidence.

We share our space on the train with a fat mom, who feeds her three kids with food purchased from a vendor who walks up and down the aisle. Meal over, she tosses all of the plastic and aluminum foil trays and drink cups out the window, littering the landscape along the tracks. Out flies the trash into the perfect green.

"What the hell are you doing lady?" I yell at her, the perfect stentorian. "You know better than to do that!"

Actually, I don't say a thing, and neither do my Western companions, but we all share one of those thoughts where your eyes don't even have to meet to get it across -- it's all said in a meaningful pause. What a pig. But this is the Third World -- that's how they do things here.

A Meeting with the Little Angels
Nov. 14, 2007
Mamallapuram, India

It smells like raw sewage and rotting garbage around the rooftop pool at our hotel in Mamallapuram, but no complaints here -- it's very nice to swim some laps and plunk the old guitar in the 85-degree sun.

I may have found PeeWee Herman's lost bicycle here on the Bay of

Bengal in east India, because the contraption I rode around to the spectacular temples was designed to have your knees bobbing up around your chin, and engineered for maximum crashibility.

But the complex of temples to Krishna spread around town are fascinating -- some are carved out of boulders the size of houses, and covered with sculptures of gods and goddesses and their wars, love-ins and grand parades.

Mamallapuram and its Hindu temple by the sea are the stars of a new marketing campaign to get more people to visit India. You see photos of the temple in all the travel magazines. But our little band of travelers is a week or two ahead of the season, and we see few Westerners here. It's almost as if we have southern India to ourselves, aside from millions of Indians, that is.

That night we visit the Orphanage of the Little Angels. Out of the darkness I hear the patter of little feet and then our party of four is engulfed by a sea of waving hands with 25 Tamil kids who live in this run-down compound. They have bright, shining faces of a dark, cherry-brown color and eyes like coffee beans in olive oil; their hair falls in crisp, raven black curls -- they're beautiful little children, ages four and up.

We shake hands with each child and they lead us from room to room, with several kids pulling each hand. It's a bit overwhelming and I'm glad I've had some experience hanging out with the kids in my wife Jeannette's day care. Here is where the tiny children sleep and do their school lessons... here the middle children... here the big children, ages 14 and up, and so on.

Florence, who is clearly dying to have a child of her own, is lovestruck. Her face is radiant.

"It's so hard to adopt a child in Germany or France," she says. "You have to wait for years and there are so many barriers and so much expense. And even when you go through all that, you never know if you will be able to adopt a child. But here, there are all these children who need someone and they are so poor. Why can't we adopt them?"

Why indeed? The government of India has put restrictions on the adoption of millions of orphans by Westerners. Right or wrong, their fear is that the children will be funneled into white slavery and used for evil purposes. In fact, that is the fate of many orphaned children in the Third World -- they are set out as beggars or used as prostitutes or slaves -- so it's a rational precaution.

But it's also a tragedy, because gazing upon Florence's joyful face, I can only imagine that she would adopt one of these kids in a heartbeat and transform that child's life with love and all the cultural riches of

Europe.

The orphanage is a collection of small, bare cinderblock rooms with little jackets hanging on the wall -- at night they throw down some mats and blankets for the kids to sleep on. These hovels serve as both classrooms and sleeping quarters.

"Some of the children are abandoned by their parents, who can't afford to take care of them," says Stefan, the social worker and restaurant owner who launched this private orphanage with his own meager funds. "But then their lives improve and they come back to get their children. Others stay until they are grown and we can find them jobs."

The place is a humid nest of mosquitoes, but the children are eager to play. Anne teaches us the Hokey Pokey, a wedding staple which is a huge success as we dance in the darkness -- it's sure to be talked about and practiced for years. My contribution is astounding the bored teenage boys with an old trick learned in the Cub Scouts where you pretend to pull off your thumb with some literal sleight of hand.

"It's not easy running the orphanage," says Stefan. "I had to borrow 35,000 rupees so the kids could have lots of firecrackers and food for the Festival of Light."

This throws us for a loop, since we figure that 35,000 rupees would be a bit less than $1,000 U.S. For that amount in India, you could buy enough fireworks to blow a small city to smithereens. Some of his other figures didn't make sense either, like the claim that he spends the equivalent of $4,000 per month to rent the appalling dump the kids live in.

"It all seemed very fishy to me," Ann says. "Imagine spending that much for fireworks, and those kids don't even have a single computer. And why would he pay that much to rent this awful place?"

But I figure it out (maybe) -- the Indians say 35,000 when they mean 3,500 -- most likely, he had borrowed about $100.

The Auroville Supermen
Nov. 15, 2007
Auroville, India

India is a land of seekers: young monks head to the Himalayas to live as hermit sadhus, seeking the meaning of life... Westerners flock to yoga retreats and ashrams... Jain priests walk around stark naked all their lives, probably looking for their dongs...

Then there's Auroville, the City of the Dawn.

In 1968, a 90-year-old woman, pretentiously named "The Mother," founded this utopian community just outside of the seaside town of Pondicherry. The town is based on the principles of guru Sri Aurobindo, who believed in the time-honored yogi practice of bamboozling Westerners out of their money with the allure of Eastern mysticism.

Just kidding, but there is a strong whiff of cash about this place, which caters to New Age Europeans. It's not like they're letting the orphans of the Little Angels compound live here -- you've got to pay to play and have the right "spiritual" attitude to boot.

Spiritual seekers flocked to Auroville from all over the world. Some contributed sweat equity, rather than cash, planting two million trees on a dusty plain. They built homes, shops and factories, and today it's a lovely place that looks like a tony ranch in southern California, with great croissants and coffee in its cafè.

The Aurovillians claim to have renounced material possessions and are advancing to a higher state of consciousness through the pursuit of art, dance and yoga with the idea of creating a new race of peaceful 'supermen.' It's the same sort of 'master race' stuff Hitler and Nietsche dreamed of, albeit dished up in a rosy wrapper.

But you have to admire what the power of culture and a little backbone can do in a messed-up place like India. There are 1,800 people living here from 35 countries. They are planning a city of 50,000 to be configured in the shape of a spiral galaxy. The new city will be powered by sustainable energy, with an organic farm and 'green' principles at work.

Personally, I think you'd have to be nuts to travel halfway around the world to live in such an obscure corner of India, but to each their own. And come to think of it, Auroville would probably be more fun to live in than Manchester, Slovakia, Cairo and a few other places I've passed through.

At the center of the project is the Matri Mandir -- a 300-foot-diameter temple which resembles a gigantic golden golf ball. Repeat: A GIANT GOLDEN GOLF BALL! It's intended to be glorious, but strikes me as chintzy, like a huge plastic Christmas ornament.

The center of the dome will house the world's largest crystal -- a perfect sphere more than two feet in diameter, to be lit by a single beam of sunlight channeled by mirrors though a hole in the roof of the dome. Someday, the superpeople will peer into their super powerful crystal in deep meditation, happy to know that they are evolving the human race to a higher level...

... Of course, other seekers of Utopia just down the road will be making the exact same claim.

In French India
Nov. 15, 2007
Pondicherry, India

The main drag into Pondicherry roars with a river of motorbikes, like a scene from an Indy version of *The Wild One*. A languid town on the southeast coast, Pondicherry was the capital of French India, going back some 300 years ago.

The French never quite cut the *poupon* in India. They established a Compagnie des Indes for trading (and exploitation) purposes, but their outfit was far less aggressive than the East India Company of the British. The Compagnie acquired Pondicherry as its capital in the late 1600s and thereafter, the French battled the British for control of eastern India.

In 1748, a British squadron bombarded Pondicherry for seven days before withdrawing.

One of the young officers at the siege was Robert Clive, who came to India at the age of 18 as a bookkeeper with the East India Company at a time when the corporation had its own private army.

Clive of India was a minor British nobleman of slight means and no military training. But he distinguished himself in his early 20s by seizing opportunities to lead men into battle and quickly became renowned for his bravery.

It was the dawn of corporate warfare, when even clerks were drafted to serve as military commanders. The brave bookkeeper led his soldiers from the front and was a born strategist. Like Napoleon, he was a rags-to-riches success who became a soldier-politician, conquering southern India and Bengal (which had a population of 40 million) for the East India Company and Britain.

During one sally against the French, 25-year-old Clive seized the city of Arcot with a small force of 200 Brits and 300 sepoys (native troops). The city was surrounded by 10,000 Indians supported by French troops, with a large number of hostile residents within the city walls. But Clive kept his enemies off balance with daring night raids outside the walls of the fort, holding out for 50 days until reinforcements arrived. This and other exploits made him a hero back home in England, and a wealthy man in India.

At one time, there were as many as 260 kingdoms in India -- many the result of the disintegrating Mughal Empire. The Brits often pitted one maharajah against another to win control of sub-continent. The maharajahs also tended to rely on mercenary soldiers, who were notorious for switching sides when the battle was going against them.

As for the French, ultimately they were outgunned and outmaneuvered. Pondicherry lapsed into a backwater of one million people that's best known today for its French restaurants and colonial avenues. Part of the city looks much the same as the French Quarter in New Orleans -- no surprise, since both towns were built in the same era.

But *vive la France*, says I, for tonight we dine at a French seafood restaurant, and my hopes are high for a bottle of zee vin rouge.

Wine is virtually non-existent in India, and in most of Asia, for that matter, beyond some sickening-sweet stuff that's on par with fruit syrup. Asia is the continent of beer & whisky, or a plainer drink known as abstinence.

Revenge of the Baffler

I've got a new "no handshake" policy.

Everywhere you go in the Third World, there's some pesky chap who wants to shake your hand. One out of 100 is sincerely interested in meeting a Westerner and wants to know where you're from. I've even been asked to pose with Indian families for photographs because I'm Mr. Exotic Foreigner.

But the other 99% are pests who just want a handout or to guide you to their shop. And these loafers spend their time picking their noses, scratching their balls and sneezing into their hands until you -- the polite foreign chump -- shows up to accept a handful of their goo.

But how not to offend the rare nice person?

Solution: now when I'm met with an outstretched hand, I touch the brim of my hat or my forehead, make a bow, and say some mysterious gobbledygook like "Badda Boom, Badda Bing!" and then do the Indian head-waggle, which can mean "do you get it?"

This throws the shakers off. Hopefully, they'll be bowing to the next foreigner they meet with a "Badda Boom, Badda Bing!" and a salute instead of a shake. My good karma deed for the day...

Elephant Geek

You never know where you'll meet an elephant in India. Out in the country, of course, but also on city streets and inside Hindu temples. They are gracious, friendly, intelligent creatures, much larger than you'd imagine when you meet one in person. Whenever I see an elephant, I go weak in the knees, like a 13-year-old teenybopper in the

You never know where you'll meet an elephant in India.

presence of a pop star.

Shocked, flabbergasted, awed, amazed, star-struck, humbled, worshipful... it's hard to describe the feelings you get when you're nose-to-trunk with one of these wonderful creatures.

Most Americans desire a million dollars, a Porsche, or a six-bedroom home with a view. My India-induced fantasy would be to own an elephant. Not that you could actually 'own' one -- at best you could be friends, serving this royal creature the finest foods and providing its daily bath.

Thus far, I've seen elephants bathing in a river, along with a stately wild tusker dining in the dark by the lights of a safari truck. I've seen a momma and her calf, browsing in the jungle.

But the best was in downtown Pondicherry, where we came upon a Temple of Ganesh. There was a huge elephant outside, his body painted in sacred markings. A twinkling light of intelligence shown in its eyes. I offered it a coin and it accepted it from my hand in the nostrils of its rough, hairy trunk. Then I bowed and it touched me on the head in a blessing.

The temple was small but fabulous -- as ornate as a baroque jewelry box -- with dozens of Hindus worshipping their god of good luck. On the walls were pictures of Ganesh in hundreds of incarnations, with multiple arms, lovers and depictions of him in many lands. Lo, the Remover of Obstacles!

Between a lane of golden pillars, worshipping Hindus packed the temple, waving their hands over the sacred flames of a candelabra carried by a barechested monk in an orange kilt -- horizontal ashes marking his forehead. The tinkle of cymbals filled the air, along with the rumble of a mechanical drum machine and the clang of an iron bell -- a tremendous racket, meant perhaps to draw the attention of Ganesh.

Vinit bought a baseball-sized yellow ball of lentils, cashews and raisins to sacrifice to the god. Ganesh got a morsel and we ate the rest. My forehead was smeared with a bar of coconut powder, indicating that I had made a sacrifice.

There is no single holy day like Sunday for the Hindus. Every day is a holy day. Many go to the temples of Krishna, Shiva, Lakshmi and other gods every day. Personally, I would go if only for the elephants.

The elephant's blessing is working so far, except for my tendency to explode from both ends at times. Our band of backpackers have all came down with cases of vomiting from different bugs than we're used to in the food and water. It's not much fun being sick combined with the constant heat, crowds, traffic, pollution, grime and hassles of traveling in India. But India isn't a place you visit for a "fun" vacation -- it's more along the lines of a hallucinogenic ordeal you come to experience.

To Give, or Not to Give?

That is the question.

What do you do when a tiny, stressed-out woman chases you around a taxi with a crying baby and an outstretched hand?

One of the editors of the *Lonely Planet* guide to India says that you should give to the many beggars here. He makes the point that there is no social safety net in India and that all good Hindus have a spiritual obligation to help the poor. Tourists should pitch in too.

No way, says Intrepid Travel, the group I'm traveling with. Under their "Responsible Tourism" guidelines, they claim that handouts to beggars are perpetuating an evil practice.

Both sides have a point.

"Many of the people who beg are -- how do you say? Doing a scam," Vinit says. "Some rent a child or a baby for a day and dress it in rags; then they pinch it to make it cry. And some pay a fee to tourist shops in order to beg out front."

Then too, evildoers like the Bombay mafia reportedly kidnap children off the streets and cut of their limbs or pluck out their eyes to make them pathetic beggar slaves, with the cash going back to the gangsters. Organized criminals set out amputees, mothers and old women, collecting their alms at the end of the day and leaving the alms-seekers to survive on pennies for their long hours in the sun.

I understand, but when I see a frail old person just a whisper from death, I can't resist digging for a coin.

On the other hand, the fat mama with three bare-ass kids in filthy rags who was parked on the steps of a Hot Bread coffee shop got nothing but my scorn. The kids were laughing and playing until a 'customer' showed up, and then the big sob story act began.

Get these kids to school, lady.

The Pilgrims
Nov. 17, 2007
Madurai, India

The Meenakshi Temple of Shiva is dedicated to the god of the destruction of evil, and a mighty castle of spiritual power it appears to be. This temple in the pilgrimage town of Madurai is the size of a baseball stadium with four 165-foot pyramidal towers decorated with beckoning, orgiastic, writhing sculptures of hundreds of Hindu gods, all brightly painted, tilting and waving their arms off the sides. Listen carefully and you can hear the babble of the gods murmuring in your ears.

Inside is the Temple of 1,000 Columns, filled with hundreds of statues of the multi-armed gods -- many of which rival the modeling of the classical Greek sculptures. There's also a mini shopping mall of religious souvenirs: merchants sell statues, bindhi forehead markings, incense, sacrificial offerings, clothing, pictures of the gods and every souvenir a religious pilgrim could ask for.

In the depths of the temple, an elaborately painted elephant accepts sacrifices of 10 rupees on Shiva's behalf. Nearby is a Brahma bull, draped in the colors of the rainbow, with glass beads and mirrors woven through its robe. The mirrors are meant to ward off the 'evil eye.' Imagine a 2,400 lb. bull with horns two feet long, and an elephant in your local cathedral.

Hundreds of people mill about inside, including many pilgrims -- these are barechested young men dressed in black skirts, with stripes of ashes on their foreheads, geeking on the universe of gods.

Imagine you are dropped on an alien planet where the sights are almost too foreign for your mind to digest. The streets quake with people jostling with bicycles, tuk-tuks and motorbikes in the narrow lanes past hundreds of seedy shops. It's the ultimate Land of the Strange -- yet you are able to walk like a tiger through the streets, feeling you somehow belong, even though every face among the many thousands is different than your own. That, in a way, is what India feels like.

When the Train Left the Station...
Nov. 18, 2007
Vallipuram, India

Busted by the Indian Army. I look up to see eight legs in uniforms and the butts of four rifles in a circle around me. But this is no shakedown -- the soldiers just want to meet the American gringo playing an impromptu show on guitar and harmonica at the train station in Vallipuram. Glad I'm playing my best harp solo at the time so as not to be embarrassed in front of the military.

I host an impromptu guitar workshop at the station for six Tamil guys, with each getting a chance to perform "That's Alright Mama" by Elvis Presley. It's a two-string strum in a 1-4-5 blues progression that any child can play with a few minutes' instruction.

My students don't speak a word of English, other than the phrase "superstar," but giggle with excitement at each chance to pick at the strings. I award the best student a guitar pick -- he's about 15 years old -- and pronounce that one day he will be "Superstar." If I ever hear of a hot guitarist from Vallipuram on the southeast coast of India, I'll know my seed has borne fruit.

Speaking of trains, it's heaps of fun of traveling on the third-class sleeper cars. There are six narrow bunks piled three-high in a compart-ment the size of a mini-van. You jam all your gear into the nearest cranny and sit on a bunk until it's time to crash, sharing the space with the Indian family across from you. There goes a stick-thin grandma, climbing up to the top bunk, with mom and two kids in the middle and dad down below... What better place is there to reflect on your life than on a hard train bunk, rumbling across India?

Also a hoot are the dusty, junky, clunker buses that seem to be held together with chicken wire. Most of these were considered wrecks 20 years ago when cities in Europe passed on their cast-offs to India. On yesterday's ride, our driver's spring-popping seat was held together with luck & twine. He stayed alert by chewing a mild narcotic known as khat, mixed with fresh tobacco leaf. A bonus was the DVD film in the Hindi language, screeching at top volume through blown speakers on the bus TV.

The worst way to travel is by private car, doing the Dance of Death on the Highways of Hell. We whipsaw in and out of traffic, passing straight into the path of oncoming cars, buses, trucks and motorbikes, with all doing the same. Every long ride includes dozens of near miss-es, tying my sphincter in a knot and curling my toes in terror.

Dinner in Tiger Country
Nov. 19, 2007
Periyar Nature Preserve, India

Looking for a fun dinner party idea? Try eating like the Indians do -- with sticky fingers. You'll soon realize why it's so important not to eat with your bathroom hand.

We visit a spice plantation, walking around a forest of allspice, tu-merac, nutmeg, cocoa, coffee, banana, pineapple, betel, pepper, cardo-man and other plants, all mixed in together in a jungle.

Our host's wife serves dinner, using banana leaves for plates. The dark green leaves are broad and stiff, well-suited to hold a smorgas-bord of fish and chicken curries, curried potatoes, mung beans, 'flat' rice, tapioca, spiced gherkins and more.

You pile these soupy curries on your rice, mush it around with your fingers to make a big gooey ball and -- *bon appetit*. I'm proud to say I tried everything, although I could only manage a teeny bit. I think that Ann and Florence were a bit grossed out, but they followed through.

One thing I don't eat, however, is the dessert made by mushing a banana into the rice mash, then dousing it with sugar and yogurt and rolling it into a ball. It looks like pastey gook.

Dinner is also a lesson in why the Indians are such litterbugs. Before the advent of plastic, they ate all of their meals on banana leaves and washed their hands with the inside of banana peels after dining. Then they wrapped up the leaf with its garbage and tossed the mess outdoors where it quickly disintegrated in the tropical heat. When plastic bags replaced banana leaf wrappers, they kept the same toss-it tradition with ugly results.

The spice plantation is in the state of Kerala, just outside the Periyar Nature Preserve, which is famous for its tigers.

"Do any of the tigers ever leave the reserve?" I ask the plantation owner.

"Oh yes, sometimes they are out in the forest right behind my house," he waves toward the jungle we've just strolled through in the near-darkness.

"Do they ever eat anyone?"

"Oh yes. A couple of years ago, one of the locals was digging a hole for yams just up over that hill. A tiger crept up from behind and nailed him in the back -- a maneater. By the time they found him, he had been dragged down into a gully and the tiger had eaten half of him."

I don't see any tigers the next day on my hike through the jungle preserve, which is home to 45 of the big cats. But I do see a large pile of tiger poop by the trail; it's big enough to do a horse proud.

Glad it's not me coming out of a tiger's ass -- it's estimated that such is the fate of about 80 Indians each year.

The Terra Formers
Nov. 20, 2007
Kerala Backwaters, India

A fruit bat the size of a cocker spaniel wheels overhead in broad daylight and flaps off into a grove of coconut palms on lazy wings. At my feet are rice fields stretching to the horizon and the canals of the Kerala Backwaters in southern India, also known as the Country of God.

One of the great themes of science fiction is that of terra-forming, in which spacemen transform hostile worlds into living planets. But over the past thousand years, humble rice farmers have done just that in Kerala, reclaiming 650 square miles of land from the sea by piling mud -- one handful at a time -- on the ancient river delta which is located between the Arabian Sea and the mountains of the Western Ghats in southwest India.

In fact, you can still see the mud diggers today, standing out in the river. They dive underwater, scoop the mud with their hands, and fill a dugout canoe. The mudders dive and dig off the bottom of the river all day long, six days a week for years until they die... Imagine having that job. I think there are positions available.

Of course, some say the land was dredged from the sea by the sixth incarnation of Vishnu. Take your pick.

We're the guests of a rice farmer and his family in a modern, American-style home with rich, red beams lining the ceiling, situated right by the river. The home was built by the farmer's sister, who is presently working as a nurse in Manchester, England. Many Indians go abroad and send money home to their families. In five years, she too will return home to her queenly palace on the river to live a life of idle luxury on the riches she has made as a humble nurse in England.

***

That night, we take a moonlight cruise through the canals and along the river in a dugout dragon boat. The boat is about 40 feet long and easily seats 11 of us, with the crew of three singing hearty Kerala folk songs, punctuated by the thump of a staff on the bottom of the boat. Many of these boats are 200 years old, with some being 75-100 feet long. The questing bats swoop overhead, hunting bugs in the night.

"Would you like a toddy?" our captain asks as we glide to the shore by the dark of the moon. We pull up to a wooden shack bar full of local men. "The toddy is made from the flower of the coconut palm," he says. "The people who make it are called toddy-tappers. They mash it every day while it ferments."

"Sure, what the hell," I say, hoisting a grimy glass that is sticky with the fingerprints of a dozen hands. "Here's to the toddy-tappers."

It smells like yeast, looks like coconut milk, and tastes like funky Sprite. But it turns out this tropical moonshine can get to be 8 proof alcohol, so I get a little buzz on (and sick to my stomach the next day).

The next morning, I rise early to greet the sunrise for a walk along the river. I see women washing their dishes by the riverbank and people bathing, brushing their teeth, and drinking straight from the river. Unfortunately, the river now has an oily film on it from the scores of giant rattan-covered houseboats full of wealthy Indian tourists from the north. Pollution has become a big problem for the farmers and fishermen who drink this muddy water.

Two duck farmers drift by in their canoes, herding a flock of thousands of quacking ducks. The average farmer has a flock of 5,000 ducks, which wander the rice fields to glean the picked-over crops, fertilizing the soil in the process. I think of those 5,000 ducks, all crapping in the river as they pass by, with people drinking the water. Strangely, I don't feel like having a glass of the stuff that morning.

Smells Like... Ernakulam
Nov. 21, 2007
Ernakulam, India

A rat darts across my path in the darkness, making me jump. Must be Ernakulam.

Ernakulam is the 'fancy' shopping and business district of Kochi, the start and end point of my circuit around southern India. Glitzy signs line MG Road (for Mahatma Ghandi), along with many upscale stores, hotels and restaurants. This town has also been chosen as the site of a new showcase IT computer center that will employ 90,000 people. It's a bustling, prosperous, rising star for India.

But the sidewalks here look like they've been shelled by heavy artillery. They are made of thousands of concrete panels, four feet long and two feet wide, laid over an open sewer. Most of them are crumbling, broken or tipping out of place, and even the tiles of newer sidewalks are soon broken and left unrepaired.

I heard of a backpacker in Thailand who fell through one of these booby traps and suffered permanent lung damage after crushing her chest on the concrete.

So each walk through the classy part of town is like tip-toeing through a roller-coaster minefield. And be sure to look up too, because low-hanging, jagged metal roofs are always ready to brain you senseless wherever you go.

Warning gals: leave your high heels at home the next time you prowl the streets of the big E.

***

This is also the place where I say goodbye to my women companions, Ann and Florence, both of whom I have come to admire.

Ann burns to travel to the most exotic, difficult places on earth. She was so enthralled by our ride on a dirty old bus that it made her vow to accept a five-month position teaching English in southern China, despite the wishes of her stay-at-home husband. She has ridden the trans-Siberian railway twice (once on a bunk beneath a strapped-in comatose drunk who vomited for two days straight), and all 'round east Africa, among other places. She's headed on to three more weeks in northern India.

Florence is traveling on to Nepal and northern India for another month, then to Vietnam and Australia, without a clue as what she will do when she gets back to Europe. Pretty gutsy, though in my estimation, she's hauling at least twice the gear she needs and is strapped down with enough stuff to break a mule.

I'm humbled by their valor. Given the hazards of traveling as lone women, their trips make mine look like a Boy Scout outing.

Comin' Up Roses

The subject of birthdays comes up and Vinit asks if it's possible to order a cake over the internet for his girlfriend in Canada. He met her a year ago while she was backpacking around Asia. Let's call her Tracey.

"Yes, I suppose you could order a cake on the internet, but why would you want to?" I ask.

"I want to order my girlfriend a birthday cake," Vinit says.

"A cake? That would be nice, but the custom over there is to send flowers," I tell him. "Women love to receive flowers on their birthday, and it's easy to arrange."

Since Vinit's Indian credit card is no good in Canada, I offer to order some roses on my card in trade for cash, planning to make the purchase part of his tip.

But Indian men are a bashful bunch, and Vinit, 28, is unsure about how to express himself on the accompanying card.

"You write something for me," he says, as we sit at the keyboard at an internet cafè tucked in a back alley in Ernakulam.

"But you've got to write it yourself," I say. "The message has to come from your heart. It has to be in your own words."

"But I don't know what to say," he shrugs and smiles with a helpless look in his eyes. Apparently, Indian men are not used to composing love notes.

He insists that I do the dirty deed, so I put on my romance cap -- read Vinit's mind -- and write:

"Dear Tracey: I love you so much. I think of you every day and wish we could be together always. Happy Birthday with all my love from India -- Vinit"

Although V is nearly as dark as milk chocolate, he blushes three more shades of red and agrees it's just right. And really, these are his words -- I have merely glimpsed them written on his heart.

Only problem is, the bunglers in Toronto send the roses that very day, instead of in January, as we ordered. Oh well, Tracey calls the next day and says she loves them.

Vinit has a problem though. His parents wouldn't approve of his marriage to a Western girl. They are searching for a good Indian girl for him to marry.

Family is everything in India. A son is treated like a prince all through childhood, never lifting a finger to help out around the house. But when he comes of age, he is expected to provide everything for his parents and the extended family -- everything. Some young men commit suicide when they are unable to find jobs and measure up to their family's expectations.

Thus, Vinit is having a new home built for his parents, with an apartment attached for himself and his someday-wife. Imagine your average 28-year-old American doing such a thing.

"But I am afraid to tell my father about Tracey," he says. "My mother knows about us, but in India, if you disobey your father's wishes by marrying someone he doesn't approve of, it's like turning your back on your family."

"Do they even know about Tracey? Have they met her?"

"Yes, we traveled around southern India together the last time she was here and they met her, but my father doesn't know we're engaged."

I don't share my suspicion, but am sure that if Vinit's mother knows, then his father is surely in on the 'secret' as well, since married couples can't resist blabbing such news to each other in an instant. But they probably also know that their son has spent only a total of five weeks with his Canadian sweetheart and it's not easy to sustain a romance between Toronto and southern India. Parents are patient.

"I'm sure things will work out for you," I assure him. "They always do when the person is right for you."

"Yes, Bob, and I want you to come to my wedding next year."

"Here in India?" I begin mentally calculating the airfare halfway around the world for myself and my wife...

"Yes, I want all my friends to come that I've met from all over the world. All the people I've met on my tours."

"Are you going to have one of those giant Indian weddings?"

"No, ours will be more on the average side," Vinit says, "maybe around 2,000 guests."

The Sick Side of India
Nov. 21, 2007
Ernakulam, India

After three weeks of kicking around southern India, I've gotten used to the place. It would be a stretch to say that India has "cast its spell" on me, but I have learned to see less of the trash and hassles, and to focus more on the colorful people, towering Hindu temples and lush scenery in this land of one billion souls.

But for every lei of marigolds to savor, there's sure to be a corresponding turd to sniff. For instance, today's big story on India CNN involved a case of "eve teasing."

This is a rosy term for the common practice of sexual harassment, up to and including rape. Oh yes, and murder as well.

Eve teasing is considered a sport by young men here, who are so sexually repressed that many reportedly have sex with each other as an outlet, not considering it to be homosexual. Young men hang out in packs, and as a result, young women tend to travel in groups as well, perhaps for protection. You never see Indian couples of the opposite sex holding hands or displaying affection in public.

The police tend to consider eve teasing as harmless fun. Just a boys-will-be-boys kind of thing.

In today's case, a man on a passing scooter thought it would be great fun to shove an 18-year-old college student into the path of an oncoming bus, where she was crushed under the wheels. She lay in the street face up for an hour before her body was recovered. The police declined to investigate, saying it was only a case of eve teasing. One officer told the press he wouldn't intervene in such a matter even if a woman was being raped before his eyes.

This drew outrage from the women college students shown on CNN, but big grins on the faces of the Delhi police who endured their pummeling.

Reports of gang rapes are common in India's press. In Bombay, the big story during the week I arrived was of a telephone call center girl who was raped by two taxi drivers in a remote field, before having her head bashed in with a rock.

And although it's true that the people of India clearly love their children above all else (for many, children are their only treasure), it's also been estimated that 20% of all Indian children are sexually assaulted, mostly by family members.

No doubt, there are similar statistics in the Western world. So, is it true? Tough to say, but if so, that means that in a population of one billion people, then some 200 million Indians have been raped or sexually abused as children.

***

Speaking of the media, friends back home comment in their emails that I must be hearing a lot about the devastating cyclone that killed

3,000 people in Bangladesh and resulted in 280,000 people losing their homes. It's all over the news in the States.

Far from it -- there's barely a peep about the tragedy on TV in India, or in the papers. My impression is that many Indians feel that overpopulated, poverty-stricken, Muslim Bangladesh is a huge pain in the ass and wouldn't mind if the entire bedeviled country were washed out the sea. In 2005, India began constructing a 2,500-mile steel wall along the border of its Muslim neighbor, hoping to keep the Bangladeshis out. They are the illegal migrants of the subcontinent.

***

Here's another sick thing about India. On the way to Kerala, our driver passes a man who appeared to be in his 80s who had fallen down the stairs of his home and was lying unconscious on the pavement, just inches from the road.

"Shouldn't we stop?" I ask.

"No, someone will come," the driver replies. He doesn't even consider the idea of stopping, and I doubt that any of the other motorists passing by gave any thought to stopping either.

In America, every car on the road would have slammed on their brakes, mashing their cell phones on speed dial to 9-11 if they saw an old-timer lying in the road.

But in India, such a sight is someone else's problem, or your own tough luck. India is notorious for bringing out the best and the worst of humanity.

Goa

The Land of Make Believe,
Nov. 22, 2007
Calangute, India

What the fuck am I going to do for 12 days in Goa? I wonder somewhat dejectedly as my cab makes the 30-mile trip from the airport to the beach town of Calangute.

Perhaps this is a tactical error, but when I conceived of this trip, I planned for a Goa beach break to be a respite from travel after two-and-a-half months on the road. Still, 12 days sounds like a lot of loafing for an action monkey like me.

But Calangute looks like a fun town, even though it's considered

The wreck of the River Princess on the beach in Goa.

dreadfully uncool by the international backpacking community. There are swarms of Western tourists here and I'm ready to see my ethnic cohorts again after swimming in a sea of Indian faces for three weeks.

Calangute is also a good base for day-tripping around the State of Goa, which runs for nearly 100 miles along the Arabian Sea.

I had half expected Goa to look like Cancun, Mexico, with 20 miles of high-rise hotels rimming the beach. Instead, it's the same old squalor and anarchy of India, with small hotels, shops and cafes crammed into the narrow lanes paralleling the beach along with hundreds of touts and hustlers. And instead of pretty topless girls in string bikinis, the human scenery here is mostly paunchy Russians and Brits who look like walking conch shells, stuffed into sleeveless tee's, skimpy shorts and thongs that only a stripper would wear back home. I think the Europeans owe Americans a sincere apology for claiming that *we're* fat. Haven't seen so many fat people since Christmas shopping at Walmart last year.

With Calangute as a model, it's hard to imagine why Goa is such a big deal, much less one of the most celebrated beach breaks on this half of the planet.

But my heart melts at the sweetness of my room, which is on the second floor of a courtyard hotel, with a balcony overlooking the pool and a garden of ivy, palm trees and hibiscus. There are cool terra-cotta tiles on the floor and furnishings of rich teak and rosewood.

Here is a place to fantasize about being a writer in the tropics in the tradition of Robert Louis Stevenson in Tahiti, Jack London in the South Seas, Mark Twain in Hawaii, and Ernest Hemingway in Havana. Obviously, I'm in the little leagues compared to those chaps, but I am smoking from the same bong, so to speak, by sharing their tropical sojourns.

But what if I fall prey to dissolution -- or worse -- tropical lassitude, which is the fate of all drunken writers who head south and go native? No worries -- after a month of sitting on my ass on trains and buses, my body has gone soft and craves exercise. I plan to walk for miles on the beaches each day, swim, and practice my rusty yoga.

Dinner proves to be a delight. The chef at an outdoor cafè called Electric Cats presents me with a tray of tiger prawns the size of bananas, along with langostino lobsters, fresh tuna and other fish. He is my new best friend in Goa, along with Mrs. Varma of the Varma Beach Resort. I choose a pound of sweet and sour prawns, some veg fried rice and garlic naan, washed down with a pint of the 'strong' variety of Kingfisher beer. The shrimp are so fresh and full of iodine that I believe my body could withstand the fallout from a nuclear blast.

I think I'm going to like it here.

The Last Hippie Tribe
Nov. 22, 2007
Anjuna Beach, India

When it comes to spectacles, you can keep your Taj Mahal. My choice is the Wednesday Flea Market at Anjuna Beach.

Talk about your Magical Mystery Tour: It's like driving into a big rock festival, down a long dusty road lined with tuk-tuks and motor scooters. Then you come to hundreds of tents and stalls, filled with the treasures of India, China, Tibet and Southeast Asia. You see leathery Gujarati tribal women dressed in the colors of circus clowns with their faces dangling with what looks like a pound of metal jewelry. There are also small workshops along the way where custom clothing, textiles and jewelry are being hand-crafted by members of the last hippie tribe. Cows wander through the throng, which pulses with the techno and trance music of the world-famous Goan raves. The music provides a backbeat for the constant refrain: "Jus' loook, my fren', jus' loook..."

Back in the '70s, an international group of hippies founded a colony near the village of Anjuna, living naked, doing heavy drugs and screwing their brains out with a different partner or three every day. It was the ultimate free love dopetopia.

Many are still going at it in the same spirit, with new young recruits from Europe and Australia.

But lest you're tempted to say "coulda', woulda', shoulda'," remember that there there are no handouts in India and even hippies have to eat. Solution? They launched a flea market on the beach, selling homemade crafts. It has since drawn vendors from all over Asia.

And talk about characters. My own hair falls something like 14 inches when I let it down, qualifying me for an audition with Led Zeppelin, yet I look as conservative as a lawyer in a three-piece suit compared to the groovy cats drifting through the market. Many are as picket-fence-thin as the Indians, covered with freaky Asian tattoos, and have matted dreadlocks that fall to the waist. And of course, they're shirtless with dozens of bangles, piercings and who-knows-whats-who-knows-where.

I do my bit, buying a sphere of marble carved with elephants to be used for burning incense, and a couple of fabric lanterns. But I could use $1,000 and a mini-van to haul away more booty. Even a non-shopper would be hard-pressed to resist this wonder.

Thanksgiving Day
Nov. 22, 2007
Calangute, India

Today finds me on a 10-mile hike up the beach under a pulsing sun. The beach is a glory here -- an anesthetic balm to soothe the roar of commerce beyond the palms. Lathered with two handfuls of sunscreen, I am nonetheless nut brown within a couple of hours.

Back home my family will be dining on turkey, sweet potatoes and pumpkin pie in the American holiday of togetherness. Missing holidays is the price you pay for backpacking around the world. On my trip, I'll miss celebrating Halloween, Thanksgiving, Christmas, New Year's Eve and my wife's birthday as well as my own, with all the heavy freight of friendship, love and family that go with them.

At a beachside cafè, I offer a silent prayer of thanks for this trip and for the blessing and safety of myself and the people I love back home. The prayer is a daily ritual for me, but it seems to have more weight on this day of Thanksgiving. *Namaste.*

Stuck in a Rut
Nov. 23, 2007
On the Beach, Goa, India

Have established a routine here in Goa: I dodge an obstacle course of touts to score a cappuccino in the a.m. and then head for my 10-mile walk on the beach wearing my funky cowboy hat.

I wander past thousands of Europeans lounging in sun beds along what I call Cellulite Alley. Most seem to be in training to become Goodyear Blimps, and when you do see the extremely rare beach beauty, it's like a gift from ocular heaven. Some of the Western men have beer guts that are so huge they look like they're about to give birth to twins.

But there is glory here as well -- I find fishermen hauling in their catch from 30-foot wooden boats and filling bushel baskets with flopping silver. There are young Indian women splashing in the waves, fully-dressed in their saris. And young men walk hand-in-hand, sometimes three abreast, without a clue this looks gay to a Westerner. British tourists play cricket on the beach with Indian teenagers, and cows ramble up and down the shore.

Just offshore is the wreck of an old freighter, The River Princess, that has run aground and is rusting away in the tropical sun. A sea eagle glides past the word MOCKBA (Moscow) painted on its bridge while swimmers splash in its shadow.

Lunch is always the same: a handful of cashews, some bananas from the women peddlers on the beach, and a diet Pepsi.

There's a steady string of hustlers, but I've learned to play nice, declining offers for a massage, or a beach chair, or a necklace or bananas, and asking for nonsensical things I know they can't produce, such as chocolate cake or ostrich feathers. "I'd like an Australian girl in a string bikini. And could you make her a blonde?" I tell one perplexed tout who's anxious to know what I might desire. This produces the Indian head wiggle and his immediate disappearance. "Badda boom, badda bing!" also sends the hand-shakers running like rabbits. I've learned to cage my snarl, until I get dead tired, at least.

By the time I'm ready to drop from sunstroke, I head to Bobby's Beach Shack, where they greet me as "the boss." With drinks and a big American tip, my daily meal of seafood and rice runs about $10. Then it's back to the hotel for happy hour on the balcony and hit the internet cafè for some writerly moments.

Kinda' boring, but I'm forcing myself to live with it.

You learn a lesson about time in a place like Goa: If you wish to live for 1,000 years, go traveling alone. It's sheer relativity: time whips around like a spinning top when you're home doing the Same Old Thing for weeks on end. But time slows to a grind when you're alone and far from home, and you live longer by dint of its stretching. With only your own thoughts for company, time shifts into its lowest gear, plodding forward at the speed of ennui.

And what is ennui? Boredom.

On the road, time towers over you as a mile-high glacier, grinding over the tundra of your thoughts, which grow barren from too much inner absorption. Back home, the weeks flicker by like a thumb fanning the pages of an open book, but all alone in the wide world, my days feel luxuriously long, the weeks stretch on like months, and the months feel like years since I've been gone.

Jungle Rot
Nov. 25, 2007
Calangute, India

Mr. Varma, who has traveled the world, says it's terribly difficult keeping his hotel up to snuff in the tropical climate. It makes this dumb gringo realize why much of the Third World looks like hell.

"There are two monsoons per year in this part of India," he says. "Terrible rains that last for weeks and flood all the streets and houses."

This results in a relentless, creeping rot. Then there is the blistering sun, the constant chewing of the bugs, and the humidity -- not to mention shoddy, adulterated building materials and bad paint. Even the concrete for the sidewalks is often mixed with salt water in India, which guarantees their ruin.

"I paint my hotel fresh each year from top to bottom to try to keep it nice, but it's never-ending," Mr. Varma says. He also has a staff of maids and three men constantly polishing and cleaning from dawn til dark every day of the week. It's a tough way to make a rupee.

Beach Culture

When we backpackers aren't trolling old temples and palaces, we fall back on making pithy observations. Here are some of the latest:

-- It seems like half of England visits Goa each year, just as Americans flock to Florida. Many come again and again, some staying for months at a time. There are special English restaurants and the Brits all cozy up in their own hotels over baked beans and tomatoes for breakfast. Also, an Englishman or Aussie will do almost anything for rice pudding -- haven't a clue why.

-- Don't even dream of heading out after 5 p.m. in malaria-prone India without lathering yourself with Odomos, the leading mosquito cream. I've learned to coat my feet as well because the mozzies bite right through the web of my shoes and SmartWool socks.

-- The Indian head wiggle can mean anything: yes, no, maybe, don't bother me, maybe someday, tastes good, get lost crazy tourist, etc...

-- If there are waffles on a menu in India, you can bet your last rupee they haven't actually served one in years.

-- A 500 rupee note ($12.50 U.S.) throws most shop owners into a tizzy, running next door to try to make change. Unfortunately, this is what the ATMs distribute. Even a 100 rupee note ($2.50) can be difficult to break.

-- Contrary to what you've heard, I've yet to discover a filthy bathroom in India. They're all as clean as in the U.S., although they are just holes in the ground with footpads on either side (and a bucket for splashing the backside). Even the legendary nightmare of a bus station john looked like it had just been sprayed with a firehose and 20 gallons of disinfectant. I've seen worse in in the restaurants of downtown Boston and Chicago.

-- Westerners in Goa tan themselves to crisps, but on TV, Nivea is selling a skin-whitening cream to Indian men. Perhaps they have Michael Jackson Disease. Maybe that's also why the women go fully clothed in their saris when they swim -- everyone wants to be as pale as possible in India.

-- The men of India wear the oddest outfits to the beach after the age of 25 or so: dress shoes, neatly pressed slacks, a fancy leather belt, and either a dress shirt or a buttoned-up sports shirt. Sometimes, you'll see a man in a full-blown suit. All this in the 90 degree heat with many Westerners (such as myself) dressed worse than beggars. But when they decide to swim, the Indian men strip to their underwear.

-- Yes, Goa is a bit of a trip, but this lonely traveler wouldn't mind bumping into a few Americans, who are as rare as snowflakes in India. On the beach, I see the flags of Israel, Denmark, France and those of other countries fluttering proudly in the breeze, and it makes me wish the Stars & Stripes were here as well.

On the other hand, I guess if I wanted to see Americans, I wouldn't be on the far side of the world, now would I?

My brain is whirling like a carnival tilt-a-whirl each day, trying to keep pace with the kaleidoscope visions of this country. India keeps you spinning. No wonder this is the land where meditation was conceived. Twenty years ago, I learned Transcendental Meditation, but was appalled to discover years later that my "top-secret" $150 mantra was the name of a Hindu god, even though I'd been assured there was nothing religious about TM. Now, I try meditating to the universal mantra of "Om," the sub-sonic sound of life.

It's about as effective as a cat jumping up and down on your head.

Daytripper, Yeah

You can go almost anywhere on the public bus in Goa for 10 rupees (25 cents) or less, provided you don't mind being mashed into human jam with your fellow passengers in the tropical heat.

It's quite easy to get around India because there are skads of Helpful Harrys helping you to navigate even the maddest bus stations.

In recent days, I've kicked around some old Portuguese forts at Aguada and Anhora -- big blocky structures high over the sea, that no doubt had many a teary-eyed soldier looking west to a sweetheart in faraway Lisbon, back in the day.

At Little Vagator Beach, I find out where all the pretty girls have been hiding and suffer an hour at a beach bar, contemplating a smorgasbord of bare buns and breasts with the pangs of a starving man. I'm glad Jeannette is joining me in Thailand next week because, brutha' -- it don't matter how nice the beach is -- if there's no woman around, it ain't no paradise.

In fact, the pangs of loneliness are what you suffer from the most on a round-the-world trip. I psyched myself up for this eventuality, but 16 hours a day to fill with your own company gets old, no matter how charming you might be in a group, and time drags like a broken clock when you're talking to yourself in your thoughts all day. Yes, loneliness is a bit of an ordeal.

***

I offer a Marketing 101 lesson to some of the vendors on the beach so that they too can someday become a rich know-it-all like me. Most are selling some variant of beach necklaces made from beads strung together.

"Look," I point out, "you're selling the same jewelry and t-shirts as hundreds of others that I meet all day long. And it's stuff that most tourists don't want to begin with.

"You need to sell something unusual and creative that no one else is offering," I add. "Try painting some landscapes -- no one's doing that here, and the tourists would buy them to take home. Learn to play the sitar or carve palm trees in coconuts -- anything that's different that will set you apart from the other vendors."

"Yes, but do your want to buy a necklace?" a young woman responds, oblivious to my tutorial. It's like explaining algebra to a goat, without a word sinking in. The illiterate vendors plow the same track each day without a clue as to how to break free of it.

A Visit With St. Xavier
Nov. 26, 2007
Old Goa, India

St. Francis Xavier is tougher than Death itself. That's why he's still a tourist attraction in Old Goa, 450 years after his demise.

Old Goa was known as the "Rome of the East" back in the 1600s. This was the capital of Portugal's empire in India and its commerce rivaled Amsterdam at the time. But it was built next to a marsh filled with mosquitoes and pestilence; as a result, a cholera plague killed 200,000 people in the mid-1600s. No problem, said the Portuguese, who kept on building. Other plagues came along, killing just as many people, and eventually the place became an abandoned city of ghosts.

Today, it's filled with churches and cathedrals and is a World Heritage Site. Its biggest attraction is Mr. X.

Born in Navarre, Spain in 1506, Francis Xavier was a brilliant, daring adventurer who distinguished himself at Paris University. There, he met Ignatius Loyola, and the two founded the Jesuits, aka The Society of Jesus -- a courageous group of wandering priests who journeyed to the most exotic and difficult places on earth to spread the gospel -- and also to plunder and burn 'heathen' temples. (Actor Robert DeNiro dramatized their conviction in *The Mission*)

Being popular wasn't always part of their gig. One captain in the 18th century called the Jesuits "a pack of the most atrocious hypocrites in the world," and the "most zealous bigots," who were infamous for their murderous Inquisition.

Xavier had a traveling bone and arrived in Goa in 1542, moving on to Ceylon, Japan and Malacca at a time when this was like heading to Mars.

Then, a miracle happened -- he died off the Chinese coast in 1552 and was packed into a coffin with four bags of quicklime to speed the breakdown of his body. But when his corpse arrived in Goa, it was found to be completely intact. Two priests even claimed there was

The paradise of Palolem Beach.

blood in his arm when they inspected a small wound. His incorrupt-
ible body was proclaimed a miracle.

The Catholic Church was skeptical, sending physicians and specialists to see in Xavier had been embalmed or was simply a really great
piece of wax-work, as some claimed. But the facts of his living death
held up and he was canonized as a saint. In fact, his right arm was amputated and shipped to the Vatican, where it picked up a pen, dipped it
in ink and wrote "Xavier" before a college of cardinals and priests.

Parts of Xavier's corpse were chopped off for religious souvenirs.
The right arm was divided between churches in Rome and Japan, and
his internal organs became relics at churches all over Asia.

But what's left of him can still be seen in profile high up in a glass
coffin atop a marble altar in the Basilica of Bom Jesus in Old Goa,
along with photos of the old chap. They bring him out for show-and-
tell with the public every 10 years -- with the next viewing in 2014.

I must say, he looks pretty good.

***

Also here in Old Goa is the Church of St. Catherine, whom we last
met at the monastery beneath Mt. Sinai. Her church was established
here because the Portuguese landed on this spot on St. Catherine's Day
-- each saint in the Catholic pantheon has their own special day.

St. Catherine was a member of the Egyptian nobility who converted
to Coptic Christianity at a time when the Roman Empire was feeling

threatened by the new religion. Family members tried to get her to renounce her faith, but instead, she converted them to Jesus.

Finally, the Romans gave her an offer she couldn't refuse: either get back to worshipping the pagan gods of Jupiter, Juno, Minerva, et. al, or off with your head. She chose the latter and was declared a saint for her trouble.

By the way, Old Goa is perhaps the only World Heritage Site on earth that has a large number of poor families living on sidewalks in the park and even in the churches. The Basilica of Bom Jesus had many elderly women lying on rags along the walls -- apparently, it serves as a nursing home for destitute women. It's the only church I've seen in all the world that actually lives up to its mission of caring for the poor, instead of being a gross welter of gold -- so score one for the Jesuits.

Three Days in Heaven
Nov. 28, 2007
Palolem Beach, India

Palolem is said to be the most beautiful beach in Goa, and that's saying a lot. The *Times of London* lauds it as one off the 10 most beautiful beaches on earth, and who can argue? I made the 70-mile trip this morning to the southernmost tip of the state and find a mile-long crescent of the sweetest paradise imaginable. A surrealistic curtain of druggy palms slouch down the beach, like they've been watered with mescaline and are making their rubbery way to Nirvana.

It sinks in -- I've reached Nirvana on the far side of the Earth... A Hindu god stares at me with faraway eyes, his face etched in a boulder just off the beach: "How's it goin', man?"

And rather than the hassle and hustle of Calangute, the first two creatures I meet are a friendly pig and a cow walking down the dirt road leading to the village.

Rather than staying at a hut right on the beach (which would be far too romantic for single me), I opt for a genteel aging mansion back a ways, where my room has a marble balcony overlooking a jungle courtyard. It seems to be occupied by old farts in my demographic, only from Europe of course.

This is a necessity because on the beach I see a lithe Israeli girl in a black bikini who is as dark as Kali the Destroyer, and surely the most beautiful young woman in India. I tear my eyes away with a ripping sound, and would rather have my thoughts focused on things like banana pancakes and fractured conversations with cranky Germans.

Places like this are why Ulysees made his men cover their eyes and stuff their ears when they sailed past the Sirens.

It took three bus rides and half a day to get here, with the longest stretch being a screamer. In India, no bus leaves the stop until it is crammed full with passengers, and our conductor on the trip from Margao to Palolem was a master of cramology, packing our mini bus to the rafters. Although the bus was only a few yards long, I swear there were 50 people onboard.

One consequence of this is that you get to know the body parts of the Indian people much more than is desired. One woman rubbed her crotch against my upper arm in such a languid up-and-down motion that I thought she was trying to get off. Then another woman did much the same. Maybe it's good luck to grind on a foreigner... Oh well, better that than a dick in your face, I always say -- which is a distinct possibility on these slam-packed rides.

But it was anything but 'sex on the bus' for me, because we were packed in so tight whipping around the winding roads that it was like being in a rolling coffin, with no way out if the bus rolled. The only sensation I felt during my pussy shoulder massage was one of terror.

I'd like to feel proud of myself for 'winging it' in India, but the truth is I feel more like a frightened little crustacean most of the time, fearful of peeking out of my shell. Fortunately, necessity gives me a poke each day to make me scuttle out.

On the other hand, even the toughest, young backpackers tend to travel in twos and threes, so I feel entitled to a wee bit of bragging rights for going it alone in places that would give most Midwesterners the heebie-jeebies, although Palolem certainly isn't one of them.

Rolling Double-5s
Nov. 29, 2007
Palolem Beach, India

Woke up this morning with a 55-year-old man in my bed, and to my surprise, the man was me... It's the 333rd day of the year -- November 29 is my birthday.

Fortunately, 55 is the new 25, and I'm proving it on this trip. (Just like the $50 bill is the new $20.)

Thought of a bunch of maudlin, mopey stuff to say about getting old, but I'll spare you, since everyone mulls over the same junk in their time. I like to imagine that this trip is a "last fling at youth," but that would be kidding myself.

Last night, for instance, a group of young people wandered past my hotel going home from the beach bars at 4:30 a.m., laughing, talking and setting off every dog in the village. Those were the days, my friends -- we thought they'd never end...

...but they do. Unlike some of the younger travelers, I tell drug dealers to fuck off when they come around, muttering their wares on the beach. Half of it is being married -- If I were single, I'd be inclined to try some Ecstasy and alley cat around to the clubs until sunrise; but to quote Popeye, "I yam what I yam..."

Meanwhile, pineapple juice has replaced beer in importance. And instead of head-bobbing into the wee hours in a disco, I'm looking at my watch around 9:30 p.m. each night, thinking about beddy-bye.

You can't get much older than that.

The Cow in the Cafè

You know you've finally reached the Land of the Strange when a friendly cow wanders into the restaurant and no one on the staff gives it a second look.

After weeks of eating spicey curries and greenish glop made with veggies and lentils, I decide to get a little crazy and order a pizza at an Italian restaurant just off the beach to celebrate my birthday.

Looking up from the menu, I was startled to find that one of the sacred cows from the village had wandered through the open-air doorway and was watching the chefs working at the grill. It had a friendly piebald face along with black, 10-inch-long horns, and a bemused look in its eyes that bordered on being a smile.

No one shooed it away -- apparently, this smiling cow drops by each evening to stand inside the door and welcome guests to the Little Italy Restaurant. It stood in the doorway for nearly an hour watching the chefs prepare dinner (all seafood, no beef, by the way) before one of the cooks waved it out the door. Like, getouttahere...

And then -- wouldn't you know it -- another cow walked in, like it was her turn in the kitchen. An even bigger cow, with longer horns...

Over the Moon

O, my friends, read no further unless you wish to hear of a lost soul, living the Jimmy Buffet dream of "wasting away in Southern India."

For the second night in a row, I have a dinner of prawns nearly the size of lobsters, this time cooked in a delicate white wine sauce and served by candlelight on the beach at one of the dozens of outdoor restaurants lining the bay. Groovy people from all over the world are my tablemates -- all in swimsuits with long hair, tattoos, and heavily draped with Indian beach beads.

The sound system is superb -- they're playing electronic Goa trance music, and then a reggae-dub version of Pink Floyd's "Dark Side of the Moon." Perfect. I have two glasses of sugary port wine -- a crude, but effective potion that's similar to the homemade 'Thunderfoot' vintage I made from Concord jelly grapes several years ago -- it kicks my ass over the moon.

By day I kayak on the Indian Ocean and wade a quarter mile through the shallow sea along a sandbar to a secluded cove, bathing in my underwear and doing yoga... broiling under the 90 degree sun. The scenery is beyond spectacular -- swaying palm trees (is there any other kind?) skirt the beach, beyond which stretch distant misty mountains. An armada of arrow-prowed fishing boats rigged with wooden outriggers are perched on the sands, waiting to be sent to catch my dinner. Hawaii would blush with envy.

It's not hard to imagine moving here. I could easily perform on guitar at a beachside cafè -- a cinch with some Bob Marley tunes and that old Eagles' hit, "Hotel Goa, India." Accompanied by a guy on a "boooiinnng" Indian tabla drum, it would be easy to be a hit on the beach. Days baking in the sun... nights plucking strings... Writing the Great Indian Expat Novel...

In short, I'm lonely and bored out of my gourd with paradise and can't wait to get out of this place. And I'm dying to see my blond angel Jeannette again. Counting the days... counting the hours... this place is way too mellow for a AA-type like me. Counting the minutes...

The Disunited Nations
Nov. 30, 2007
Palolem Beach, India

Finland, Denmark, Spain, France, Belgium, Australia, New Zealand and scads of Brits and Russians... I look at my hotel registry and wonder where all the Americans are in Goa. Apparently, they are as rare as penguins here, but the manager assures me that a few Yanks show up every so often.

Yeah, sure. Anyway, here's the rundown on who shows up:

Most of the English travelers arrive on package tours and charter flights, although some come to live here the entire winter, renting homes near the beach along with motorbikes. They are an affable bunch -- in fact, I think the word "affable" was coined to describe the Brits, who always seem lit with a jolly vibe.

One of the biggest surprises of this trip is how many Russians there are floating around the world. The beaches here are packed with them, since the Russian economy is booming. A pretty blond real estate agent from Moscow tells me that a small two-bedroom apartment there now rents for $2,500 per month, and did you know that Russia now has more billionaires than any other country? The New Russia has money.

I attempt to speak in my rusty college Russian, but it turns out she majored in English. This is her first trip to India -- she usually visits the resorts of the Red Sea and Chechnya.

"But isn't there still a war going on in Chechnya?" I ask, remembering the terror attacks on a theater in Moscow and at an elementary school on the Russian border which resulted in lethal shootouts a few years ago.

"Oh no, that's all over," my Moscow friend assures me with a wave. "Many people from Russia vacation there now."

"That's the funny thing about the world," I say. "You think a place is dangerous only to find that it's all history a couple years later and everyone's getting on to better things. How do you like Goa?"

"It's okay, but it's very dirty here," she replies. "I like the Red Sea better."

We're so used to thinking of the Russians as being a scroungy bunch in the States that it surprises me that she'd be so particular.

"We don't have many Russian travelers in our country," I say. "In fact, I can't remember ever meeting a single one."

"Yes, we would like to visit America, but the visa is very hard to obtain," she says.

True enough. Post 9/11 America has become a prickly destination for foreign travelers, or should we say "non" destination, because of the stringent entry requirements. It's another way we've walled ourselves off from the world.

"If it's any consolation, I wanted to visit Russia on my trip, but couldn't get in because it had the toughest visa requirements of any country on my list," I respond. "The Russian authorities require that you travel with an official tour group."

"Yes, but try getting into America if you want difficult," she says. "There is no way."

***

Then there are the Israelis -- a bedraggled bunch of long-hairs who look like the species of Midwestern 'freaks' who were my contemporaries back in 1970. The young Israeli men all seem to labor under surly expressions with pasted-on scowls. But for all I know, they think the same of me.

Many young Israelis blast off for India as soon as their two-year compulsory military service is over. Fresh from the Israeli Defense Forces, they compete with the Aussies for the title of the world's scrappiest backpackers in Third World backwaters from India to Brazil. They arrive here with a chip on their shoulder the size of a saw log and a crying need to party their brains out. Many are not too keen about having to serve in the military at the behest of the religious fanatics and right-wing zealots who run their sorry sandbox of a country.

Even though Americans are nowhere to be seen, our presence is felt. For starters, we're easy to find on Indian TV with HBO, CNN and Hollywood films and TV shows. And I hear the Euros bad-mouthing America about the war. Of course, there are so few Americans here that other Westerners simply assume that none of us are within earshot.

Over breakfast at my hotel, a Canadian couple are going off in this vein, never dreaming that a native of the Great Satan America is sitting RIGHT NEXT TO THEM!

"People ask us if we're Americans and I say, 'are you *kidding* me?!?'" the woman squawks to the hotel manager. "No way!"

I want to remind her that if it weren't for America, she'd probably be speaking Russian right now and slaving on a Soviet grain collective out in Alberta. But it's none of my business what she thinks.

On the other hand I have to agree with her husband when he says, "Imagine how much good the Americans could have done in the world with all the money they spent on the war, instead of killing all those people in Iraq."

Touchè.

The Pig Loo
Dec. 1, 2007
Bogmalo Beach, India

One of the sights I missed in Goa is the "pig loo," which is found in local homes.

This is a squat toilet which is attached to a drain pipe that runs straight to the pig sty behind the house. You take aim at the hole, make a deposit, and the pig gets a nice snack at the other end, along with a drink of flush water. "The sound of contented snuffling is an unusual accompaniment to a normally solitary activity," reports the *Lonely Planet Guide to Goa.*

"The pig loo solves the problem of sewage disposal, waste water and pig food all in one go and arguably does its bit to promote vegetarianism."

Is America ready for the pig loo? Dunno, but happy am I to have abstained from eating meat in India... especially pork.

Tinkerbella
Dec. 2, 2007
Bogmalo Beach, India

There's a new attraction on Bogmalo Beach in Goa, where a well-tanned gringo strums a tiny guitar by the sea and poses for photos.

This is a place where the Indians come to vacation, staying at shabby hotels and dining at plastic tables on the sidewalks at convenience shops set back from the beach. For some, it's a thrill to have a photo taken with a foreigner, especially one wearing a lady's sun bonnet rimmed with Bedouin beads that looks kind of like a cowboy hat.

For those who sit and listen, the troubadour explains in grave tones that one must always wear a cowboy hat in order to play American country-western songs such as "She Thinks I Still Care" by George Jones. All who stop by are invited to pose with the guitar, whose name is Tinkerbella.

Just off the beach is a row of shops that he calls Desperation Gulch. Each little cubbyhole is much the same as 5,000 other shops he has already visited, filled with carved marble elephants, statues of an angry dancing Shiva (said to be bad luck to have in the home), beaded handbags and t-shirts that are so dull and unimaginative that their design can only be described as "cruddy."

As any shop owner anywhere in the world will always tell you, business is always "bad." Here? Very, very bad.

The cowboy can't help but feel sorry for the folks in Desperation Gulch, some of whom are at the point of tears for a sale. He gets the feeling that many haven't had a sale in days -- maybe even weeks.

"Cum in, my fren'... jus' loook, no buy... jus' loook..." is their mournful refrain.

The cowboy makes a last feeble attempt to help the local economy, scouring a few shops for unwanted souvenirs on his last night in Goa. A few rupees are spilled in the attempt, but his heart just isn't into it.

***

Speaking of music, I was sitting in a beachside cafe when a Christmas song came on over the sound system. What the heck are they playing that for? I wondered. Then it dawned on me -- oh, right, it's December. Over this-a-way, it feels like the Fourth of July.

Did you know that many Hindus celebrate Christmas? With 333 million gods in their religion, it's a cinch to add Jesus, Virgin Mary and Santa Claus to the mix as an excuse to celebrate.

The Checkout Counter
Dec. 3, 2007
Delhi, India

India has been good to me. It's hard to describe how difficult the "Land of Contrasts" is, but on the other hand, everyone here has knocked themselves silly to help me at every turn. I never got lost (much), never felt threatened -- and was always treated like a king, even though I look like a slob -- what's not to like?

So, thank you, Helpful Harrys.

India is a separate planet, alien to ours in thought and action. It travels in its own orbit in a distant galaxy with its own gods and pop stars, barely aware that we Westerners even exist. That's why it's such a fantastic place to visit.

And the Indian people are a very sweet bunch. Even when they're ripping you off for double or triple cab fare, they do it with an endearing smile.

And they are so crazy polite, sir. Some Bollywood stars who were making a film in London were shocked to be subjected to racial slurs by British teenagers driving by on the street where they were filming. It made the national news here. Such a thing would never happen in hyper-polite India.

No doubt, one has to be polite to live in a place half the size of the U.S. with three times our population -- 1.1 billion people. That's basically the problem with India: it has about 700,000,000 too many people, so relatively few have meaningful jobs or full-time work, despite all the blather in the press about their booming economy.

Currently India has a middle class of around 350 million; but that still leaves 750 million people struggling with poverty. For many, those numbers add up to menial jobs in a country where triple-handling every task has been institutionalized.

For instance, in one town, I was the only customer at a hotel bar with seven waiters. So one guy took my order, another brought my beer, a third opened the bottle, a fourth brought me some snacks, a fifth asked if I wanted another drink, a sixth reloaded the snack tray, and so on -- that's India.

The little bit of Delhi I saw on a night's layover was depressing beyond words, with people tramping through the dust and filth with little hope for the future. Northern India is the poorest part of the country and the poverty is horrific when it's in your face instead of a distant vision on TV or in a magazine. Ultimately, it gives India an ominous atmosphere. If this place ever blows, it's going to make the Holocaust look like a marshmallow roast.

But things could be worse -- like Pakistan.

Speaking of which, most Indians don't seem to have the affliction of consumer envy that is the pox on happiness in the U.S. and Europe. They don't sit around feeling sorry for themselves because they're driving a moped instead of a Toyota. Happiness in India gazes in the other direction: they're thankful for what they've got -- even if it's only a bicycle -- and thank Krishna they're not in the terrible mess of the family next door.

But still, my prescription for a brighter India would be to stop popping kids out of the collective womb like this was some kind of chinchilla farm and bring the numbers down. Increasingly, that's the norm for the middle class, with many couples opting to have two children, the same as in the West.

Unfortunately, that's not the case down on the street corner, where you find mothers who look like children themselves, only with three kids in tow. And despite all the hoopla about India's booming economy, I wonder if these hundreds of millions of semi-literate people will end up steering India's destiny in a downward spiral by the sheer dint of their numbers.

I spend my last night in Delhi, happy to be heading east at first light to Thailand.

Bangkok

I Tripped on a Cloud and Fell Eight Miles High...
Dec. 4, 2007
Bangkok, Thailand

Okay, my mind is officially, totally blown. I score a room on Khaosan Road in downtown Bangkok and it is so far over the top I'm flabbergasted, jaw dragging on the street -- it's two hits of acid, sharing a mug of tequila with a talking giraffe -- that's what sleek, prosperous Bangkok feels like after a month of submersion in raggedy India.

Bangkok is bursting with backpackers from all over the world. My bus into town was packed with them, and hundreds of us are hanging out on Khaosan Road, which is a half-mile of neon lights and hundreds of bars, restaurants, shops, outdoor vendors... all selling very interesting, if useless, things, like toy frogs and jig-saw Buddha wall hangings (mental note -- buy a dozen t-shirts). I'm numb... sensory overload... duh... holy crap! Part of my being bowled over is a result of leaving Planet India behind and getting back to a place that looks like the world I remember.

Khaosan Road is a backpacker's version of the Vegas Strip crossed with Willie Wonka's Chocolate Factory, all under the smiling gaze of a golden Buddha. Like Amsterdam, Khaosan Road is a vortice to the travel dimension and a rendezvous for backpackers -- a place to trade info and tall tales with kindred souls who are fresh from faraway lands ranging from Brazil to Botswana.

The party is an international affair. Next to me at a streetside cafè is a heavily tattooed French couple in their 40s -- he with shoulder-length hair and a silver earring nestled in the gray, she a svelte blonde heading into the twilight of her beauty. On my other hand are three German men in their early 20s, bumming around the world with no reservations in any sense of the word, their packs piled on the sidewalk. I pick up the accents of Australians and Brits passing by on the street. A trio of Danish girls drift by, mingling with the Thai street vendor women who sell mad tribal hats in rainbow colors.

I peel the wet label from a bottle of Chang beer, pasting the twin el-

ephants to the table as a plate of stir-fried noodles arrives. God, it's hot out here -- at least 95 Fahrenheit, with the hammer of the sun pounding you toward the shade -- it feels more like 130 degrees coming off the black goo of the abused pavement.

I've had 60 days of this heat and six months of summer, following the sun on my way around the world. Back home they're suffering from the cold, black night of early December, where it gets dark at 5 p.m. Like the saying goes in Asia, it's the "same, same, but different" back in America.

If they only knew what they're missing.

The World's Biggest Birthday Bash
Dec. 5, 2007
Bangkok, Thailand

There's something spooky about being jammed like jelly into a crowd of more than a million people. I decide that if all hell breaks loose, I'll climb the nearest tree and wait for it to blow over.

By dumb luck, I've arrived in Bangkok on the eve of King Bhumibol Adulyadej's 81st birthday. The Thai people are nuts about the king -- even more so since there was a military coup here last year and he represents a sense of stability. Actually, the king okay'd the coup before it went forward -- no one does boo here without his permission. There are billboard-sized posters of his face all over town and arches over the main roads that are foiled in gold with his picture.

The king is not exactly Mr. Charisma -- he's a bookish-looking old man in gold-framed glasses -- but to the Thai people, he's got the pizazz of a rock star. Or at least they pretend that he does, because bad-mouthing the royal family will get you tossed in prison.

Throughout the day, tens of thousands of people line up along the streets, hoping to get a glimpse of His Majesty as he glides serenely from one gold-plated palace to another in his gold stretch Mercedes limo, accompanied by a motorcade of around 50 red Lexus and Mercedes sedans.

But the real show was tonight, when an ocean of the Thai people filled a 150-foot-wide avenue for miles -- all dressed in yellow to honor the king (yellow, of course, is the color of Monday, which is the day His Royal Highness was born on). Tens of thousands of soldiers marched down the street -- all as thin as whips and looking snazzy in their high-peaked hats. Then came dozens of marching bands and an endless mob.

The evening brings out a crowd of 1.5 million, all packed in shoulder-to-shoulder. The cops ordered thousands of us in my section to sit in the filthy street next to one of Bangkok's skunkiest sewers. Yessir -- you don't argue with these guys unless you crave a whipping with a baton. Then the king floated by in his limo (same ho-hum show as during the day) and everyone lit candles and sang the national anthem. Thousands of gentle faces were bathed in the golden glow, and then lit from above as the sky exploded with fireworks.

Templeitis
Dec. 6, 2007
Bangkok, Thailand

Wrenching the hell out of my left knee means I'm stuck taking a sucker tourist's tour in a tuk-tuk, which is an enclosed three-wheel motorcycle. I hobble around like a three-legged dog, declining offers to buy hand-tailored suits and diamond rings, accompanied by the sinking expression of the tuk-tuk driver, whose kickback depends on me buying something from the places he insists I visit. Here's some of the stuff I soak up on the way around town:

-- Down on your luck? In Bangkok, you can buy a wooden cage of sparrows, a bag of live fish or a turtle to release at a Buddhist temple to bring you good fortune. Guaranteed to work, every time.

-- For those on a budget, dinner on the street is pad thai noodles with a spring roll and a skewer of chicken -- all cooked in a wok at a vendor's cart for under $1. Delicious. If that doesn't suit you, why not try the stir-fried grasshoppers, locusts, or some especially fat, gruesome grubs?

-- One of the "perks" of being a Western traveler in Asia or Africa is getting charged at least triple what the locals pay. I was steamed at getting soaked for $25 to watch a kickboxing tournament in Bangkok while all the homeys got in for 50 cents or less. The boxers are as ripped as washboards and beat the snot out of each other with slashing kicks to the head and knees to the gut and other unfortunate places. I'm sure they must be wearing cups, or they'd have mashed potatoes going on "down there," if you know what I mean.

-- I see some of the infamous sex tourists on the street. These are middle-aged Western men, hooked up with Thai women who are often one-third their size and one-third their age. Apparently, many impoverished families in the north sell their daughters into an informal slavery to the bars and brothels of Bangkok. Some of the women look happy to be tagging along with these losers -- others, pretty glum. Some guys are here shopping for wives, having struck out back home.

-- Living in hotels is getting old. I miss my soggy pup tent from Europe. And I can't even brag that I'm staying in cheap dives, since for $25 you get a fairly swanky place in Asia. Bonus: last night, a heavy metal Thai band playing downstairs at my hotel kept me awake for hours. Like American metal, the "singing" was all yelling, screaming and grunting in a bombastic way in the Thai language. It sounded so hilarious that I laughed myself to sleep.

-- Somewhere, Buddha is smiling, because he's got the most bitchin' temples any disembodied spirit could ask for. They're like golden gingerbread castles with psychedelic spires and curlicue ridge lines. And, inside -- whattayaknow -- Buddha is at home and waiting to greet you with an upraised palm.

Here Comes the Sun
Dec. 8, 2007
Bangkok, Thailand

A blonde halo and a smile materializes in the arrival zone at Suvarnabhumi Airport and my lovely wife Jeannette steps into Asia.

Three months without having the old man around has been good for Jeannette: she has lost 10 pounds as a result of not being subjected to my home cooking, and has a sleek new haircut. She is, in short, a vision of loveliness to a love-starved travel bum.

Jeannette has been doing her homework. Do I know that the map of Thailand resembles the shape of an elephant, which is the symbol of the country? And that the temple towers are shaped like spires because this is meant to impale demons when they fall out of the sky? I do now.

Many people say that marriage is difficult and that one has to 'work' at it. That has never been true of us. We resume our 16-year-conversation as if there has never been a pause in the months we've been apart.

"It's funny, but it doesn't seem like we've even been apart," I say over beers and a plate of shrimp rolls.

"I know," Jeannette says. People ask if I miss you and I've had to say no because we've been able to talk almost every day on the phone. I was worried for the first two weeks that you were gone, but after that I knew you'd be alright."

"We have a connection where we always feel like we're in touch, no matter where we are."

"I think it must be love," she says.

My absence has been good for Jeannette, who has enjoyed what all women crave, according to a medieval tale: sovereignty -- or the right to run your own life without some guy calling the shots. Back home, she's plunged into remodeling a room in our house and having the place painted. She's been busy with her friends, family, and her yoga classes, thoroughly enjoying her independence. I imagine that most wives would love to have their husbands take a leave of absence to enjoy the same sensation.

Jeannette has the gift of eternal youth. Although she is 55, she looks 20 years younger and has even been mistaken at times for the wife of our 27-year-old son, Nathan. In fact, she could give most women in their 20s a run for their money. A Capricorn, she has the sign's blessing of looking older in youth and younger in her later years. From the moment I first saw her at a square dance years ago, I've been drawn by her inner golden glow.

And did I mention that she is also brave, funny, wise and kind?

But it's not all a second honeymoon. After a cold November of early evening darkness and the onset of winter back home, Jeannette is bursting with enthusiasm to hike all over town, including lengthy excursions into the markets until late in the evening.

"Jeannette! I'm sick of this shopping crap! I've been marching around these markets for months, and it's gotten really old."

But my pouts and pleas are all in vain.

Like recovering nicotine addicts who resume smoking again with the first puff after 10 years of abstinence, we are soon back in sync with the American style of travel, leaving a roostertail of cash in our wake.

Fortunately, Christmas shopping in Thailand is a bargain. Everything seems to cost about 25 percent of what you'd pay in the States.

The Death Train
Dec. 10, 2007
The River Kwai, Thailand

Three days of hanging out in Bangkok (City of Plums -- City of Angels) gets pretty old, especially the mad scene around "Chaos-San" Road, which quickly loses its charm and takes on the aspect of a three-day-old burrito, seasoned in the sun.

Before Jeannette arrived, I took a day-trip to the River Kwai. The famous bridge built by slave labor during World War II is actually a tiny affair compared to the wooden whopper in the film by David Lean, which was shot in Sri Lanka. It's a low-slung railway bridge of steel, crowded with tourists; it's a wonder that a dozen of them don't fall through its gaping holes each day. The original bridge was bombed several times during WWII.

The trip includes a ride on the "Death Train" which runs to Burma, with the tracks laid by starving prisoners of war. The Death Railway took the lives of 16,000 allied prisoners of war, who now lie in a carefully manicured cemetery. The sacrifice of more than 100,000 slaves from Thailand, Burma, India, China, Indonesia, Malaysia and Singapore is barely noted. Many lie in unmarked graves, or have simply decayed beneath the cover of leaves out in the jungle.

Today, the train is a tourist attraction filled with laughing teenagers, squealing with delight as they bounce along over rails built on the backs of 120,000 dead slaves.

The Pickpocket

No trip to Bangkok is complete without a tour of the famous Patpong red light district. The street gives new meaning to the word "skanky," with several hundred young prostitutes and hustlers standing around during the early evening with no business in sight. It's like strolling through a garbage dump, buzzing with human flies.

On a streetcorner, I check out the menu for one of the live sex shows. You can see "pussy ping-pong ball" (a variation of a cherry-pit spitting contest) or "pussy banana," or a dozen other kinky acts for $12 per show, plus drinks. Thanks, but no thanks.

But, while looking at the menu of kink, I notice someone is trying to pick my pocket.

Yes, indeed -- it's a baby elephant who is trying to get the orchids from our pina coladas out of my shirt pocket. Yum-yum! He stuffs them in his mouth and wanders off down the road.

Later, my delight is crushed when I learn that these city elephants -- which are employed to tempt dollars from tourists -- are the victims of animal abuse, raised in a stressful urban environment on a poor diet, little water or chance to bathe, and deprived of the family structure that is necessary to a young elephant's development. Animal rights activists have tried to get the Thai government to take action against the urban abuse of elephants, but obviously, with no luck.

Thailand

The Buddha Barns
Dec. 11, 2007
Chiang Mai, Thailand

The overnight train to Chiang Mai in northern Thailand goes clickety-clack, bumpety-bump and rumbly-tumble for 300 miles all night long, providing little in the way of sleep.

Chiang Mai is a backpacker's playground, serving as the gateway to Laos and Myanmar, where the government is busy cracking heads in an uprising of Buddhist monks. It's also the jump-off for treks among the scores of hill tribes who live up yonder.

It's claimed that Chiang Mai offers some 300 Buddhist temples, and each one has a golden, smiling Buddha inside. Bangkok also has more than 300 temples and an ocean of gold paint.

Yet I think that if I see one more of these buddha barns (or for that matter, any more dusty old churches or palaces) I'll go batshit. But that's part of the job description here on Planet Backpacker: inspecting tarnished old temples and snapping photos of burnished old buddhas that you'll never look at once you get home.

Life on Planet Backpacker
Dec. 12, 2007
Chiang Mai, Thailand

What could be finer than riding an elephant up a jungle trail under the cool green mountains of northern Thailand? Far below, a river crashes in a torrent through a jungle canyon, while palm trees along the trail explode with the green fire of the sun. I'm swept away by a vision beyond my dreams.

It's just another day on Planet Backpacker, and one of the best, I might add. They're not all this good: sometimes you're covered with mosquito bites, wondering if you'll contract Dengue fever (aka: "bone-crushing fever"), or you get stuck for eight hours in a dismal airport. Or you find yourself scrambling around after midnight in a strange town and an unfriendly neighborhood, looking for a place to crash.

But that's the gig, and I've gotten to know the backpacking brother-and-sisterhood quite well in the past three months on my way around the world. Planet Backpacker is a world with its own customs, capitals and highways.

Many backpackers are college-aged, with some taking a gap year off from school. Others are celebrating the completion of their undergrad degrees before heading on to med school or to complete their masters. Some of the younger members of the tribe appear to be from well-to-do families, with their trips financed by the Bank of Mom & Daddy.

"I had to work on weekends at uni and I hated it," one young adventurer confides to another on the River Kwai trip. "It really got in the way of my socializing."

I want to ask how the kid how he managed to come up with the money to spend four months traveling around Asia if he only worked on weekends? But that would be rude, and the answer seems evident.

But there are a surprising number of older professionals on the road

-- people like me who've saved for years in order to see the world. I've met lawyers, bankers, physicians and a gourmet chef -- with ages ranging from the 30s through the 60s -- who've abandoned their careers for six months or a year to see the world. Most say their stint isn't long enough to see all they could wish for. Travel is addicting.

Planet Backpacker has its own dress code: The women all seem to wear pedal pushers and tank tops of a solid color. You often see the ladies lugging the heaviest loads: a huge pack on their backs and a bursting daypack strapped out front. Often, their packs look bigger than their bodies -- full of more tank tops and pedal pushers, I suppose.

For men, standard garb is a pair of knee-length camo shorts and a t-shirt featuring the logo of the local beer for whatever country you're in at the moment. And of course, both men and women wear flip-flops and bead necklaces from the miles of souvenir markets you encounter everywhere you go.

You used to have to be a bit of an Indiana Jones to bum around the world with a pack on your back, but no longer. Over the past 10 years, the travel industry has flexed its muscles, making remote trips as easy as banana pancakes. There are thousands of travel offices in Asia which can book anything from an elephant safari to a three-day trip to Cambodia or Laos in a matter of minutes. Want to ride an overnight bus halfway across India? It will pick you up at your hotel. Want to float down the Mekong through Indochina on a bamboo raft? It is easily arranged.

Occasionally, the real world intrudes, such as when I went to pick up Jeannette at Suvarnabhumi Airport and was shocked to bump into regular folks. What am I doing in this ridiculous outfit? I wondered, that being camo shorts, a beer t-shirt and a fake tiger tooth necklace. Why don't I get a decent haircut and wear some grown-up clothes and start acting my age?

But thoughts like that always bring to mind Jim Morrison's great quote about our time on earth: "No one here gets out alive." You may as well act out your fantasies, bub -- they won't last long.

Animal Planet
Dec. 13, 2007
Chiang Mai, Thailand

Back in the days of old Siam, monkeys were employed to knock coconuts out of trees. A good monkey could fetch 800-1,000 coconuts per day.

But then mechanized harvesters came along and put the monkeys out of work. These days, monkeys have to go to school to learn the trade. We visit a "monkey school" near Chiang Mai and Jeannette cradles a baby that's as jumpy as a spring trap. One of these monkeys clearly has his Ph.D in collecting though, because he whips up a palm tree and showers the ground with flying coconuts.

A visit to Thailand is a trip to Animal Planet. I have a live cobra dumped in my lap by "Snake Man," who clowns around during a visit to a snake farm. The cobras flare their hoods and strike repeatedly at Snake Man, who manages to dodge them (when he's not picking them up and sticking their heads in his mouth, that is).

An announcer at the snake farm coos seductively into the micro- phone: "Ooooh, be ca'fu' Snake Man... Ooooh, don' let cobwa bi' you Snake Man..."

The cobra in my lap is a good six feet long and as big around as my arm, with a soft, silky texture. It has a shocked "what the hell?" look in its black, doll eyes. And it's loaded to kill -- we watch Snake Man milk it for poison after my lap dance. Its fangs have been filed down to nubs, but still, I'm glad he had a good grip on its head, because I jumped about a foot.

Snake Man has to dive head first into a dark pool to retrieve a python, which it an unpleasant experience even for him, because these critters bite. He comes out of a pool bleeding, with the snake hissing and snapping at the air.

And did you know that a King Cobra can grow to 18 feet long? Not something you want to find in your bed on Sunday morning...

There's also the Tiger Temple near the River Kwai. The preserve is run by Buddhist monks who line up tourists 100 deep and give them five seconds with a staked-down tiger on a short leash to have their photos taken. A tourist in his early 20s, who obviously has too much money for his own good, coughs up $50 to pose with a doped-up ti- ger's head in his lap. Hey, tough guy!

Some practices at the Tiger Temple are pure animal abuse: a monk jerks a baby tiger around all day long to rouse it enough to make a good photo for tourists. The cub looks stressed and irritated, but of course, no one seems to notice.

The biggest thrill in Thailand, however, is an elephant ride. Tourism has literally saved the nation's elephants.

From 1945-1975, some 200,000 wild elephants were slaughtered by poachers as Thailand entered the modern world and people ditched their age-old traditions in order to scrape up money for the new con- sumer products which flooded the world after WWII. The old trainers, called mahouts, nearly died out along with the animals, since elephants were no longer used for logging, warfare or other jobs. They were only good for the money gained from their tusks.

But when elephant-adoring tourists began coming to Thailand in 1985, the people here began to see their value. By the early '90s, elephant rides were all the rage, and today, they're a "must" for every tourist in Thailand. As a result, there are now 50,000 wild elephants protected in parks around the country, and 5,000 "house" elephants working in the tourism business.

Elephant riding is addictive. Jeannette leaps out of the howdah and straddles the elephant's neck on the stroll through the jungle. Ours is the biggest tusker in the bunch and I call him Big Boy. Every 10 seconds he rears back his trunk and demands another banana. We purchase two bunches because our tender says nothing makes an elephant crankier than when you mess with its food and water. Really cranky elephants get their point across by stomping people; and when an elephant stomps you, he means business.

In India, there was a newspaper photo of an elephant going nuts. He threw his American rider from his howdah, and then knocked over a truck. But Big Boy is good to us and floats like a raft through the jungle -- well worth two bunches of bananas.

The Human Zoo

There's also a bit of a 'human zoo' in Chiang Mai in that most of the trekking companies take you for a stroll through the hill tribe villages. Some of these treks go on for several days.

It's a disturbing trend, marching through these villages to gape at the ragged inhabitants, similar to the slum tourism now popular in the ghettos of Mumbai, the favelas of Rio, and the townships outside Johannesburg, where you pay a guide to steer you through the wreckage of humanity.

The hill tribes are made up of dirt-poor refugees from Burma, southern China and Laos. They live in palm huts up in the hills, with most of the women selling handicrafts to trekkers and the men working with the elephants, or poling bamboo rafts full of tourists down the rivers. The hill people seem to be happy working in the tourist industry -- but it's appalling to walk through the villages and gawk at these people like they were monkeys.

Poo-poo Phuket
Dec. 15, 2007
Phuket, Thailand

If you go traveling around the world in search of paradise, you are likely to be sadly disappointed. Every time you see a beautiful beach or a waterfall in a travel brochure, it simply means that the photographer was able to sweep thousands of tourists out of the way long enough to grab a shot before they all came flooding back again. We travelers tend to love beautiful places to death.

Such is the case with the island of Phuket in southern Thailand, which proves to be a blend of shock and disappointment.

The town of Patong Beach on the western side of the island suffered heavy damage during the tsunami of 2004. You wouldn't know it now though, since there's not a trace of the 28-foot monster that swept through the beach restaurants and up the streets into town, carrying away hundreds of people.

I had expected Patong to be a touristy place, but thought there would be some sandy lanes and secluded beaches to enjoy, like in Goa. Instead, we find a hyper-developed strip of hundreds of shops and restaurants, packed like a train wreck into a two-mile strip of beach, with thousands of tourists from all over the world: Russia, England, Germany, Australia, Sweden and India.

All of the tourism and development run amok makes it seem as if the Thai people are an afterthought. You feel like you're on a beach in the Twilight Zone -- nowhere, actually -- you could be in any tropical resort town in the world: Mexico, Tortola, Costa Rica, the Mediterranean... there's little "sense of place" here. Many of the bartenders have dreadlocks and deep, chocolate complexions -- you get the feeling you're in Jamaica.

So, the island of Phuket is kind of a downer -- and far from a paradise -- but as Mick Jagger once said, "If you try sometimes, you just might find, you get what you need, oh baby."

So we do as the Romans do and go with the flow, engaging in what passes for bloodsport in Patong: shopping, dining by the sea, and sharing a hookah of apple-flavored tobacco at an Indian café. Jeannette finds the ultimate bargain dress shop, with frilly frocks for $3. She is known as "Madame" in Thailand, by the way (pronounced "Ma-dahm"). Everywhere she goes, shop owners want to know what Madame would like.

Adventures in the Skin Trade

You can't help but notice that there are hundreds of prostitutes in Patong, many walking around with old goats from the West.

A typical scenario is sitting in a restaurant next to some fat old dude with a gray crewcut and hair growing out of his ears, with flesh the texture of rice pudding. And there at his arm is an 17-year-old Thai bar girl... Oh, and a Scandinavian family with a bunch of little kids at the next table. It's a bit surreal.

The sex workers are petite, trim, and uniformly dressed in skin-tight mini-shirts and high-heeled sandals. It must be a shock for the groups of young Western women we see looking a bit forlorn out on the street. Even the pretty blondes are being ignored by the young guys who have their whores in tow. And to make things worse, the Thais have can-celed the sale of booze for two days because of the national elections, so even the disco scene is a flop.

Yet there can be an emotional price to pay for being a sex tourist in Thailand. Many of the women aren't outright whores: they serve as professional girlfriends, like the *jineteras* of Cuba who hook up for a week or so with some free-spending tourist.

Some men fall desperately in love with their paramours and are tenderly milked of their money with sweet words and adoring eyes for their "big, big lover." Back home, many of these guys are invisible to the opposite sex, so it's not hard for them to fall head over heels. The more fetching bar girls get stacks of foreign mail each day, along with cash to help them get through "secretarial school" or whatever. And of course, many Thai, Laotian or Burmese girls dream of marrying a rich sugar daddy and being whisked away to the land of shopping malls and mini vans. You see these odd couples sitting silently at restaurant tables, each mesmerized by the narcotic of their private fantasies.

Typically, a customer pays the bar a fee to take a girl to dinner, and if a night in his hotel transpires, he must pay a hotel guest fee as well. In our hotel, the fee was 500 baht to bring a visitor to one's room -- about $15 U.S.

Our hotel also charges extra if you get a new tattoo, because the ink from a fresh tat tends to bleed on the sheets.

The Lady Boys

There are also plenty of male prostitutes walking the streets, this be-ing a gay mecca. A major attraction is the "lady boys" -- transsexuals and transvestites who are dead ringers for their sexy sisters, with long, sleek hair, full breasts, girlie outfits and thongs. Some are dressed in tu-tus, ball gowns and wedding gowns, advertising for a local bar.

On a street full of nightclubs, a flock of five lady boys dance to the sounds of "Ice Baby, Ice" for a huge crowd gathered outside Dclub Crocodile. Some idiot tourist hands his baby to them to shake up and down on the platform. Classic. But then, you see all kinds of European and Australian families with children and infants walking through this red light zone late at night. Many of the kids look exhausted.

But there's always some quality that gives the she-males away: they walk a bit too suggestively or show a bit too much ass or have mannish faces... Jeannette and I have fun guessing who's a lady boy -- ultimately you can tell if they have an Adam's apple. These "ka-thoey" (as the Thais call them) cover their necks with scarves or heavy jewelry so as not to give away their secret, and some even have their Adam's apples surgically removed. Since this protrusion is basically a man's larger larynx, I'm not sure how they manage to remove it and retain the ability to talk.

I can only wonder how many drunken sex tourists have woken up after a night with one of these 'ladies' with an unpleasant 'crying game' experience to savor. And possibly a sore ass.

James Bond Island
Dec. 17, 2007
The Andaman Sea, Thailand

With the theme song to "You Only Live Twice" blasting in our imaginations in full stereophonic, symphonic glory, our ship sets sail for James Bond Island, an upside-down flower pot which is where *The Man With the Golden Gun* was filmed in 1971.

This island archipelago is where the beauty of Phuket and southern Thailand lies hidden. Misty isles and karst formations rise in the haze of the sea. Once, these islands hid the pirates of Thailand and were the home of sea gypsies for hundreds of years. Today, their descendants usher boatloads of tourists.

We're ferried to and from the ship by inflatable sea canoes. On a couple of islands, we travel hundreds of feet into sea caves, some with ceilings so low we have to lie down in the canoe to worm your way through tunnels. It's a bit claustrophobic -- with the stench of the ocean, the heat and humidity, you feel like a turd in a sea god's rectum.

One sea cave is filled with thousands of sleeping bats, which hang

"I would never dare to wear this back home,"Jeannette said.

from the ceiling as our canoe glides beneath them by the light of a flashlight. The cave has a horrible, hideous stink -- like the concentrated B.O. of 100 jock straps that have been worn for a month on jungle maneuvers -- only worse, I imagine. "Don't open your mouth and look up," our captain warns. Aye-aye sir! Scary place...

I hate the place and can't wait to get out. For a moment, I even consider reappraising Batman as my favorite comic book character... surely Batman must know how bad a bat cave smells.

At the mouth of the cave, a group of young men are diving frantically into the dark water.

"What happened?"

"This guy lost his wedding ring!" a swimmer cries. "His hand was dangling over the side of the boat and it just slipped off. And they just got married a couple of days ago." With that, he slipped like an otter beneath the sea in the darkness of the grotto, searching for the band of gold on the ocean floor.

The Teeny Bikini
Dec. 18, 2007
Phi-Phi, Thailand

Jeannette looks adorable in her new teeny-weeny string bikini, which cost $7 at a street stall -- about what you'd pay for lunch back home.

"I would never dare to wear this back home," she confides of the little wisp of cloth, held together with more imagination than string, "but it's okay to wear it here where I don't know anyone."

Such a garment (or lack of one) is perfect for the paradise of Koh Phi-Phi Don ("Big Phi-Phi Island"), which is reached via a 30-mile boat trip across the Andaman Sea. The island is shaped like the head of a Viking battle axe, with our guest house room located at one end of a broad sweep of beach on the town side.

A nice bonus is the addition of about 10 young drunken Germans who move into the two rooms next to us and keep everyone up past 4 a.m. True, they could take their party down to the beach, which is the logical place for it, but would much rather sit outside our door, smashing beer bottles and braying teen witticisms half the night. We bang around as much as possible that morning to wake them up.

But here are scenes of tropical splendor fit for a Hollywood movie: in fact, *The Beach*, starring Leonardo DiCaprio, was shot just a coconut-toss away on Phi-Phi's little sister island. It's about a group of backpackers who go looking for a secret island paradise in Thailand and find that their neighbors are a cutthroat gang of pot farmers.

What does paradise look like? Long-tail dragon boats roar across the bay, powered by 10-foot-long propeller shafts attached to V-8 auto engines. Rock towers leap from the sea. The aquamarine shoals are lined with palm trees, frangipani and hibiscus flowers. The lanes through town are filled with Westerners walking around half-naked or strapped with backpacks. The cafès brim with prawns, lobsters and fish still wriggling on ice. At night, fire dancers whirl batons and bolos filled with kerosene on the beach while the bar blasts Limp Bizkit, LL Cool

J and Bob Marley's remixed reggae at a thumping volume that pounds through your heart. Would you like some "merrywanna" to go with your beer? The friendly barman can supply.

But it's too hot to do much of anything but melt. A tough day here is dining by the waves over shrimp pad thai and pineapple shakes and trying to decide whether to get a massage or hang by the pool... Or should you go for a chocolate banana crepe instead? Hmm...

The Killer
Dec. 19, 2007
Phi-Phi, Thailand

The Tsunami Memorial Garden on Phi Phi is a pleasant place, full of flowers and overlooking the sea. Here are 127 plaques in memory of the people who were washed away on Dec. 26, 2004. Photos of happy couples and young family members turning amber under the sun, so close to the Equator. The victims are a mix of locals and tourists from Europe, Australia and South Africa.

It's impossible to know how many people were killed by the tsunami, which radiated across the Indian Ocean from Sri Lanka to Indonesia, but estimates run as high as 800,000.

Phi Phi was virtually destroyed, with the tidal wave sweeping across the narrow isthmus between a popular beach and the main part of town. There's still debris piled up along the back lanes. More than 8,000 people were swept away in Thailand.

Yet today -- just three years later -- the restaurants, shops and hotels have all been rebuilt and you would hardly know the killer wave even came to call. There are Tsunami Evacuation Route signs around town, but you have to wonder -- which way would the wave come from? If the sirens sounded here, you might be running towards your death.

Feeling Krabi
Dec. 21, 2007
Krabi, Thailand

It's an easy ferry ride to the province of Krabi back on the mainland, where swarms of travel agents stand by to attend to every need.

"Landing in a new place always makes me anxious," I say to Jeannette. "You feel like you're lost in a good book, and then you look up to find that you're sitting in a jungle or on a strange beach, instead of the cafè where you started reading. And you think, how did I get here?

And how did the plot get so strangely twisted? You know you're on an adventure, landing in all of these foreign places, but you feel disoriented."

"Mmm-hmm," Jeannette says, tuning out my soliloquy to watch the bustle on the pier.

The best thing about the beach at Ao Nang is its long row of palapa-covered massage huts. The huts each have about 10 beds in them, and ladies calling out: "Mass-aage... Mass-aage, ma-dahm." We surrender to an hour-long coconut oil massage for $10 per hour. Back home, this would cost $60 or more.

Thai massage is a full-contact affair -- my masseuse uses her legs, elbows and body weight to give me the works. It's much better than the ayurvedic massage I got in India, which involved a bucket of warm oil, a skimpy loincloth, and a masseur who appeared to be gay. Not my trip.

The scenery here is out of a dream. Stone muffin tops and mushrooms rise hundreds of feet from the sea. Limestone extrusions of stallagtites writhe in fantastic shapes off the cliffs like the drippings of a gravy pan. It's a mescaline dreamscape.

The beach town of Rai Lay is a rock climber's fantasy and many make pilgrimages here from all over the world. A whip-thin blonde clings to the side of a cliff, the muscles of her back rippling as she climbs high above the trees.

This island also sports one of the many penis-shaped mountains seen throughout southern Thailand, which are always good for a laugh.

This phallic feature is the root of an old legend: In a cave on the beach, there is a temple to a sea goddess who grants favors to fishermen. Whenever their wish comes true, they must return and place a present in her temple. She prefers lingams, so the cave is filled with hundreds of carved wooden penises, including some that are buried in the sand, standing six feet tall.

Monky Business,
Dec. 23, 2007
Bangkok, Thailand

"It is what it is." -- *Zen*

A young monk looks shell-shocked in his orange robe and shaved head as stares from the gates of a temple, like he just swallowed a frog.

Ninety-five percent of the Thais are Buddhists. In the old days, all young men to become Buddhist monks for a year prior to marrying. Today, many teens still become monks, but for a three-month period after high school. Some young women sign on as nuns. The kids live in a skein of monasteries, engaged in chores or religious rigamarole and living off donations made at the local temples.

Legend has it that Buddha was born 2,500 years ago in the Himalayan foothills of India to a royal family. King Shuddhodana Gautama and his wife Maya tried bearing children for 20 years with no luck. Then one night, Maya dreamed she saw a white elephant enter her womb through the right side of her body -- sure enough, she was pregnant with a child who would change the world.

The infant was named Siddhartha, which means "every wish fulfilled," but his mother never lived to see her prayers come to flower: Maya died a few days after the birth. Soon, a hermit holy man came calling: he had seen a strange glow about the palace from his home in the mountains. He told the king that if his son grew up and remained at the palace, he would become a great warrior and subjugate the entire world; but if he left his royal lifestyle for a religious calling, he would become a Buddha -- the savior.

Sure enough, at the age of 29, Prince Siddhartha gave up the comforts of the palace to live the life of an ascetic in the forest for several years, meditating on the meaning of life.

And life, the young prince found, was relentlessly harsh and unfair.

One can't help but wonder if young Buddha suffered from clinical depression, since he always seemed to find something to be gloomy about. Life was a bummer: he felt sorry for an unfortunate worm plucked from a freshly-plowed field by a bird. Palace pleasures were a drag. And there was nothing to be happy about in the vigor of youth because old age and sickness were waiting just down the road. Perhaps if a supply of Prozac had been available to young Siddhartha, there would have been no Buddhism.

After many adventures, he evolved a philosophy that people are naturally bound to suffering, which springs from a desire for things beyond our limits: even the rich have an itch, so to speak. The only way to happiness is to get beyond the desire for luxuries, lust and comforts. One must find the 'middle way' with not too much and not too little of anything.

By being reincarnated through many lives, a Buddhist feels he can move toward nirvana, which is a perfect state of mind that is free of desire. Beyond nirvana is the extinguishment of the self, or the ego, and "poof" -- you're outta' here and all the pain of living. But first you

Naturally bound: the Buddha in the tree at Ayutthaya.

must evolve through many lifetimes from that of an animal to that of a woman and then a man (of course), and then to something approaching a god or a saint in the form of a bodhisattva.

The bodhisattvas may progress to a state of full-blown Buddhas, but only after all who suffer on earth are saved -- a long haul indeed.

It's a fairly simple tale, but like the Hindus, the Buddhists can't resist elaborating on their myths beyond all sense of reason. Any trip to the Orient reveals scores of saints who've become Buddhas, parallel worlds, time travel, Buddharealms, and various demons, servants and sidekicks who complicate the cosmology. Oh yeah, and their own version of the apocalypse, which is as wacky as that of the Christians. There's also a Cosmic Buddha who reigns over a triple universe of one billion earths, one billion magic mountains and one billion heavens. Imagine what the Asians would do with Jesus.

The Buddhists were chased out of India by a long list of invaders, including the Mughals, who were Muslims. Today, there are few Buddhists in India -- most of the religion is found in Southeast Asia, Japan and China.

Currently, there's a film in the works which makes the claim that young Jesus journeyed to India and was influenced by the ideas of the Buddha, who lived 500 years before he was born. It's possible, since no one knows what Jesus was up to between the ages of 12 and 30. And 2,000 years ago, many Jewish traders traveled by camel caravans and ships to India. For all we know, Jesus traveled to India, bringing back ideas which humanized the vengeful Yahweh, god of the Old Testament.

On the other hand, you'd think that if JC made the trip, there would be some rumor of it in the books of the New Testament. And even though much of the Bible was rewritten in the fourth and fifth century by Christian revisionists, you'd think there would still be hints of a trip to India in the Apocrypha, which are the "lost" books of the Bible. Plus, it's no stretch to believe that Jesus could have evolved his ideas on his own, and there's no hint of Buddhist-style reincarnation in the New Testament.

But the idea of a swashbuckling young Jesus traveling to India way back when should make for an interesting movie. Perhaps Buddha will make an appearance. The fact that they were born 500 years apart shouldn't be much of a problem for a Hollywood screenwriter or the credulous public.

The Missing

Where are the Americans?
Dec. 23, 2007
Bangkok, Thailand

You hear American music everywhere you go in Asia, and you see American films and TV. There's a "Texas Hold 'Em" pinball machine in the restaurant at my hotel, and a McDonald's downstairs. But one thing you rarely find are any living, breathing citizens of the United States.

Over the past two months in Asia I can count the number of Americans I've met on one hand -- and it might as well have been a hand with two fingers at that.

I don't mean the kind of tourists with luggage on wheels who stay at the Radisson and buy packaged bus tours on the order of "Ten Days in Thailand." I mean Americans who are missing from the ranks of the estimated 100,000 or so backpackers of all ages and nationalities who are kicking around the planet at any given moment.

In general, Americans seem as scarce as frog feathers in the developing world.

Peering at the registries of hostels and guest houses across Asia, I found page after page of Russians, Brits, Finns, Swedes, Irish, French, Germans, Aussies, New Zealanders, South Africans... but only here and there a solitary signature with "U.S.A." written in the nationality column. The same was true of gatherings of backpackers in bars, cafès, tour sites and other hot spots -- lots of Westerners from other lands, but none from the United States.

Nor is my evidence entirely anecdotal. Intrepid Travel, an international tour company which guides the backpacking set to exotic locales such as Vietnam, India and China, reported in 2006 that just 17 percent of its customers were from the U.S. and Canada.

There were mobs of us yanks in Prague, back in the Czech Republic, but after Central Europe, it was as if the people from Tennessee, Texas, Alabama and Ohio all dropped off the map. I saw a tour bus of Americans in Egypt, with my countrymen hidden behind black windows and sheltered in a fortified Hilton on the Nile behind armed guards -- they might as well have been traveling in a Thermos. And there was another monster tour bus at a jungle reserve in southern India, but otherwise, zip.

Back home, I know several Americans who've backpacked around the world, so it seems odd that 2007 feels so empty.

Then-Senator Barack Obama observed during the 2008 presidential campaign that a "lack of curiosity about the world outside our borders" led to the Bush administration's ideological response to the disaster of 9/11. Perhaps that lack of curiosity is endemic throughout the country. But I can't help but wonder if it's also simple fear that keeps Americans locked in their own country, or confined to hermetically-sealed, all-inclusive resorts in Mexico or package tours in Western Europe.

Many other Westerners routinely travel as backpackers through the Mideast, India, Africa and Asia. They bypass tour groups in favor of the rock-bottom rates of guesthouses, or seek out cheap destinations such as Malaysia. For these visitors from Europe or Australia, traveling on local trains and buses and mingling with the people of other lands leads to a greater understanding of the world.

By contrast, the stay-at-home American is dangerously ill-informed. Our perceptions are shaped mostly by what we see on television. Our vision of the world is invariably that of Africans hacking at each other with machetes on TV, or crowds of Muslims burning cars over the latest slight to Muhammad. And it's always raining suicide bombers on the airwaves in America.

Perhaps it's no surprise that we're afraid: as Michael Moore pointed out in *Bowling for Colombine*, the American media is obsessed with spreading fear of everything from killer bees to Chinese teddy bears. Our rap and heavy metal music oozes warnings of a dangerous world, essentially telling young people to stay inside and travel no farther than the screen of their video games. You'd think this scared-silly rap & metal stuff was written by quivering jellyfish. Teen films such as the *Hostel* series are frantic in their warnings of foreign travel. Our newspapers are filled with hair-raising abductions and bombings. And on television, foreigners invariably have evil motives -- our fears roil like an episode of *24,* with Snidely Whiplash villains in the guise of Arab terrorists and the Russian mafia lurking inside the friendly neighborhood ice cream truck.

Given all that, who wouldn't be afraid to travel?

Indeed, it's entirely possible that you could travel overseas and be kidnapped by a terror organization such as FARC, or by a criminal who's hijacked your cab in Mexico City, Lima or Jakarta.

On the other hand, you could stay home and be one of the more than 42,000 Americans who are killed in vehicular accidents each year, or one of more than 15,000 who are murdered within the borders of the U.S.A.

It's a wonder we're not a nation of agoraphobics.

Reality Bites

Europeans, Australians and other Western travelers operate from the assumption that the world is their playground and there's nothing to fear -- they don't seem to give the hazards of traveling in the developing world a second thought. But many Americans assume that the opposite is true, and with few acquaintances who've "made the trip," they have nothing to fall back on but the frightening images of our media and their own anxieties.

And those Americans who do travel often meet only the most unpleasant people in other countries: the cynical, aggrieved, pesky merchants who harangue tourists at the souvenir markets lining the docks of cruise ships, or in the bazaars of Cancun or Jamaica.

So imagine enduring many American travelers' biggest fear: you're rushed by two dark-skinned men in a lonely place in a Muslim country with no chance of escape.

But this is no mugging -- these guys just want to shake your hand and say how thrilled they are that an American is visiting their country. They practically have tears of joy in their eyes.

This happened to me several times in Egypt and also in the Kingdom of Bahrain, where an innkeeper assured me that Americans are the "best of the best" among foreign travelers, and wished there were more of us stopping by. A Thai cab driver said much the same as we endured the long crawl through a Bangkok traffic jam.

Why? Because people are curious about Americans and hope to make a connection. Are we really like the characters they see in our movies and TV? Are we all rich? Could a possible contact lead to a new life in America?

Then too, in the Muslim lands, millions fear they're being left behind by the world. They reject terrorism; they want peace and trade, like anyone living anywhere. Many would love to have more Western visitors, and of course, our dollars.

In street-corner conversations conducted at levels just above a whisper, I've met Muslims who chafe under the prison of their medieval religion, which -- like any fundamentalist faith -- is basically a cult of sexual repression. Yet they feel powerless to resist a state religion in which the literal translation of "Islam" is that of "submission."

Consider that public stonings, decapitations, floggings and the amputation of limbs for religious offenses are still practiced in Saudi Arabia, Pakistan, Sudan and Afghanistan. I met a Pakistani backpacker living in London whose mother warned him not to return to his own country because it was too dangerous. Even in the more secular countries, such as Morocco, an offense on par with chewing gum during the fasting month of Ramadan can get you a visit from the 'religion police' and a month in jail. Who wouldn't want to get out from under that grind? Who wouldn't hope that more Western tourists might bring changes and a better life?

One of the things you get asked everywhere in foreign lands is, "Where are you from? Australia? England? Germany?"

I always answer "America," and love to catch the reaction, since our country isn't exactly leading the popularity parade these days. I don't mind hearing people vent if they have a problem with my country. I'm here to listen.

But some Americans are fearful to admit where they're from. And who can blame them, considering the wave of anti-Americanism sweeping the world?

It's not unusual to meet Americans who claim to be natives of Canada, England or Australia when traveling overseas. There is the occasional American who actually brags about pretending to be a Canadian as a cover. Perhaps they're afraid that someone will say something mean in the marketplace, or assault them for the crime of being from Minnesota or Delaware.

This is an overblown fear because the dirt-poor citizens of the Third World are so used to living under incompetent, corrupt governments that Western politicians look like amateurs by comparison. They must contend with corrupt, autocratic leaders like Hosni Mubarek ("the last pharaoh") in Egypt, Robert Mugabe in Zimbabwe, or Pervez "Mush" Musharef in Pakistan. And you have to wonder if the Spice Girls couldn't run India better than its fanatical Hindu politicians.

Most of the poor people of the world could care less about American politics -- they're too busy worrying about the struggle to survive. It's tourist dollars that matter to them, along with the visitor's desire to spread them lavishly.

In fact, I've met many Third World citizens who love Americans, because we are inclined to be big-hearted and don't pinch every nickel like travelers from many other nations. Some Western tourists bargain so hard in the markets that it verges on being cruel, considering that the tourist stuff for sale is a matter of pennies to us, but means a great deal to poor merchants.

At a shop in Egypt on the Red Sea, my roommate paused for a

moment when asked where he was from. It was just long enough to prompt the Muslim shopkeeper to give us a friendly lecture.

"Why are you afraid to say you are from America?" the shopkeeper asked. "We know you have bad leaders, just like us. But that's just politics. Your people are good, just like our people are good. Even the Israelis come here and we know they are good people. You must always say with pride: 'I am from the United States of America.'"

The Time Crunch

A big part of the reason you don't find many Americans bumming around Asia, South America or Africa is because we simply don't have the time off.

A citizen of western Europe gets four-to-six weeks off to go "on holiday" each year. The French get as much as eight weeks off, including the entire month of August. In Australia, it's practically a national imperative to take six months or a year off sometime during your life to go on a walkabout through the Third World. In Denmark, you get extra time off if you agree to have more children to bolster the declining birth rate.

By contrast, the average American feels that taking a two-week vacation is really pushing it. We're like the workaholic Japanese in that respect -- they too get an average of two weeks off, and must spend part of that time visiting family.

Thus, Americans who *do* travel tend to take expensive week-long vacations close to home or to Europe, Mexico or Hawaii, spending lavishly to cram as much fun as possible into seven days before heading back to work.

The American travel industry even pushes the wacky idea of the three-day weekend in the tropics, where you bring home a half-tan and ugly memories of your time in the airport and on the plane.

This also tends to make Americans more destination-oriented, or intent on achieving a goal, rather than wandering at will around the world. For instance, even back home in rural northern Michigan I've met a fair number of people who've visited an Indian ashram to study yoga.

Then too, 75 million Americans are homeowners and have mortgages to pay, unlike the European apartment-dwellers I met. Many Western backpackers have a cavalier attitude about ditching their jobs or apartments; some are even searching for new homes in foreign lands. By contrast, Americans are homebodies at heart.

I've also known many Americans (including myself) who had the wherewithal to purchase a home while still in our 20s. That is virtually unheard of in Europe. Perhaps that's why our cousins overseas are the travelers while we prefer to sit on our nests.

On a Mission

Other Americans are more inclined to do mission work than go skylarking around the world. In 2007, the Peace Corps had more than 8,000 volunteers working around the planet. Thousands more volunteer as missionaries, or contribute medical and nursing skills through groups such as Doctors Without Borders, which has as many as 27,000 volunteers.

In Michigan, my friends Chris and Susan Skellenger funneled their skills as landscapers into 11 Oaks, a low-tech "bucket" irrigation project they created to help subsistence farmers in Lesotho, a small landlocked country in southern Africa. Another couple from my town, Chris and Jody Treter, travel to Ethiopia and Chiapas, Mexico each year to purchase coffee from poor farmers for their Higher Grounds Trading Company.

Then there is Hanley Denning, an educator in her 20s, who arrived in Guatemala in 1999 to study Spanish. Appalled by the sight of families rooting in the Guatemala City dump, she established Safe Passage, a program for kids who live and work in Central America's biggest landfill. Starting with 40 children, her program mushroomed to help hundreds of kids and their families. Denning was killed in a car crash in Guatemala in January, 2007, but her work lives on.

A Matter of Pride

The far side of the world could use more Americans spreading goodwill to repair our country's reputation. To win the 'War on Terror' we could use more American travelers touring the mosques of the Mideast, and fewer soldiers with automatic weapons kicking down doors.

As an example, I enjoy buying souvenirs from craftspersons along the road, usually paying full price instead of haggling, or bargaining just for fun and then giving the peddlers what they asked for originally.

Sometimes you buy things not because you want or need them, but just to support the cause of the locals, sitting in the heat and dust of a benighted land. It's a game a middle-class American can easily afford to play.

I was buying some trinket jewelry from a wizened old Bedouin woman at a windblown oasis deep in the Sinai desert. It was just junk, but

I wanted to make a connection. Perhaps she was younger than me, but her skin was as parched, brown and wrinkled as a camel's nose and her dark eyes peered out of deep folds, brutalized by the sun.

One of the other backpackers in our party from London said, "You shouldn't buy from them -- it just encourages them to sell to the tourists. You should give your money to charity instead."

"Hey, give them a break," I shot back. "You are a millionaire or a multi-millionaire by comparison, and these people have nothing."

I'm not sure that anyone on the bus agreed with me, but I think that charity would have crushed the dignity of this Bedouin nomad, who was proud of her work. Instead, she made a clever necklace with her own hands and sold it at full price to a passing tourist. Now, she can tell all her friends about her big sale and impress her husband as well. And the whole family will eat better because someone bothered to reward her industry. In return, I have an exotic hatband and a memory to last a lifetime.

My only regret after making those small purchases is that I didn't look into that desert woman's eyes and say, "Thank you for selling your jewelry to an American."

But that, of course, would have been silly.

Bangkok Blues
Dec. 23, 2007
Bangkok, Thailand

Back in Bangkok, Jeannette and I check into the Buddy Lodge on Khaosan Road. It's our final splurge -- the best hotel on the strip, with a rooftop pool that makes a pleasant oasis from the heat smoldering like a wet electric blanket.

The frog ladies are still here -- women in traditional stovetop Thai hats who walk up and down the street, scraping wands over the backs of carved wooden frogs to produce a croaking sound. And the usual suspects are still on the scene, hoisting backpacks and wearing beer-brand tee-shirts and Billabong shorts. We mill through the crowd of Johnny Depp lookalikes, gangs of hulking Germans, lithe European girls (surely members of a lost Scandinavian volleyball team), and sun-blackened Thai men in tattoos and dreads, as skinny as sticks. Not a pleasant place to be if the Thai rebels in the south ever get it in their heads to plant a bomb in a pad thai cart...

Then there's the stink plastering your face with a drizzling accumulation of grease and the sun smashing you with hammer blows be-

Chew enough betel nut and you too can have brilliant black teeth.

tween the eyes. The black tar flooding the pavement is thick enough to be flipped and fried if only you could peel eons of spilled Pepsi, snot, and the skids of drunken flip-flops from its surface. The sticky-sweet, warm stench of rotting garbage reminds you not to breathe too deeply.

Legless beggars and anxious dogs crouch in the middle of the street with pleading eyes amid the crowds. Women braid hair entwined with tinsel. Hope dies in the eyes of vendors as you give their price a pass. Periodically, Thai cops in stormtrooper uniforms, CHIPs helmets and honeybee sunglasses sweep the street clean of pad thai carts and chicken BBQ stands to appease the restaurant owners along the strip. The cart owners scurry their stainless steel kitchens down a narrow alley, returning as soon as the cops leave. If they get caught, the cops can seize their carts. A tuk-tuk hustler bugs you to catch a ping-pong pussy show, oblivious to the fact that you're strolling with your wife. *Kob kuhn krab* (thank you), but fuck no, senor. Just another day in Asia -- you've got to love it.

We brave another hour-long cab ride for a last pass at the Night Market where Jeannette piles up more Christmas booty. The trinkets are stuffed into her luggage as tight as Santa Claus's happy bag.

Jeannette gets one last chocolate banana pancake, fried on a street-vendor's wok. And then a final gift -- a tin elephant bracelet from a frog lady who remembers me from two weeks ago out of all the thousands of tourists who've passed through since then. Guess it was meant to be. Merry Christmas.

At 4 a.m., December 23, Jeannette and I share our 'Christmas breakfast' at Starbucks at the airport and then she's gone -- back to the West, family, home and Christmas. I love that girl.

By the miracle of the earth's east-west rotation and her crossing of the International Date Line, Jeannette will make the 27-hour, 12,000-mile flight home in the same day, arriving in Michigan at 9 p.m.

I get a spooky feeling of disconnection and loss as I walk back to the bus stop -- a stray dog again, feeling lost and alone on the other side of the world. The sentimental strains of Christmas music hang leaden weights on my heartstrings, dragging me down with waves of guilt and loss for not being home for the holidays. Bah, humbug. Where are you, Sir Laugh-A-Lot?

So long, Thailand. I'm leaving on a jet plane, don't know when I'll be back again. But if and when I return, it will be with your name already written large in black magic marker on my Lucky Travel Hat. *Kob kuhn krab*.

Vietnam

Christmas Eve, Vietnam
Dec. 24, 2007
Hanoi, Vietnam

Christmas in Vietnam starts with a bang -- a furious argument on the streets of Hanoi that threatens to spiral into flying fists and a visit from the cops.

I should have known better than to take an unmarked, gypsy cab from the airport, but a guy at the travel desk vouched for the driver and we headed into town.

Hanoi is a gray, chilly place, a far remove from the Death Valley temperatures of Bangkok. My first impression is of an Asian Grand Rapids, Michigan. The Talking Heads song rings in my thoughts: "This ain't no party, this ain't no disco, this ain't no fooling around."

There are literally millions of motorbike riders on the streets, with all the riders wearing the new "rice cooker" helmets which were recently mandated by law. There are 22 million bikes in this land of 85 million people, so the helmet manufacturers must be doing handsprings.

We pass a vast billboard depicting a blood-red B-52 Stratofortress bomber going down over a city filled with explosions. It's a horrifying image, full of anger and pain. From the date: "1972" and the number "35" I deduce that this is in celebration of the 35th anniversary of the plane getting shot down, with its wreckage on display at the city's famous B-52 Museum. The B-52 carried 60,000 lbs. of high explosive and rained death on Hanoi from 55,000 feet -- it is still the largest bomber in the world.

For 12 days of Christmas in 1972, President Richard Nixon and Secretary of State Henry Kissinger ordered the bombing of Hanoi, which was to be the last battle of the U.S. war in Vietnam. The North Vietnamese had turned down America's final offer at the Paris Peace Talks, knowing that an anti-war Congress had been elected with a vow to cut funding for the war when they took office in January. So the Nixon administration ordered the bombings which destroyed bridges and factories, but also hospitals and neighborhoods filled with civilians. The raids sacrificed the lives of several B-52 crews, shot down over the city.

But the North Vietnamese high command had the bejesus scared out of them by the bombings -- which had finally brought flaming hell to their door -- and went back to the bargaining table, signing an agreement to end the war. Yet they considered themselves to be the winners of the air battle. They figured they'd paid in blood to end the war.

We got to our destination and the driver and his tout indicated that the hotel was down a side street and that I should pay them, get out, and walk there. This told me they weren't on the up-and-up, so I leapt out of the cab with all my gear and said we'd walk the rest of the way to the hotel and pay in the lobby.

I'm not that tough compared to some of the gritty French and German backpackers I've met who'll eat anything and stay anywhere, but I do have a fuse like a blasting cap when it comes to cab drivers trying to rip me off, which is endemic in Asia. Several times I've pushed the ejector button on cabs, playing their game on my own terms.

As it turned out, these crooks were directing me down the wrong street, possibly in hopes that I'd be so confused looking for the hotel that they'd be long gone by the time I figured out they had overcharged me. When I refused to play along, they wanted me to get back in the cab. No deal.

"There's no way I'm getting back in your cab!" I yelled, walking off down the street with my pack and guitar. "You lied to me and now there's no trust. No trust!"

There ensued a loud, angry argument in which I insisted on walking in the correct direction of the hotel, with them following me in the car -- screaming, yelling and gesturing the whole way. I've heard that you're not supposed to act like a drama queen and make a fuss in Asia because someone might "lose face," which is considered to be an intolerable insult, but to hell with that.

Sure enough, the hotel clerk told me they were charging me two-and-a-half times the local rate and the driver was a bad character. I gave the driver half of what he wanted and indicated that he should buzz off. He was mad enough to spit nails, but I don't think either of us wanted a talk with the police, so eventually he ripped the money from my hand and left. Then a happy smile settled on Bubby's face.

So, what to do on Christmas Eve in the 'Nam? The local restaurants were pretty scroungy, but I found a nice "pho" noodle joint and had chicken soup. Then I squatted on the sidewalk with six men playing Chinese checkers and watched awhile. Oooh, my aching joints.

A young police officer in a dark green uniform came over for a friendly talk.

"Where you from?" he asked in ragged English.

"America. I'm from northern Michigan in America. It's up on the big Lake Michigan. Do you know it?"

He shook his head yes, but I suspect he didn't have a clue.

"My uncle also live in America," he said. "He live in Mexico City."

"You mean he lives in Mexico?" I asked.

"No, he live in America -- in Mexico City," he responded.

Before turning in, I saw an old man outside my hotel who was missing a leg. Probably a casualty of the war, and perhaps this man was younger than me, but had grown old before his time as a result of all the injuries and insults to his life. He gave me a wary glance and I felt a stab of guilt for what my country had done, so long ago. I realized that I would be seeing many people here missing limbs and would have to get used to it.

As I fell asleep, I wondered what it would have been like to have lain in bed on a Christmas Eve long ago, listening to the anti-aircraft guns and SAM missiles exploding far overhead as a B-52 Stratofortress delivered its flaming death.

Out of the blue, a dozen Australians appeared in Santa outfits and Victoria's Secret angel wings....

Christmas Day
Dec. 25, 2007
Hanoi, Vietnam

I'm hopelessly lost within minutes of leaving my hotel, which is in an obscure part of town, far from the tourist zone. Soon, I'm wandering down alleys full of women chopping raw beef on mats on the sidewalk, or bearing up under crossbeam poles with baskets of oranges and melons dangling from either end. People burn trash in small metal stoves on the pavement; a woman roasts ears of corn on a charcoal grill; there is a brisk trade in lottery tickets; and hordes of people set up produce for sale.

You can't walk more than 50 feet without having to step into the street because the sidewalks are filled with vendors, idle men, or barriers of parked motorbikes. A parking spot on the sidewalk runs the equivalent of six cents.

But then, most of the streets of Asia are built around the same model. You walk 30 feet down a sidewalk, then step into the street to get around a cab or motorbike, then back up the curb to avoid getting run over, then down in the street because a repair shop has got a transmission laid out in pieces on the sidewalk. Up, down, round and round.

And the streets are like fording a river filled with a never-ending school of metal fish on two wheels. Thousands of them. To cross this stream of motorbikes you must step into the current and slowly walk forward with the conviction that they will flow around you. Don't even think of making a sudden move.

The Vietnamese are even lazier than Americans when it comes to walking. In Hanoi, they've all but obliterated any chance to stroll the sidewalks. "Do you want a ride?" you get asked at every street corner by the cyclo taxi men. They can't imagine why anyone would even want to walk through town.

Apprehending Apprehension

I don't mind getting lost. I have all day and night to pound the streets of Hanoi. My only regret is the lack of a compass. There's no sun under Hanoi's gray ceiling, so I can't tell which way is north or south.

It's not hard to be apprehensive in such an alien place. Everyone passing by is wearing a helmet -- and some are wearing surgical masks because of the air pollution. And there are many police in heavy green uniforms trimmed in red. I have the eerie, almost subconscious feeling of being in a police state, but that's precisely what the Socialist Republic of Vietnam is.

But I remind myself that to these people, this scene is no different than a day at my hometown farm market. So I compose a pleasant expression and offer friendly waves and smiles to the people who greet me on my walk through town.

You have to use the Socratic Method of one question following another to analyze fear when traveling. Will people give me a hard time because I'm an American? After all, the war in Vietnam killed three or four million of their people. But would I give a Vietnamese person a hard time in my country? No, of course not. And who won the war? Vietnam. In their eyes, I'm probably more to be pitied than censored.

Soon, I get my bearings and master the layout of the city. I make my way to a park at Ho Hoan Kiem Lake in the heart of Hanoi and find a cappuccino and chocolate cheesecake waiting for me at a lakeside coffee shop. Other Westerners hove into view at the north end of the lake. I've tracked them to their lair in the maze of shopping lanes known as Old Town.

The Helpful Harrys of Hanoi trail in their wake. Would I like to buy some books, postcards or a map? Would I like a taxi ride on the back of a motorbike? Would I like to help a poor student? Where would I be without these guys... "Thanks, but what I'd really like is to be left alone," I tell one guy who waves a map in my face.

Out of the blue, a dozen Australians appear, marching down the street in Santa Claus outfits, shouting season's greetings. Some of the women are dressed as angels with Victoria's Secret wings. "Merry fuckin' Christmas!" a skinny Santa bellows in my ear. It's good to know the season hasn't been forgotten in Hanoi.

***

Speaking of which, I had promised that I would attend church here on this holy day. The French occupied Vietnam for about 100 years, so there are both Catholic and Protestant churches in the city. I make my way to the old St. Joseph's Cathedral, built in 1886, only to find the crumbling stone edifice barred and fenced off -- it has become a tourist attraction. Outside are mobs of Vietnamese school kids, dashing amid a carnival of balloon vendors and nativity scenes.

But the old bell still tolls a single chime from the steeple and I make my way to a quiet bench in the shadow of the cathedral, offering a Christmas prayer of thanks for my wife, family, friends and all the blessings in my life. It is a very long list.

Aladdin Sane
Dec. 26, 2007
Hanoi, Vietnam

Hmmm... how much money should I get out of the ATM? As usual, a motorbike driver is hovering over my shoulder, anxious to know if I want a cycle taxi ride the second I'm done with my transaction. I know he's harmless, but he breaks my concentration.

ATMs are the backpackers' lifeline, with cash available almost anywhere on earth, and it occurs to me that I'd be screwed if one of these machines gobbled my card or it was stolen.

But 200,000 dong seems like a lot of money so I hit the payout button. Walking away, I realize I've just withdrawn the equivalent of $12 -- about one-tenth of what I had intended.

It's all part of the culture shock of getting used to a new place, and there's plenty of that sensation to go around.

A young soldier waves to me at the Temple of Literature and asks if he can have his photo taken with the funny looking Westerner wearing a cowboy hat. Hell yeah.

Soon, I have half a platoon of Viet soldiers lined up with our arms over each others' shoulders in a grip & grin shot. They're all smiling from ear-to-ear. It's an eerie feeling, because a generation ago, these kids would have been mortal enemies of the cowboy in their midst.

But bygones seem to be bygones. Despite my recent gripe over a lack of Americans in Asia, I see some apparent former U.S. soldiers visiting Hanoi and being treated with respect by the locals. If anything, the Vietnamese seem bored with us. For the young, the "American War" is ancient history. Most of the people who fought in it are dead.

Not that the Vietnamese have forgotten the war. The Museum of Fine Arts has many propaganda oil paintings of soldiers struggling against the "American aggressors" (sample painting: "The Enemy Burned My Village"). And there are also paintings of peasants enjoying the "fruits of communism," painted after the war when three million Vietnamese starved to death, despite this being one of the most fertile countries on earth.

Those tough times prompted the communist rulers to reinstate free market principles, and in 1995, full diplomatic relations were restored with the U.S. Our first ambassador, Douglas Peterson, had been a POW here.

In Russia, they've pulled down most of their statues to Lenin, but he still rules in Hanoi, with a tall statue in a park, striding toward the Army History Museum. The museum is a Disneyland of Destruction, full of dismal relics and photos.

Included is the destruction of the "impregnable" French fort of Dien Bien Phu in 1954. Viet Minh General Vo Nguyen Giap brought 55,000 men to the battle and used 200,000 porters to haul cannon up into the mountains above the fort, the heights of which were thought to be impossible to climb with artillery. Thousands of porters pushed bicycles laden with as much as 700 lbs. of supplies for hundreds of miles down the Ho Chi Minh Trail (these pack bicycles were later used to the same effect in the war against the U.S.).

Between the bombardment, attack, and a bomb tunneled under the fort with a ton of TNT, the French suffered a humiliating defeat, not to mention 95,000 killed in the war. They got out of Vietnam, and President John F. Kennedy got the bright idea to send us in their place.

Vietnam was divided into North and South by the Geneva Accords of 1954, which ended the war against the French. The country became the checkerboard for the global chess game against communism. But the Soviets and the Red Chinese were smarter than us: they funded a proxy war, using the Vietnamese as their pawns.

Of course, that's not how they tell it at the Army History Museum, where the now-hated Soviets and Chinese aren't even mentioned. Also known as the B-52 Museum, its yard is filled with captured U.S. planes, helicopters, tanks and other weapons. Included is the wreckage of the B-52 I saw on the billboard on the way into town, piled up in a tattered pyramid.

There are somber American and French citizens here, reflecting on the past. Me too. If you wish to be enlightened on the madness and futility of war, Vietnam is the place to get your overdose.

***

But the culture scene is not all gloom and doom. Hanoi has the best TV I've found outside of America, with HBO, Cinemax, CNN, BBC and many other English channels at my hotel, along with free wifi.

There are also excellent coffeehouses -- Vietnam is the land of coffee in Asia. Today, I had a *croque monsieur* with french fries at an outdoor cafè, serenaded by Dido on the loudspeaker. It's not what you'd expect of communist Hanoi, with that big statue of Lenin waving at you from across the street.

But I'm beginning to suffer from travel fatigue. Not from traveling, but because I'm constantly harassed to buy things wherever I go. Since I walk a great deal, I'm a target for every itinerant peddler, taxi bike driver and "student" selling postcards in Hanoi (not to mention Thailand, India, Egypt...). It's debilitating to have to constantly wave people away while trying to maintain a sense of humor. If there's one thing I've discovered on this trip, it's that most of the people in the world are very, very poor, and it's easy for them to see a rich Westerner as a meal ticket.

Fellow Travelers
Dec. 27, 2007
Hanoi, Vietnam

On the top floor of the Van Mieu Hotel in Hanoi, I connect with another group of backpackers for the trek across Vietnam.

Nine of our party are from Australia, with their numbers drawn from Brisbane, Sydney and Melbourne, along with two recent emigrants from New Zealand. Our leader is "Beerlao" Bill Raymond, a Kiwi, from Wellington. The lone Americans are Katie -- a potter from Oregon, and myself.

I detect a murmur of surprise from the Aussies when they hear that there are two Americans with the group. People from other Western countries are invariably polite, but sometimes you catch a vibe that Americans are looked down upon. We're oddities in this corner of the world.

Part of the fun of traveling with Intrepid Travel is meeting backpackers who've been everywhere imaginable: Tanzania, Tibet, Ghana,

Laos, Brazil, Kenya, Bali, Mali... It's a good way to gather intelligence for your next trip.

And the beauty of such a group is that you see 10 times as much with one-tenth the hassle if you tried going it alone.

Intrepid is based in Melbourne, Australia, and specializes in adventure travel for small groups of no more than 11. Canada has a similar outfit called GAP Adventures.

The company was started in 1989 by Darrell Wade and Geoff Manchester. The two led a group of 12 across the Sahara in 1988 and realized that there was a business opportunity in smoothing the way for backpackers interested in seeing the world's more exotic destinations.

They started with a single trip to Thailand in 1989, with one partner leading the tour and the other running the business office back in Australia. The business evolved around taking local buses and trains (rather than expensive tour buses), and staying in the same hotels frequented by the natives of each country.

The trips include 'home stays' and dinners in the homes of locals, along with offbeat lodgings, such as our felucca cruise in Egypt. These keep the costs down and add to the authentic flavor of each trip.

The idea was a hit. As of 2006, Intrepid Travel was offering trips in 96 countries, with more than 50,000 backpackers. They have a staff of over 100 and offer 471 trips, ranging from "Basix" low-budget travel for young adults to a "Comfort" level with more amenities. Trips run from 6-60 days.

You're bound to meet a lot of Australians on an Intrepid trip: 40% are from Down Under, with just 17% from the U.S. and Canada. Women make up 62% of travelers, with 38% male. It's also a good option for single travelers, with each trip tending to have several onboard. In fact, the majority of travelers I've met on my three trips with Intrepid have been single.

The group leaders are also a 'trip': "BeerLao" Bill Raymond is a native of New Zealand with shoulder-length hair who invariably wears a red t-shirt emblazoned with the popular Laotian beer brand.

Bill is the sort of renegade expat you find everywhere in the travel world -- running a hotel, leading fishing charters or whatever -- who figured out long ago that the 9-to-5 grind was shit and it's better to just go on vacation for the rest of your life. These guys are all avuncular sorts who've been everywhere, done everything, but keep most of it to themselves. They'll offer an occasional wry smile when you say something particularly stupid.

Thus, Bill has spent the last few years kicking all around Asia. He says that he has no home, preferring to stop here and there in favorite places with his many friends. Vietnamese locals greet him on the street wherever we go.

In his younger days, Bill and three friends traveled across the heart of Africa from Kenya to the Rock of Gibraltar. They traveled in the back of trucks and in dugout canoes across the Congo, Chad, and the Central African Republic, and worked their way across the continent on rubber plantations and the like.

"We were young and up for anything," he recalls. "We didn't think much about it, we just went. But I doubt I'd try that now. Africa has changed for the worse since I was there."

As an example, Bill says that crossing borders in central Africa meant having all of his stuff pillaged by the customs agents. "They'd just dump everything out of your pack and go through it, taking what they wanted," he says. "And all you could do was stand there and hope they'd leave you enough things you needed to go on. They're on this power trip where they throw your stuff all over and leave it lying there on the ground; and you're thinking -- come on -- there's no need to act like that."

A Visit with Uncle Ho

"Regardless of being from different countries and religions, we are all brothers. We have suffered the same pain; the ruthlessness of colonialism. We are fighting for common goals: liberty for our fellow men and independence for our nation."

-- Ho Chi Minh, 1923

"Uncle" Ho Chi Minh looks pretty good under glass, considering he has been dead since 1969. But then, he is taken to Moscow every three or four years for a touch-up before being returned to his resting place within a glass coffin in his huge mausoleum. He's one of three dead, mummified communist leaders, including Lenin and Mao Ze-dong, who are hanging around until the "Worker's Paradise" predicted by Karl Marx sees the light of day.

It will probably be a long wait.

Ho Chi Minh was born Nguyễn Sinh Cung in 1890 to a relatively poor family, but he received a good education by dint of his father's position as a teacher, a Confucian scholar, and a civil servant in the emperor's court. As a boy, Ho was expelled from school for passing out anti-French literature to his classmates. Today, there is a statue of him in front of the old schoolyard in Hue.

He worked his way to France as a kitchen helper on a ship in 1911. There, he worked at odd jobs and fell in with the intellectuals of the day, who were fired up with the revolutionary theories of communism and socialism. He spent much of his free time studying history, philosophy and political theory in French libraries.

Yet the man who would one day fight the United States to a draw aspired to become a pastry chef as a young man. Ho is said to have worked as a pastry chef under French Chef Escoffier at London's Carlton Hotel. Legend has it that his wanderings also took him to America, where he worked as a waiter in Harlem.

By the early 1920s, Ho fell in with expat Asian nationalists back in Europe and joined the French Communist Party to rally support for Vietnam's independence.

He moved on to Moscow to study the works of Marx, Lenin, and Soviet-style communism. During his two years at Moscow's Toilers of the East University, Ho wrote magazine essays on the problems of colonialism.

But some historians claim that Ho was not a committed communist; he was simply looking for support to cast out the French overlords of Vietnam, who colonized the country in the 1860s.

Today, when Europeans badmouth America, they forget their own history -- that of King Leopold of Belgium cutting off the hands of rubber workers in the Congo who didn't meet their quotas, or the British enslaving hundreds of thousands of Egyptians to dig the Suez Canal.

The French colonialists who ruled Vietnam, Laos and Cambodia were said to be at least as cruel in their turn. The Viets were paid one-eighth what the French got for the same work, when they weren't conscripted as outright slaves. France pillaged Vietnam for hundreds of millions in treasure.

At one point, Ho appealed to President Franklin D. Roosevelt for help in getting rid of the French. Ho was an admirer of George Washington, and thought the Americans might be sympathetic to his cause. But FDR said no deal -- the French were our allies -- so Ho turned to the helpful communists.

Members of the OSS (forerunners of the CIA) stood on a platform with Ho during his 1945 Declaration of Independence from France, but no help was forthcoming.

Yet, like George Washington, Ho refused to give up on the liberation of his country despite many setbacks.

According to U.S. government records, President Lyndon Johnson did not want to get involved in a war in Vietnam, but couldn't afford to look soft on communism. Johnson had already sacrificed the Democrats' hold on America's southern states by passing civil rights legislation. Also, Johnson didn't want to be the first U.S. president to lose a war, so he was stuck with the mess John F. Kennedy started.

Johnson offered Ho Chi Minh a generous development deal of the Mekong River valley if he would back off on trying to unify Vietnam. Ho declined and escalated the war. Johnson took the bait -- he didn't want to be the first U.S. president to lose a war, and Vietnam spiraled into a 10-year fight in which the U.S. lost more than 55,000 men.

Ho Chi Minh led liberation struggles against the Chinese, Japanese, French and Americans, but died six years before North and South Vietnam were unified. Like Moses, he never saw the Promised Land, but must have known the day was coming.

Today, he lives on and is a virtual saint in Vietnam, at peaceful repose under glass in his tomb. And the Viets really pour on the syrup in his memory. But was he really a saint? Or just another despot with a great P.R. department? I imagine the folks sent to the misery of Uncle Ho's re-education camps and punishment cells had a divergent view of him. Did he have any human foibles? Any kinks? If he did, the Vietnamese have buried them deep beneath the stuff of legend. But the dead man under glass looks pleasant enough.

The Turtle and the Sword

Nearly 600 years ago a princess set sail on a lake in the middle of Hanoi. Out of the depths, a giant golden turtle arose, bearing a magic sword in its mouth.

The princess gave the sword to her father, the Emperor Le Thai, who used to it drive the Ming Chinese out of Vietnam in the 15th century.

But when the war was won, the emperor set sail on the lake and met the same turtle. "I want my magic sword back," the turtle said.

Done.

Ever since then, the giant turtles of Hoan Kiem Lake have guarded the magic sword. Once in awhile, they make their presence known, rising up from the depths, as big as manhole covers. Some are said to be 200 years old, and one was captured in 1968 that weighed 550 lbs.

And that is why the home of the turtles is known as the Lake of the Restored Sword to this day.

Ding-Dong Dollars
Dec. 28, 2007
Hanoi, Vietnam

"No motorbike, no girlfriend." -- *Vietnamese proverb*

Vietnam is a land of millionaires. But then, a million dong is only $60 U.S., so no biggie. Still, it's a bit jarring to be presented with a bill for 60,000 dong when you order a coffee and a piece of cake. It takes a moment to realize that's only a little less than $4.

It's not the fellow with the most dong who gets the girls here, however; it's the guy who has the fanciest motorbike. "The fancier the bike, the prettier the girl on the backseat," says Bill.

Ten years ago, Vietnam was a bicyclist's utopia, but once prosperity came, everyone said to hell with their bikes and bought mopeds and motorcycles. It was a bonanza for Honda, which manufactures a high-status bike that sells for around $5,000. You can also get Chinese or Vietnamese junkers for as little as $1,000.

There are now three million motorbikes in this city of 5.5 million. 'Gas stations' are found on every corner -- a soda bottle full of gasoline sits by the curb -- often tended by a child or an old-timer -- where you stop and get your go-juice.

It's said that there are illegal street races in Hanoi with up to 400 motorcycles. The bravest (ie: stupidest) riders cut their brake cables on the nighttime race through the intersections of town.

***

We travel east to Halong Bay and spent the night on an old fishing boat converted into a hotel. The bay is one of the treasures of Asia, with 3,000 karst-formation islands. These misty monochrome islands are believed to be the place where Chinese and Vietnamese ancestors go to enjoy a pleasant afterlife.

Of course, the bay also swarms with hotel boats -- photos of which have become a clichè in every travel magazine in the world, whenever Vietnam is in focus.

Nice, but touristy. I can only imagine that the hundreds of boats are probably a great irritation to the old ghosts trying to get some rest.

The Hanoi Hilton
Dec. 29, 2007
Hanoi, Vietnam

Hoa Lin Prison is an anonymous compound in downtown Hanoi which was used to imprison captured Americans during the war. It was here in the infamous "Hanoi Hilton" prison that future U.S. ambassador Doug Peterson and 2008 presidential candidate Sen. John McCain were held for for more than five years during the war.

Built by the French in 1896, Hoa Lin Prison was initially used to torture and imprison Vietnamese rebels. Then, the tables were turned on the French, who were held and tortured in their own prison by the Japanese during World War II, and then by their former Vietnamese subjects when they lost control of the country in 1954. That legacy of torture and abuse was handed down to U.S. airmen who were held here -- captives taken from more than 3,000 warplanes which were shot down over 10 years of war.

John McCain was shot down over Hanoi on Oct. 26, 1967 when a SAM missile blew off the right wing of his jet. Bailing out, his body crashed into his plane, breaking his left arm, his right arm in three places, and his right knee. But worse was to come. His parachute dumped him in a shallow lake in the middle of Hanoi, where a North Vietnamese soldier broke his shoulder with a rifle butt and stabbed him with a bayonet in his groin and ankle.

In his book, *Faith of My Fathers*, McCain says an angry mob rushed him, intent on tearing him to pieces. But a woman intervened and he was carted off to prison to be left to die from his wounds. It was only after the North Vietnamese learned that McCain was the son of a prominent U.S. admiral that they provided him with basic medical attention to save him for propaganda purposes.

McCain spent five-and-a-half years in several Vietnamese prisons without any significant surgery or treatment for his broken limbs. He endured torture and beatings that re-broke his arms, and he nearly died from dysentery. Once, he was beaten so badly that he lay unconscious on a filthy concrete floor for days on end. His imprisonment included two years in solitary confinement.

McCain was released in March, 1973. In 2000, he returned to the prison where he was held captive. By that time, he was a U.S. Senator, who helped re-establish diplomatic relations with Vietnam. Today, his photo is on the wall of the Hanoi Hilton, along with that of Doug Peterson.

McCain is critical of the civilian leaders who put America under the gun in Vietnam. President Lyndon Johnson's administration refused to allow the bombing of North Vietnam or the invasion of the country -- both of which might have resulted in the quick end of the war.

Of course, the reason the U.S. held back was because we didn't want to risk a nuclear war with China and the Soviet Union, so perhaps President Johnson took the wisest course after all. Perhaps most of us who were alive in the '70s would simply be a pile of old bones rotting in a field somewhere today if cooler heads hadn't prevailed.

Human Reminders

Saw a roast dog in the Ben Thanh Market today, well-glazed with a sugary red sauce and its canines curling from under its cooked lips. Nearby, a cage of mid-sized dogs cowered on the sidewalk, awaiting their fate. Dog is usually only eaten by men on certain ceremonial days determined by the lunar calendar. Medium-sized mutts are the meat of choice and different portions are eaten for virility, long life, blood-thinning and other nutty notions.

Traffickers also sell children in Vietnam -- illegally, of course. Boys are used to sell flowers, postcards and books out on the street corners, often until the early hours of the morning. They can bring in $700 per week to their owners. Girls are sold as household slaves, restaurant workers, and worse. Often, poor families in the country are conned into giving up their children to traffickers with the claim that they will be adopted by foreigners, or find a better life in the city. The traffickers also prey on runaways, who are both needy and easy targets.

In one of the worst areas of Hanoi -- a neighborhood noted for its heroin addicts -- you'll find the Blue Dragon Children's Foundation. Here, volunteers from Australia and America try to rescue the local street kids. They provide the kids with schooling and computers, along with fun stuff like art, yoga and hip-hop dancing.

Some of the kids are the left-behinds of parents who've been thrown in prison for selling heroin. Without the Blue Dragon, they'd have nowhere to go.

"There's no place for kids to play in this neighborhood," notes Amy Cherry, an American volunteer from Florida. "There's no playground or soccer field in this part of town and no chance just to have fun and be a kid. Our purpose is not to support them with handouts and charity, but to help them to help themselves."

Australian teacher Michael Brosowski established the Blue Dragon in 2002 after coming the Vietnam to teach English at the national university. Two months after his arrival, he met some shoeshine boys who were living on the street. Intrigued, he began teaching them English.

Since then, the Blue Dragon has worked wonders, with local kids eager to join its football team, Dragon Drummers and school.

For some there's hope, but no guarantee.

"We have some runaways who are kind of wild," Cherry says. "They stay awhile and then they leave -- they can't be tamed."

Other Impressions of Hanoi:

-- There are still human reminders of the American War here. At a bus station, an old man figured my bill with a pen strapped to the stub of his right arm. Both of his arms were blown off below the elbow during the war.

-- I unleash my inner dragon on a second occasion. In the latest, I handed a taxi driver a 50,000 dong bill and he flipped it for a 10,000 bill which looks much the same. He claimed I had shorted him. This produced a fearsome roar on my part and a refusal to pay.

He jumped out of cab like he was going to start some shit with me. But I calmed myself with some effort and turned my back on him, walking away. I remind myself to pour some water on my rage. "It's not good to get so angry," I say by apology to the women travelers sharing the cab. Still, the incident gets me shook up because I'm surprised at how angry it makes me.

It's not wise to let your emotions get out of control in a foreign land. I'm told that if you have a traffic accident in Vietnam, the judges always make Westerners pay for the damages, no matter who is at fault. One can only imagine the same spirit comes into play if an argument with a cab driver spirals out of control.

-- Speaking of money: things are cheap in Vietnam. A huge lunch at a small cafè includes shrimp rolls, stir-fried beef and noodles, pineapple upside-down cake, coffee and Pepsi for $4. Plus, French film star Catherine Deneuve used to hang out in this lunch spot while she was shooting *Indochine*, a love story of IndoChina. A liter of premium beer goes for as little as 30 cents.

You may have noticed by now that I mention food quite often. It's because that's what backpackers think about half the day when they're not looking at deadly dull old temples or wondering where to score their next beer.

-- There's nothing like a shot of snake whiskey to separate the men from the boys. This is rotgut booze with a ghastly looking cobra stuffed into the bottle, sometimes adding a scorpion for spice.

-- What's that terrible smell? Oh, pardon me. You take a shower every chance you get and wash your hands 20 times a day when traveling, but your clothes get nasty in no time, traveling on the dirty buses, trains and cabs. Oh well, I'm setting off on a journey of 1,000 miles down the length of Vietnam and my laundry will have to wait.

The Battleground at Hue
Dec. 30, 2007
Hue, Vietnam

The beauty of Vietnam unfolds on the dusty old night train to Hue, which was once the country's ancient capital.

At dawn, I lie in the upper bunk of a rocking car and gaze out the train window, watching rice paddies flow past like a river of green framed in palm trees. Here, villagers still use oxen to till the fields, or poke at clumps of soil with hoes.

Hue was the site of one of the biggest battles of Vietnam. Here on the New Year celebration of Tet in 1968, the North Vietnamese and Viet Cong reneged on their promise of a cease fire, launching a wave of attacks across the country. Hue was ground zero, with house-to-house fighting underway for 15 days in one of the bloodiest battles of the war. Filmmaker Stanley Kubrick captured the battle and the gray gloom of this rainy city in *Full Metal Jacket*.

The Vietnamese were clever strategists. First, they launched a 70-day siege of the American Marine base at Khe Sahn, which was of little strategic value in the middle of nowhere on the border of North Vietnam. Khe Sahn was besieged by 20,000-40,000 attackers. Then, after the U.S. and South Vietnamese poured troops and support into Khe Sahn from all over the country, the North Vietnamese launched the Tet Offensive with 80,000 soldiers attacking 80 cities, towns and military bases.

Some 45,000 Viet Cong and North Vietnamese were killed in the Tet Offensive, compared to a few thousand of the Western allies. But psychologically, it was a victory for them, serving to wise-up Americans that they were mired in an unwinnable war against an implacable enemy who would never surrender.

Yet the real losers of Tet were the Viet Cong of the south. The North Vietnamese never had any intention of sharing power with their counterparts in the south after the war. To remove any possible opposition, Le Doan (one of Ho Chi Minh's successors) ordered the Tet Offensive, sending 40,000 of the best and brightest leaders of the Viet Cong on a suicide mission. With the leadership of the south destroyed by Tet, the survivors had little or no say in the governance of the country once the war ended.

The old citadel of Hue was the home of the last Vietnamese emperors from 1802-1945. This royal city was surrounded by a moat full of crocodiles and girdled by six miles of thick walls. During the Tet Offensive, the South Vietnamese army holed up here, prompting artillery fire that destroyed much of the Forbidden City. Then the North Vietnamese took up residence, receiving more bombs and artillery in turn until most of the place was blown to hell. But there's still about one-third of it left -- a World Heritage Site.

The place is dripping with moss, rain and ruin. Listless Vietnamese workers tap away at renovation projects, but it looks like a long haul getting this place back up to snuff.

New Year's Eve is tomorrow, so plans are being laid to put some kind of party together with the three groups of backpackers stopping here. It's funny how concerned the Aussies get about securing their supply of beer each night -- it's really a big deal to them. I like to tip a couple or three, but could care less if I have any at all. Not so the folks from Down Under, who lay in large amounts of brew or hard liquor at every chance. Should be an interesting night.

The Perfume River
Dec. 31, 2007
Hue, Vietnam

I had vowed that I wouldn't ride on the back of a motorbike in Vietnam, since it seems far from safe. But it's impossible to face the thought of being the lone wuss in our group, so with a face blanched a whiter shade of pale and hands grasping the handhold beneath the seat like steel claws, off I ride...

... through red lights and merging traffic, down narrow alleys and along jungle paths, splashing through tangerine mud puddles and around slippery corners. A pedestrian bridge over the river is barely wider than our bike, giving me cause to fear for the loss of a knee as we speed within inches of the metal posts.

On the morning of New Year's Eve, 12 motorbikes coast in the gray-green mist down the road along the Perfume River, which winds through Hue. It's called the Perfume River because a forest of frangipani trees grows at its source, their white flowers flavoring the air.

Only a month ago, the river flooded to a depth of 12 feet, and many

poor farmers drowned while trying to save their livestock or possessions from washing away.

All day long we ride, stopping at temples and tombs out in the jungle
and coasting past rice paddies that stretch beyond the horizon. The
oxygen of the jungle charges your blood, and around each bend is a
living work of art.

Beyond the river, the mountains of the DMZ trace shadows in the
mist. Old French and American concrete bunkers guard a river bend
on a bluff that used to be called Bunker Hill. Today, it's Lover's Hill
because kids come to smooch with a romantic view.

The DMZ was the six-mile-wide Demilitarized Zone at the 17th Parallel where some of the fiercest battles of the war took place. Less than
20 miles to the west lies the border of Laos, through which the Ho Chi
Minh Trail wandered for hundreds of miles. The DMZ is still riddled
with unexploded bombs and land mines, and although there have been
international efforts to clear away the explosives, poor farmers still die
trying to harvest the old bombs for scrap metal.

At the tomb of Emperor Tu Dac, the old walls of rotting stone drip
with moss and the tea stains of time. It's as if you are walking through
a watercolor painting, with the vibrant colors of long ago diluted to
pale ghosts -- liquid pink, milk coffee and beige.

This dripping tomb and its surrounding park and riverscape was the
life's work of the last emperor of independent Vietnam, from 1829-
'83. Although Tu Duc had 104 wives and scads of concubines -- along
with a royal duty to ride one each night -- he left no children. A case
of smallpox had left him sterile as a young man.

Life has its hassles, even for an emperor. He had a horde of mandarins (minister/scholars) hovering and scheming over him at all times,
along with the intrigues of the eunuchs who guarded the harem. Villages would offer up their prettiest girls, hoping to gain his favor, and
the mandarins would search out beauties for gifts. Some guys have
all the luck.

His mating habits were recorded in detail, with much fuss and feathers given to determining his heir -- usually the child who was most
malleable to the mandarins' blandishments.

Talk about milking the stallion. But Tu Duc preferred to work on his
tomb and write poetry. Sometimes he would hunt tiny deer with a tiny
bow on the tiny island in the middle of his park.

By the end of the day, I get the hang of balancing on the back of
a 100cc Korean motorbike, but am glad, nonetheless, when the Thai
Binh Hotel hoves into view. I give my driver Thieu a whopper of a
tip for getting me back with my skin still attached -- it is New Year's

Eve, after all.

That night, our group of backpackers makes the scene at a tourist bar called the DMZ where I celebrate the dawn of 2008. Then we head down to the town's hottest disco, which would hold its own anywhere the U.S., with a green laser cutting the fog shrouding the dance floor and a cadre of cute girls from Europe and Australia dancing on a go-go platform. I get lost in the dancing and have a happily mad time, thinking how strange it seems to celebrate the New Year in a place like Hue.

Tailor Made
Jan. 1, 2008
Hoi An, Vietnam

Whenever I'm in Hoi An, I always stop in to have a new suit hand-made of the finest cashmere.

Such is the case on this occasion, when I pick out a blue pinstripe fabric and have a fitting on a side street just south of the vegetable market. There are perhaps better tailors in town and a wider selection of fabrics, but the young lady at the Hung Son tailor shop speaks good English, and that's enough for me, since things can get lost in translation in Vietnam.

I spend a frightful amount: a little over $1 million dong. However, this is only about $70 U.S. for a suit that would cost $300-$500 back home.

Having a suit made is "the" thing to do in Hoi An, a town at the midpoint of Vietnam which has 300 silk shops and tailors. Women go bananas in this town, which is the shopping capital of Vietnam; they order hand-tailored suits, blouses or silk dresses at the scores of shops you see lining the streets. Men can't resist falling prone to the fever too.

Six weeks ago, Hoi An was six feet underwater from the impact of a typhoon. A typhoon is this hemisphere's version of the hurricane, with winds of 120-200 mph. Guests in the fancy hotels on the beach were driven from their rooms, and the town is still drying out from the damage. But people are used to that sort of thing here -- they have platforms on pulleys that lift all their goods to the second floor whenever it floods.

That's Vietnam's major problem: too much water. While other thirsty nations wither from drought, Vietnam's rice fields and cities drown in the incessant rains and monsoons. The water flows down from the mountains at the same time the big spring tides occur, drowning the land. But the rain contributes to the beauty of this place -- a green dream of rice paddies plowed by oxen and the jungle-covered mountains that run along the sea, beyond which lie the sleepy kingdom of Laos.

Today, Hoi An is the wealthiest small town in Vietnam, but it was one of the poorest not so long ago. When the communists took over in '75, they decreed that all things "old" in the country must go. But Hoi An was too poverty-stricken to modernize, so it languished as a backwater with a dead economy.

But when former servicemen began visiting Vietnam again in 1989, many wandered here from Danang, the site of a former airbase just a few miles north. They loved Hoi An for its old, unruined charm and languid miles of nearby China Beach. The town boomed. It went from having three hotels and one silk shop to several hundred.

The joke about Hoi An is that it was "owned" by the Viet Cong during the war and the Americans never had a clue. Servicemen who came here from Danang airbase and Khe Sahn for R&R had no idea their dollars were going to support the war effort on the other side. The friendly waiter by day may have been stalking them by night.

Today, you can see the fuselages and fuel tanks of old B-52 bombers that have been fashioned into canoes. The Vietnamese never waste anything, or throw anything away.

Hoi An reminds me of Varadero on the north coast of Cuba, another Third World resort town with a tourist boom that few Americans know about. Huge hotels are being thrown up along the beach, and the town is packed with tourists from around the world, all in a shopping frenzy. There are fine restaurants and coffee shops, friendly people, and all the chopstick boxes, t-shirts and fabric lanterns your heart could hope for in the souvenir shops.

And of course, those suits... My only regret is not throwing a tux together as well, but that will have to wait until next time.

You Buy Something
Jan. 2, 2008
Hoi An, Vietnam

The sales technique at the shops in Vietnam is much the same as in Egypt, India and Thailand.

You sneak into a store unobserved and are mulling over which t-shirt or marble carving to buy. Suddenly, the staff spots you and comes running like the 7th Cavalry charging the enemy lines. Oh shit.

The helpful staff hovers about, misdirecting you towards everything but what you're interested in. "What you size? What color?" They begin hauling out their entire inventory. "No, no, no -- just looking -- just looking, thanks."

"Those are t-shirts," they'll tell you.

"No kidding? Never seen a t-shirt before. Is that what they look like?"

Even at bookstores, a clerk insists on hovering over your shoulder.

"This is book."

"Oh really? I didn't know that. Book, huh? I'll be damned."

In the end, they refuse to rest until they've succeeded in chasing you from the store with another sale washed down the drain.

By chance, I happened to look at the label on the $80 sweatshirt that Jeannette got me at an EMS outdoor gear store a couple of years ago: "Made in Vietnam," it says. Ironically, Vietnam is the capital of counterfeit goods, and I could probably buy a dead ringer of the same sweatshirt here for $10. You walk past tailor shops where seamstresses are copying items requested by tourists.

Copyrights and trademarks are routinely ignored in southeast Asia, and I imagine that some of you are reading a photocopied version of this book right now in a place like Bangkok or Saigon. As soon as a new bestseller comes out, it is photocopied and offered for sale in the tourist markets. Name brand items from Calvin Klein, Versacci and Rolex are copied en masse. The counterfeit shops of Vietnam are legendary, mimicking brand name clothes right down to their imperfections. CDs and DVDs? Anything you want.

"Once in a blue moon there will be a raid to satisfy the demands of foreign lawyers and their companies," Bill says. "Then a great show is made of running over counterfeit CDs with a steamroller. The next day, the same shops will be filled again with the same counterfeit CDs."

Here in Hoi An, the merchants have a rather odd sales come-on: "You buy something," they say as you walk past their shops. It's half a question and half a demand.

Souvenir shops are the pilot fish of the backpacking world. You can't go anywhere without the trinket & t-shirt shops swimming before your eyes. But what else is a weary traveler to do after a long day trudging around to dreary temples? You can only sit around coffee shops, cafès and bars for so long.

So: "You buy something." Game over.

After Dark
Jan. 3, 2008
Hoi An, Vietnam

They roll up the sidewalks at about 10 p.m. in Vietnam, with only a few cycle taxi drivers and vendors of soda pop and cigarettes hanging in for the late hours. The streets fall dark and still, with all the hubbub of the day tucked back home under the care of the grandmothers who run the households.

But hark, what's this? An oasis of light and happy voices on a lonely street means a backpacker bar is at hand.

Along with cruising the souvenir shops and sightseeing old temples, the bar scene is a "must do" every night for international travelers -- a *raison d'etre* (that's "reason for living" for you uncultured types). People compare notes from all over the world, trade tall tales, and size each other up for romance.

Being in for the long haul, I'm not keen to travel down this same track every night because nothing gets old faster than endless good times. I'm often more inclined to head back to my room after dark to read or plunk a few tunes on the guitar. Swapping tales in a bar tends to drift toward cases of oneupmanship -- a game which I play well enough -- but it all gets a bit thin after awhile.

It's funny how you see the same chaps behind the bars of every town in the world, from Hootville to Hoi An: Jim Beam is there, along with Jack Daniels, Bacardi, Gordon's London Dry Gin, Havana Club, J&B, Kahlua, and always a dusty bottle of Malibu coconut rum that looks like it hasn't been poured in years. Different bar, same cats, every time.

But the beer brands change faces everywhere you go from Cusco to Kyoto: Tiger, Biere LaRue, 333, Chang, Beerlao, Kingfisher, San Miguel, Imperial, Saigon...

***

Three days in Hoi An is a pleasant respite from traveling. I rent a junker mountain bike (60 cents for the day) and ride along China Beach and through the back roads of town, zigzagging between the other bikes and bouncing through potholes and mud puddles. What could be better than being an American riding the backroads of Vietnam on a mountain bike? I can't imagine. How I wish I had time to ride all across Vietnam on its backroads, over the mountains to Laos and beyond.

At one stop, a cheerful old lady in a palm leaf hat chatters and grins

Despite the pain of her past, there is much love in Nan's life.

from ear-to-ear, baring her teeth which are a shiny jet black from chewing betel nut -- a mild narcotic.

I learn again how wrong you can be making assumptions about people in other lands. I thought the women of Vietnam were wearing surgical masks to ward off air pollution, but actually, it's to avoid getting a tan. As in India, the most desirable complexion here is that of a pale face. Darker skin means you're a peasant who works out in the fields. Occasionally, you'll see a woman riding her bike with her face completely swathed in a cotton wrap like a burn victim, with only a thin slit for her eyes, peering out from under a palm leaf coolie hat.

Another fun fact: the Vietnamese fishermen never carry lifejackets, life rafts or safety equipment of any kind when they're out on the wild sea, because that of course, would bring bad luck. But they do take one important safety measure: they paint eyes on the prows of their boats so the watercraft will know where they're going.

And hey, don't go sticking your hand in that open-weave upturned basket with the sparky-looking rooster inside. These birds are raised to kill in the local cock fights, with their spurs embedded with razor blades. They're juiced with amphetamines before the fight, and if one manages to crawl from the ring, it's only because the other is bound for the stew pot. Many of the gamblers pledge the only thing they have of value in the fights: their motorbikes.

A Hard Life
Jan. 5, 2008
Hoi An, Vietnam

There's a weather-beaten woman with a broad smile who runs a snack cart outside the Au Hoi Hotel. She's as sweet as a peach, inviting all passersby to buy a soda or a box of crackers -- anything to help make ends meet.

Nan clowns around with my guitar at a rollicking concert outside the hotel the morning we depart. She has a smile that could rouse the dead.

But Nan, 42, has had a rough life and there's a bitter stab on her face as she volunteers her story. "I was only a year old when my mother and four members of my family were killed by American bombs," she says out of the blue, with her dark eyes suddenly bitter. "My mother was killed, and I was just a baby."

Nan gets up at 5 a.m. to cook breakfast for her children, ages 5 and 16. Then she's on the job from 6:30 in the morning until 10:30 at night, seven days a week, even in the cold, drizzling rain. I find her late at night, exhausted and sleeping by her cart on the street.

She lives next door to the hotel with her father, who is 86 and addled by Alzheimer's. His face is as grave as a street-corner Confucius. He takes my hand with a look in his eyes that is both wary and shy.

I want to tell Nan that I opposed the war in Vietnam and marched in protests, vowing not to go if drafted. At that time, some 40 years ago, it seemed obvious to many protesters in America that the war in Vietnam wasn't much different than our own Civil War and that we were the foreign meddlers. The people of South Vietnam didn't generate millions of Viet Cong guerrillas because they loved the good old U.S.A. and its puppet government in Saigon -- they wanted their independence and reunification.

But America's politicians and military believed that there was a "domino effect" with the communists threatening to engulf the world one country at a time. That theory turned out to be dead wrong. Today, you're hard-pressed to find anyone in America who even knows why the war was fought. The only dominoes that fell were our soldiers and people like Nan.

My words go unsaid as being too trivial and lame to mention. I can't imagine the horror of Nan's upbringing -- her family murdered by bombs, her home destroyed -- and the years of famine and poverty which followed the war.

Vietnam wasn't off the hook after the Americans left -- they launched right into a war with the Khmer soldiers of Cambodia and their Chinese allies. It's estimated that roughly one-third of the people in Vietnam died in the course of all the fighting in the years from World War II through the 1980s. It's a wonder they're not as grim as stone.

"Why do you think these people seem so happy after all they've been through?" I ask Bill later that day.

"It's because they made a decision to put the past behind them. After the war, the survivors felt that had been part of a lost generation," Bill says. "They felt that they had missed out on the good life and the benefits of the modern world. So, they decided to put the war behind them and poured all of their dreams into making a better life for their kids.

"That's the reason you don't find bitterness here today -- they don't think about the past -- they think about their children and the future. For the Vietnamese, the past has nothing to offer but pain."

***

Nan's is one of many sad stories you hear everywhere in Asia. It's stereotypical, but there does seem to be a sense of fatalism and futility in Asia -- perhaps even a lack of imagination -- where people don't seem to believe that they can break free of their lives of drudgery.

A 15-year-old beach vendor in Goa told me his father died when he was a year old and he had to drop out of school to support his family. He claimed he was selling necklaces so his sister could go to school. Yet he couldn't imagine doing anything to benefit himself other than begging people to buy the same ratty necklaces peddled everywhere.

Similarly, a taxi driver in Bangkok said it would be simply impossible to move a few hundred miles north to a better life in Chiang Mai. He didn't have the money to make the move. And so on.

Often, I've felt like an amateur psychotherapist, assuring people in India, Thailand and Vietnam that they have a good country, great climate, excellent food and friendly people. And no snow piling up three feet high, like where I'm from. Would I trade places with them? Hell no, but I've tried to diplomatically suggest that the route to a better life is through education, attitude and imagination.

But those ideals are hard to convey in the space of a few minutes, especially if just surviving the day is a struggle. For these folks, filling a rice bowl is a a grinding, daily concern that trumps any high-flying thoughts of attending university.

And I wouldn't presume to tell Nan these things. The next morning I see her on her motorbike, taking her baby girl to school. Her child is cute as a doll, riding on the front of the bike and snug in a fluffy winter hat. She looks well fed and happy, and it seems clear that despite the pain of her past, there is much love in Nan's life.

The Night Train
Jan. 6, 2008
Danang, Vietnam

I wait three hours for the train to arrive in Danang -- a typical experience in Vietnam, where sometimes the trains don't arrive until the next day. The station is packed with travelers, with their luggage jamming the aisles. We pass the time watching a clip from a Mr. Bean movie that plays over and over again on a big-screen TV.

I wander across the street from the station and find a restaurant that serves roast frog with chili, BBQ pigeon, and steamed goat meat with ginger. There's also a dish called "inside of duck with lemon juice." The Vietnamese love their duck innards.

It's tempting to order the roast frog just to see what the critter looks like, but hey -- maybe next time.

It's a 10-hour trip to Nha Trang, so I settle into the top bunk and finish reading *Once We Were Soldiers... And Young*, by Lt. General Harold Moore and journalist Joseph Galloway. It's the story of the battle in the Ia Drang River valley in November, 1965, in which a battalion of the U.S. Army was wiped out.

The 450 troops in the 1st Battalion, 7th Cavalry were dropped into the heart of a stronghold of 2,000 North Vietnamese soldiers in an area that was only accessible by helicopter. Some 305 were killed in the Pleiku campaign, with many horribly wounded. Many of our guys were cut off in an ambush and lay wounded in the jungle where they were methodically shot by execution squads of Vietnamese soldiers.

The book is nearly 400 pages of who got shot where, man-by-man. If you've seen the film starring Mel Gibson, you've been served a weak tea compared to the bloodbath described in the book.

I watch the jungle roll past the train, knowing I could never begin to grasp what it must have been like to lie flat in the elephant grass with the bullets and bombs ripping the air, inches overhead. All is at peace outside my window -- a lush green land of red dirt roads and skinny people riding between the crooked checkerboards of glimmering rice paddies.

At midnight, I stare at the train ceiling and wonder what the heck I'll do when I get home, harnessed once again to the plow of existence. Funny, but I can't imagine doing anything out of the ordinary -- no grandiose trips in the near future, no big dreams -- I just plan to enjoy getting back to my family and friends and settling in like Bilbo Baggins with no particular itch to scratch.

I think of Jeannette, and how she is the most fantastic, brave companion anyone could ask for. Marriage is a covenant of trust and conviction, and although we all give lip-service to the idea of offering our partners the freedom to follow their dreams, I know that few wives would give permission to their husbands to go wandering around the world for months on end. She is a rare and beautiful flower.

The Kingdom of Champa
Jan. 7, 2008
Nha Trang

Nha Trang is a seaside town with a broad boulevard along a coastline that could be any tropical resort on earth: a more laid-back version of South Beach comes to mind, while the Aussies say it reminds them of the hyperdeveloped stretch of coast in their country that's known as Surfer's Paradise.

Today, mixed in with little old ladies grilling lobsters on the boardwalk, there are elegant seaside restaurants offering Italian cuisine. You'll also find boat tours which offer a chance to swim in the South China Sea and enjoy a ride in the "basket boats" used by fishermen. They're literally waterproofed baskets the size of small hot tubs.

There's also a $500 million VinPearl resort across the bay, built by (I kid you not) a Ukrainian uranium mining company on a former military island. The resort is reached by an aerial gondola that stretches for two miles high above the water.

When Ho Chi Minh City (formerly Saigon) has its version of spring break, this town is packed to the palm tops with Vietnamese tourists.

But once upon a time, Nha Trang was the last stronghold of the

Cham, whose Champa Kingdom reigned here for 1,500 years.

The Cham were sandwiched between the Lac Viet tribal groups of the north, and the Cambodian empire of the west. The Cambodians were great city builders: they built Angkor Wat in the jungle with slave labor from Thailand. In 1200 A.D., it had a population of two million and was one of the biggest cities on earth.

But the Cham were seafarers, traders and pirates. Word has it they loved nothing better than to swarm down on ships passing by their coast for a round of rape, pillage and murder.

I've heard two stories of how the Cham fell and Vietnam became a single country. In 1471, they were defeated by a Viet army from the north, and the last remnant of their kingdom around Nha Trang disappeared in 1720, when the royal family fled to Cambodia.

A more romantic story has it that the king of the Viets married a Cham princess and united their armies. The army marched on Cambodia and took over the rich Me Kong River valley and the wealthy trading city of Sai Gon. That's how modern Vietnam got its start, 300 years ago.

As for the great Cambodian Empire, once it lost the Mekong and Saigon, it dwindled and died. Angkor Wat was abandoned, vanishing beneath jungle rot, vines and moss until it was rediscovered by archeologists hundreds of years later.

It's said that to this day, the Cambodians and Vietnamese still can't stand each other, and that Cambodia and Laos are now under the covert control of Vietnam through political machinations.

The American Remnants
Jan. 8, 2008
Ho Chi Minh City, Vietnam

A ruined man in his 50s walks up to me at the American Remnants Museum in Saigon and asks to shake my hand. It seems rude not to, given that he has lost both arms above the elbow, so I grasp the tender stub of his right arm.

"Where are you from?" he asks.

I look him in the eye and notice that his right orb is a wet snail, boiled away in the blast that took off his arms.

"America."

"Can you buy a book to help me out?" He has a stack of photocopied guidebooks under his left arm.

"No thanks."

I walk off and he calls out "Happy New Year" after me. We're on the brink of the Year of the Rat in southeast Asia.

It's a kneejerk reaction on my part, due to a mix of horror and my resistance to being manipulated with a guilt trip. But of course I feel mean and like shit almost immediately and walk back to try to find him. What would it hurt to buy a book from an old vet?

But of course, he's gone.

Amputees hang around all of the tourist sites in Vietnam. That, and people who suffered horrible birth defects as a result of our spraying Agent Orange all over the countryside -- a chemical defoliant meant to clear the jungle of trees, but which also affected the people who breathed its toxic fumes or drank its poisoned waters. These include men with arms the size of newborn infants, or geeks twisted into knots and lying on the pavement. When Americans get on their high horse about Saddam Hussein using poison gas to kill his enemies in Iraq, they forget our own chemical war crimes with Agent Orange.

Evidence of the efficacy of Agent Orange in twisting humanity into monsters is found at the museum. Along a dark wall, you come face-to-face with pickled birth-defect babies floating ghastly and silent in jars of honey-colored brine.

The American Remnants Museum used to be called the American Atrocities Museum. When relations softened between the countries it was renamed the American War Crimes Museum. Then, in the spirit of political correctness, the "Remnants."

And maybe that's the best way to put it, considering that armless vet hanging around the ice cream stand.

This is clearly a propaganda museum, and I can only wonder what a different view might reveal of Vietnamese brutality, but the exhibits are damning:

Here are heroic photos of American troops in combat, taken by Pulitzer Prize-winning photographers. But there are also photos of U.S. soldiers torturing or beheading prisoners, or dragging people to death behind tanks. There are photos of napalm and white phosphorous victims with their faces melted away. Photos of little children, begging American soldiers for the lives of their parents.

Here too are photos of the victims of the My Lai Massacre, and of nearby My Khe, where on March, 16, 1968, up to 504 people, including women, children and old folks were systematically murdered by U.S. troops in an orgy of torture, rape and mutilation.

A BBC News report from the time offered this take on the massacre:

"Soldiers went berserk, gunning down unarmed men, women, children and babies. Families which huddled together for safety in huts or bunkers were shown no mercy. Those who emerged with hands held high were murdered. ... Elsewhere in the village, other atrocities were in progress. Women were gang raped; Vietnamese who had bowed to greet the Americans were beaten with fists and tortured, clubbed with rifle butts and stabbed with bayonets. Some victims were mutilated with the signature "C Company" carved into the chest. By late morning word had got back to higher authorities and a cease-fire was ordered. My Lai was in a state of carnage. Bodies were strewn through the village."

The bodies strewn in the fields of My Lai aren't propaganda photos shot by the Vietnamese. They appeared in American magazines, such as *Life*, and in U.S. newspapers. These images appeared regularly in the U.S. press in the '60s and '70s and were a major reason American opinion turned against the war. As a result, the U.S. military instituted rules to control the free-ranging press in future wars, "embedding" reporters with the troops in Iraq with a show of allowing access to the war, while keeping their cameras and questions far from the action.

But the Vietnamese unwittingly deal themselves a *riposte* at the museum, which features a replica of the "tiger cages" of Con Son Island, where Viet Cong prisoners were packed into cells, often awaiting torture. Open grates at the top of the cells made it possible for the jailers to urinate and defecate on the crowded prisoners, on top of whatever else they cared to throw in.

One teenager was tortured by having his legs amputated one joint at a time over several months -- an old favorite in Asia, going back to the days of pirates and evil emperors. Legend has it he refused to give up the names of Viet Cong members of his family and village, if he ever knew of any in the first place.

Of course, the Viets neglect to mention that the tiger cages were maintained by their own countrymen in what was then South Vietnam, and not by the Americans. In fact, it was a visit by two U.S. Congressmen, Augustus Hawkins and William Anderson, in 1970, that exposed abuses at the prison in *Life* magazine and the U.S. press, prompting the Vietnamese to clean up their act.

But overall, the American Remnants Museum is a grim place with a grim message: war is hell.

A Visit with the Viet Cong
Jan. 9, 2008
Cu Chi, Vietnam

The old Viet Cong stronghold at Cu Chi is a museum now, but once, this area was riddled with a 35-mile network of tunnels that hid up to 16,000 guerrillas, complete with underground hospitals, kitchens and war planning rooms hacked from the clay.

Set in the jungle to the west of Saigon (aka Ho Chi Minh City -- which, like the recently-named Mumbai, is rarely used), Cu Chi features an American tank which was blown up by a land mine in 1967. Amid the craters of B-52 bomb strikes there are tents housing animatronic Viet Cong guerillas performing tasks such as sawing through unexploded bomb shells to make homemade mines. It's like the robotic Hall of the Presidents at Disney World, with a guerrilla twist.

You can also shoot five rounds from an AK-47 for around $6. Word has it the Viets used to let you shoot your own chicken for the BBQ, but animal rights activists put the kibosh on the fun. Not far away in Cambodia, they went one better: for $200, you could blow away a cow with a rocket launcher.

Here, the cruelty of the war comes home again with a display of the vicious booby traps of the Viet Cong: there are pits full of bamboo stakes dipped in manure, and handmade metal barbs on revolving axles which pierced the bodies of those unlucky enough to step on them. As your weight sank down, the iron barbs plunged inexorably deeper.

The highlight of Cu Chi is a crawl through the tunnels dug in clay that seems as dense as concrete. The tunnels have been widened to accommodate fat Westerners, and it's no big feat to crabwalk 30 yards through one in the pitch black.

The Viet Cong lived down here for months at a time, surviving on pulped cassava root. Overhead, the bombs of the B-52s shook the ground like the sledgehammer of the gods. The VC's bed partners included snakes, centipedes, bats, mosquitoes and big nasty spiders.

"Oohh... I ahbso-lute-ly hate spidahs!" shivers Erin, a gorgeous Australian of 25 who's backpacking through Borneo, Vietnam and Cambodia. But Erin and other young members of our group decide to give a second tunnel a go. It's longer -- about 300 feet -- narrower, and so dark that you can't even see your hand if you hold it an inch from your eyes. Sure enough, there are frightened squawks as the party nears the end of the tunnel, and they deliver a huge, frisky spider at least two inches in diameter, who emerges on the neck of a young photographer named Max.

The daughter of an Australian Air Force colonel, Erin is a superwoman with the dash of a natural-born leader. If she were a man, perhaps she'd be the captain of a football team or a combat pilot.

As a kid, she excelled in many sports but had a special talent for cycling and became one of Australia's top women racers. She had a shot at the 2004 Olympics in Athens. Unfortunately, a young admirer was clowning around and jumped on her back one day while she was talking with friends on the campus of her university. "People said they could hear this terrible 'snap' all around the area because the weight of his body tore all the tendons in my knee," she recalls.

Years of ceaseless training and Olympic dreams vanished in an instant, replaced by extensive surgery and months of recovery and rehab. But Erin didn't crumble; instead, she became a world traveler, backpacking throughout South America and Africa, where she volunteered in an AIDS clinic for children.

Early on, she notices I'm wearing a wedding ring.

"Oh yes, I'm married," I say, going through the long, much-repeated explanation of why I'm out roaming the world while my wife is back home with other obligations. "My wife met me for a couple of weeks in Thailand. And what about you? Do you have someone?"

"No," she says. "I haven't been with anyone in quite awhile. The guys in my town don't seem to be interested."

"Well I find that hard to believe," I reply. "I would think the men would be chasing you up one street and down the other all over town."

"Well I wish!" she says, "But if that were true, I'd be here with someone now. Not that I don't have opportunities, but most of the men I meet just want sex, and I can tell right away what they're thinking."

I can well imagine that's true, because Erin is a vivacious blonde with a wide smile, an outrageous sense of humor, and the curves of a centerfold. At the bar on New Year's Eve, some Italian guy tried painting her tonsils with his tongue before she pushed him away, laughing.

It strikes me that Erin has more testosterone than most of the guys she meets and they're simply afraid to ask her out. Guys looking for a kitty are easily frightened by a tigress. She's in the same league as Tomb Raider Lara Croft. On the other hand, being good-looking, lots of fun, and a daring adventuress are hardly drawbacks, so I suspect that Erin won't have to wait too long for Mr. Right.

It turns out that she has a low-grade, simmering rivalry with a 19-year-old brunette in our group for the affections of Max, 21. A brilliant commercial photographer for an Australian company that specializes in skateboard wear, Max is on vacation with his mom, dad and sister and it's the family's first big trip outside of Australia. Max is arrestingly handsome in the blond Australian surfer tradition. He has a girlfriend back home, however, and could seem to care less about any female attention on the trip; his time is occupied by a passion for photographing Vietnam.

"There's someone on this trip who thinks I'm after Max," Erin says in a confiding moment over a beer, her blue eyes flaring. "But that's not true -- believe me, if I were after him, she wouldn't have a chance," she snaps.

I definitely believe it, thinking Max, if you only knew...

Max is quite a sweet guy, by the way. His right arm is covered with tattoos, which I disdainfully think of as being trendy -- I imagine that they are the usual demons, skulls and Celtic horseshit that most walking palettes choose to ink themselves with in America. But when I ask to see his arm, Max reveals a touching scene that represents his mother and father silhouetted in the doorway of their farm in the Outback, with the beams of a red Australian sunset in the background. The tattoo covers his arm from shoulder-to-elbow -- a stunning act of love.

***

As for Saigon, it's an exciting town with an ocean of motorbikes coming at you from every direction, filling the streets with a constant roar. Cobwebs of electrical lines hang in dense shrouds just overhead along the streets. You sit at little sidewalk cafès at toy picnic tables on tiny plastic stools designed for preschoolers, watching the millions go by.

It's a shop-til-you-drop town and looks to be very prosperous, considering the wreck of Vietnam a few years back. There are Gucci and Longines stores on the fancy avenue that leads to a huge tourist bazaar at the heart of the city.

Here too is the Continental Hotel, where Graham Greene wrote *The Quiet American*. He also hung his hat at the ritzy Metropole in Hanoi. It sort of bursts your bubble to know that Greene, Josef Conrad and Somerset Maugham lived and wrote in such fancy digs. Aren't writers supposed to live in squalid, bug-ridden hotels, thick with tropical heat, lassitude and angst? Hmmm...

Pass the Goat Dick, Please

Steamed goat penis or beef cock "with Chinese medicinals" are among the menu items at the Bo Tung Xeo Restaurant in Saigon, where our group of 12 backpackers has a rollicking dinner after wrapping up our trip across Vietnam.

Although it's a Tuesday night, the cavernous place is packed with locals sitting at long tables. The joint is dense with the greasy smoke of hibachi grills set in ceramic pots on every table, where you BBQ your own meat and veggies.

I'm afraid I haven't been much of a conversationalist during our trip: Sometimes I can't quite make out what what my fellow travelers are saying with my tin Midwestern ear. I've mastered the sound of the Australian accent, but the burr of New Zealand is hard to catch at times: "Bahwb, awh ewe hahving a gude tayhm?" might be a sample phrase to digest. Then too, I'm a bit deaf from listening to too much loud music in my wayward youth, and it's generally louder than hell in the roaring streets of the 'Nam, making conversation difficult.

But the folks from Down Under are a lovely bunch -- "full on," as they say -- and I invite several to stop by for a visit if they ever make it to that remote outpost of America known as Traverse City.

But I digress: here are some of the menu choices at Bo Tung Xeo:

-- pork brain soup
-- fried suckling pig heart with garlic
-- fried cuttlefish teeth
-- sauteed frog stomach with garlic
-- stewed snake with lemongrass
-- minced snake
-- grilled bloody cockles
-- sauteed field rat with coconut
-- raw oyster with mustard
-- crispy fried small intestine of pork
-- goat in hot pot
-- eel with rice gruel
-- fried cricket
-- deep fried scorpion (yum!)
-- ... and let's wrap it up with the udderly delicious grilled breast of she-goat, shall we?

Bon appetit.

To Wave a Flag

After dinner, we all head to an Aussie bar next door. It looks like a typical waterhole in America: dart board, pool table, sports TVs on the wall, beer brand mirrors... The Americans and Australians are kissing cousins when it comes to some things.

Close to midnight, my brain is a furry brown blanket soaked in 333 beer. I'm sharing a cab to the airport at 6:30 with Holly, an Australian of mixed Maori descent by way of New Zealand. Holly shows no sign of slowing down and ends up heading out with the others to party 'til the wee hours.

But this is the Aussie kids' last night of fun in Vietnam, with some headed home and others on to Cambodia. And they do love their booze.

There's a big Australian flag hanging from ceiling to floor in the bar. It bears a Union Jack tucked into a field of blue that's spangled with the Southern Cross. The Aussies get the idea to pose together in front of their flag, their faces lighting up like a shopping mall Christmas tree.

"You'd never see Americans doing that," I say to Bill. "We'd never pose like that in front of our flag."

"No, never," adds Katie, the only other Yank in our group.

"It just wouldn't be a cool thing to do."

I fly the flag at home through the summer, but it's not something I want to prance in front of like a country-western singer, least of all in a place like Vietnam. There's too much power -- and too much pain -- in the American flag to trivialize it as a background prop the way politicians do. The American flag is a symbol of freedom and liberty from tyrants, but too often, it has fallen into the hands of politicians bent on exploitation and war, or right-wing flag-wavers who have more in common with the Ku Klux Klan than Thomas Jefferson.

I tell Bill that I'm still shook up by the American Remnants Museum. Even though I was against the war as a teenager in the '70s, I still feel sick that my country was to blame for so many pointless deaths, amputees and homeless kids. What value does patriotism have if it's not balanced by atonement when your country loses its way?

"It's hard to square those atrocities with how I was raised," I say. "Every American is raised to believe that we're the good guys of the world, and that we hold ourselves to a higher standard than undemocratic nations. When the reality destroys the myths you grew up with, it's not easy to accept."

Ours is the flag that freed the slaves, but also the flag that denied blacks their freedom in the first place. It's the flag that saved Europe and Asia during World War II, but also the banner that flew over American Indian reservations, Vietnam, Iraq and Abu Ghraib. Unfortunately, it's not much respected in the world today due to the oil men who've held the White House these past eight years.

"Yes, but let's face it, if it weren't for America, most countries wouldn't do fuck-all to lend a hand when there's a problem," says a Kiwi at our table. "You don't see any of these other countries helping out. They sit on their hands and wait for the Americans to clean up the mess."

I'm surprised that anyone has a kind word to say about America, since overseas, these conversations tend to go in the other direction.

"I guess everyone loves to make America the whipping boy until the shit hits the fan," I say.

I remind myself that we're the ones who led the way in kicking the Taliban and al Qaeda out of Afghanistan. And we did save the Kuwaitis, the Kurds, the Bosnians, the folks in Kosovo, and tried to lend a hand in Haiti and Somalia. And when Vietnam fell in 1975, millions of boat people fled the country, many with the dream of reaching the shores of America.

Sometimes we get slapped for our efforts, or blasted for not intervening in places like Darfur or Rwanda, but the world has become a safer place under the Pax Americana, even for our country's critics. That's the flag I stand in front of.

Malaysia

"Same, Same, But Different"
Jan. 10, 2008
Georgetown, Malaysia

I have a cracking hangover on the flight out of Vietnam, a condition aided by too little sleep that no amount of coffee can cure. But then, hangovers are an occupational hazard for backpackers the world over.

Georgetown on the island of Penang isn't the fun place it's cracked up to be in the guidebooks. I stroll around town, wrapped in a blanket of heat and humidity, dodging some listless whores down on Love Lane, one of whom looks like a guy in a skimpy polyester dress. Sure enough, these are lady-boys from Thailand who haunt this corner. In contrast to their flamboyant brothers, the Indian girls who prostie themselves tend to stand in the shadows and hiss at men passing by.

Love Lane was the old red light district when the Brits ran Penang. It had three brothels, a gambling house, an opium den and a mah jong parlor. Now, it's full of cheap backpacker guesthouses.

Georgetown is Malaysia's second largest city after KL (Kuala Lumpur). It reminds me of a tropical Kalamazoo, with everyone so fagged out from the heat that they've developed a permanent slack-shouldered zombie shuffle.

But I can't complain about the digs. I'm staying at the wonderfully seedy Western Oriental Cafè, a guesthouse near Love Lane that runs $6 a night. It has a padlock on the plywood door, an antique fan, peeling paint on the plaster walls, and a friendly feel with travelers from all over the world. There'll be no Raffles Hotel for this scribbler.

But there's a price to be paid for the luxury of staying in a grungy backpacker pit. For starters, there's no top sheet on the bed and no towels. I wonder if there are lice... And it's hot at night here on the Equator -- steamy hot -- in a tiny 8-by-10 foot room with a fan that's so far up the 12 foot ceiling that no breeze reaches me.

Mosquitoes are included in the room rate, but not, unfortunately, toilet paper, which I find out to my surprise the next morning during a visit to the communal john. And, wouldn't you know it, in Saigon I ditched the roll that I'd been carrying around for the past four months, assuming it would no longer be needed in a spiff place like Malaysia.

But *Predator* is playing on the DVD next door, a film enjoyed in the company of all-male, beery backpackers who look like they don't have much tread left on their tires. What with the atmosphere and all, you can't ask for better than that.

***

"Excuse me, are you a writer?"

I look up from the computer screen at the guesthouse and meet Daniel, who has noticed me posting a column to my newspaper back home.

Daniel and Rosemary of Olympia, Washington are on a trip that includes India, Thailand, Vietnam, Laos, Malaysia, Indonesia and New Zealand. It turns out we've already crossed paths in Ooty, Mysore, Goa and Chiang Mai. Small world.

I'm surprised to find Americans staying at the same dive as me -- it's not like this is the Holiday Inn. Like every other backpacker in the world, Daniel is also writing a travel blog and wants me to check it out.

"You know, you're one of the only American backpackers I've met the whole time I've been away from the States," I say.

"Yeah, you don't find too many of us out here," Daniel says. "We're heading on to Bali."

"How long will you be gone?

"At least six months."

Daniel invites me to read his mindsay.com blog, where I find a kindred spirit. Months later, I find that his words sum up what backpacking around the world is all about:

"We've been students and teachers; volunteers and paid workers; campers; hikers; bikers; surfers and beach bums; mountain climbers; honored guests and proud hosts; penny pinching tramps and lavish splurgers; friends; lovers; clever navigators of the unknown and marks for the unscrupulous... We sought and found repeatedly the variety and sense of discovery we felt escaped us too often back home."

***

That evening, I find an open-air cafè, pleased to be the only *ferringhi* on the premises. Dinner is a plate of saffron rice with shrimp caked with a paste of smokin' hot minced chiles. Billy Joel is torturing the clients with "Uptown Girls" on the P.A.: "And when she's walkin', she's walkin' so fi-yi-yine..."

Georgetown seems to have its share of Western down-and-outers; I wonder if some of the old-timers in the cafès and cheap guesthouses are the so-called heroin hippies, in for the long haul in southeast Asia.

I attempt a world-weary countenance, which comes easy as a result of three hours sleep last night, following our farewell party. Scribbling notes in the cafè, I realize that a lot of this blog has been devoted to food. It reminds me of one of my favorite books, *Islands in the Stream*, by Hemingway, where the protagonist (Ernest in the guise of a great oil painter) is continually asking the boys on his boat in Cuba for a sandwich and a mojito. Like every other page it's: "Boy, bring me a sandwich and a mojito." I love the book because you don't know if the old fart is making fun of himself or dead serious.

"You want beer, you want beer?" a bar doorman calls out on the main street in a sing-song voice as night falls. "You want girls? You want girls? You want young, young Chinese girls? They make you massage all night." With his sing-song voice and rolling banter, he could be a rap artist.

The offer sounds pretty good right about now, I muse. But instead, I drift over to an English pub and have an overpriced stout beneath the blare of a soccer game on TV. France versus Argentina.

In the distance is the call of the *muezzin*. This is a Muslim country -- in fact, Malaysia and Indonesia have the most Muslims of anyplace in the world. They too have their share of Islamist radicals.

That proved to be a bit of a problem on Oct. 12, 2002, when three bombs went off in the tourist district of Kuta on the Indonesian island of Bali.

A suicide bomber strolled into a tourist nightclub with a backpack full of explosives and blew the dancers to bits; meanwhile, a large car bomb was exploded outside another popular nightclub. A small bomb was also set off outside the United States consulate in Denpasar. The bombings killed 202 people, of which 164 were foreign tourists. Another 209 people were injured.

The culprits were members of Jemaah Islamiyah, a violent Islamist group. Three of them were sentenced to death.

Bali's tourism industry still hasn't recovered: with 88 of their countrymen killed, the Aussies moved on to Thailand and Vietnam to party. But they do sell a nice "Fuck Terrorist" t-shirt in Bali now, in hopes of setting the record straight.

Speaking of which, after the 9/11 attack in 2001, Malaysian officials had the bright idea to declare that this multicultural country of Indians, Chinese, Malays and Buddhists was officially a "Muslim" country, even though the religion is practiced by roughly 60% of its citizens -- hardly a mandate. And even that percentage may be a false reflection of the country, since if you are born a Malay, you are officially classified as a Muslim whether you believe in Islam or not. Under the 'laws' of the Koran, which informs the country's Shariah courts, the apostasy of changing one's religion is grounds for death. Talk about arm-twisting.

Tourism from Europe and the U.S. dropped like a bomb after Malaysia's Muslim moment and has been in the pits ever since. But many Muslim vacationers from the Arab nations have arrived to help fill their shoes, with scads of them flocking to the brothels and bars near the Thai border, a notorious region which serves as Asia's "Wild West."

It turns out that the Muslims are as hypocritical as the followers of any organized religion. Who could imagine?

Malaysia also has a charming way of greeting visitors in its in-flight magazines and customs declarations:

"BE FOREWARNED DEATH FOR DRUG TRAFFICKERS UNDER MALAYSIAN LAW."

And that's a *mandatory* sentence, brother, if you're caught with as little as 200 grams of marijuana. Malaysian drivers are extra careful when they cross the Thai border because sometimes druggers attach bags of dope under the cars of passersby at cafès or gas stations and then follow them over the border. If the unfortunate Malays are caught by drug-sniffing dogs, it can be curtains for them, with no way of explaining their way out.

It's said that there are billboards in Malaysia featuring photos of drug dealers hanging by their necks -- a modern version of the medieval custom of putting the heads of criminals on pikes outside of town.

As a popular saying goes in Asia: "Same, same, but different."

The Dangerous Land, Part II
Georgetown, Malaysia
Jan. 10, 2008

It's surprising how many people I've met on this trip who believe that America is way too dangerous to a place to visit.

They're just like the Americans who are afraid to travel overseas.

Today, I met a couple from Britain who are traveling through Malaysia, Indonesia and New Zealand. Previously, they spent six months traveling through Southeast Asia, and have basically been on the go each year since the late '70s.

"Have you ever been to the States?" I ask.

"No. Isn't it dangerous there?" they respond. They're afraid to visit.

This is the third or fourth time I've heard this sentiment from seasoned travelers. And come to think of it, if you were passing through Newark on your way to New York, or the ugly parts of Chicago, Detroit, Miami and Los Angeles, then America would indeed seem to be a dangerous land. The murders of European tourists who stumbled into the gangland neighborhoods in America have been well-publicized overseas.

On the other hand, Manhattan is absolutely wallpapered with Europeans and Asians, especially since the value of the dollar has dropped by 35 percent in the past five years and everything in America seems dirt cheap to visitors. So perhaps I've met the only handful of travelers in the entire world who are afraid to make the trip.

I met a little boy in India who assumed that since I was an American, I loved to get into fights. I assured him that we much prefer to play guitars in America, rather than shooting each other.

***

Fear of the unknown has a powerful grip. I'd like to go to sub-Saharan Africa someday, but get wildly different opinions from people who've been there. Some say it's quite dangerous, and others say there's no problem. The same deal for Brazil. Travelers to both places have told me they've been held up at gunpoint and feared for their lives. World traveler Erin told me she survived a bus hijacking in Brazil, a police massacre during a tour of one of the favela slums of Rio, and then a shootout in a bar.

"We were getting a guided tour of the favela when a van of police pulled up and just started shooting people. Our guide told us to run. Then, later that day, we were on the upper floor of this nightclub and heard someone shooting at people on the first floor. We ran out the fire escape at the back of the building to get away."

Similarly, Beerlao Bill said he wouldn't care to return to Africa today, because he understands it to be quite a bit more hazardous than when he crossed the continent 17 years ago.

But you really don't know until you go, do you? Erin had also been all around Africa and thought it was fine, as had Anne and Florence, my companions in India. And I have no doubt that if Bill were presented with a ticket to Mombassa or Dar Es Salaam, he'd be on the plane tomorrow.

Bill also told the story of a young tour leader, Mike Matsushita, who vowed to visit all of the places in Asia listed as being dangerous in the guidebooks.

"He wandered all over Asia, visiting hot spots and war zones and never had a problem," Bill said. "Then, on a trip to London -- one of the safest places in the world -- he was riding the subway when the terrorist bombs went off and killed him." That was on July 7, 2005.

Fear of travel is a virulent virus of the mind -- a meme. Mexico, for instance, is widely held to be a dangerous place, with a higher murder rate per capita than the U.S., according to a United Nations report on violence. Yet I've traveled for hundreds of miles across Mexico on local buses on several occasions and never felt the least threat. Wouldn't travel in Brazil and Africa be much the same?

The Muslims claim that everyone's fate is written down in the great Book of Destiny and no one can predict when they'll die. Only Allah knows, so you may as well roll the dice.

Speaking of Muslims, I wandered around Georgetown today, looking for a t-shirt to present to my pal George, for whom this town is surely named. No such luck. But they do have a couple of popular styles for the many Islamic tourists here, decked out with the smiling face of that great Muslim hero, Osama bin Laden.

But I'm pleased to see that Osama is tucked into the clearance rack, apparently with few people buying his act.

Last Stand at Ferringhi Beach
Jan. 11, 2008
Batu Ferringhi, Malaysia

Hippies discovered the island of Penang in the early 1970s and were followed by hordes of backpackers, drawn to the beauty of Ferringhi Beach on the north shore.

Well, not really: a daring British chap named Captain Francis Light "took possession" of the island in 1786 to serve as a refitting station for the trading ships of the East India Company.

It was the perfect location -- halfway between China and India -- and just past the pirate-infested Malacca Strait that divides Malaysia and Sumatra. Penang and the star-shaped Fort Cornwallis became a good place for ships to resupply for the long trip back to London.

The Sultan of Kedah gave Penang to the British East India Company, based on an understanding that the Brits would help defend his kingdom from the armies of Burma and Siam. But unknown to the sultan, Captain Light didn't have the authority to make such a deal. So after the British dropped the ball and failed to defend Kedah, a lease arrangement was worked out instead.

The British brought 'convicts' from South India to build their fort and to slave in their plantations. (One can imagine the ease with which native peoples were enslaved as convicts in those days.) Then Chinese refugees arrived here from the turmoil of wars in their country during the 19th century. The Indians became known as "Clings" because of the large metal ball and chain they wore around their ankle. Many of the Clings converted to Islam as an affront to the cruelties of their British masters.

But for our purposes, it was a brave band of hippies who made Penang the tourist resort it is today. Westerners flocked in their footsteps to Batu Ferringhi -- "Foreigner Beach."

Those old hippies would think they were tripping if they could see the place today. A vast wall of development runs along the shore and up into the hills, crowding out what was once a paradise with high-rise hotels and chain stores. And the sea is a greasy, greenish-brown gravy of pollution that few dare to swim in.

I nearly turn around and get right back on the bus to Georgetown when I arrive in Batu Ferringhi with my gear. But after bumbling around a bit, I manage to find a row of old guest houses on a lane just off the main beach. Miraculously, this dirt road paralleling the beach has survived the tsunami of development, and although its guest houses are in a prime location, they offer the cheapest rates in town.

I settle in at Baba's Guesthouse for $13 per night, staying with a Malay family. A grandma is cooking at a wok in the kitchen downstairs and the kids of the household are hypnotized day and night by cartoons on a flatscreen TV, like you'd expect to find anywhere on earth. Same, same, but different.

Next door is a mosque with a chap in the tower delivering the call to prayer with the enthusiasm of a professional yodeler at 4:30 in the morning. He's got a great voice, but he does go on forever. Dinner is at the local *halal* restaurants, meaning the chicken is prayed over in thanks to Allah before it gets its head lopped off.

But my second-story room faces the sea and there's a pleasant veranda just outside my door. A caged dove sings "Coo--cuckoo-coo" outside my window, telling me it's a great place to roost. It's a good place to lounge on the beach and enjoy hikes in the jungle with my monkey and butterfly friends. Sometimes a fool gets lucky.

The Lucky Travel Hat
Jan. 14, 2008
Batu Ferringhi, Malaysia

"MALAYSIA" -- the last country is inscribed in felt-tipped marker on my lucky travel hat, signifying it's time to go home. Eire, England C2C, East Europe, Der Donau, Egypt, India... a ring of been-there-and-gones runs round my head.

It's not much of a hat -- just an old army flopper that got its first outing back in 1999 when Jeannette and I hiked the Bright Angel Trail to the bottom of the Grand Canyon. We got a big laugh out of our matching jungle hats, because at mid-day, when the temp hit 115 Fahrenheit, we stretched out for an hour or so in the cooling waters of Bright Angel Creek. We filled our hats from the creek, plopped them on our heads, and watched twin streams of water spout out the vent holes on either side.

Since then, I've worn the hat to Alaska, Costa Rica, Greece, Peru, Hawaii, Isle Royale, China and many other places, writing each name on its khaki face. By the time I reached India, the Lucky Travel Hat had matured into more of a relic than a practical head cover. I started adding memento pins from each country: an ankh in Egypt, a coconut sun in India, an elephant in Goa, a Buddha amulet in Thailand, lucky money from Vietnam.

A relic is an inanimate object which brimmed with power before its energy was spent -- a work of magic that's been retired to a shelf. So it is with my hat, which has grown so august with bric-a-brac and markings that it's become too silly to wear out in public except for ceremonial occasions, such as if I ever have an audience with Queen Elizabeth.

If such a trip can transform a hat, then what about the person who wore it? I feel that my trip around the world has made me more patient with others and less concerned over matters of spilt milk or lost time (not good qualities for a newspaper editor, however). In some way that can't be expressed, I too have become a relic of my travels, ready to be hung up on a wall as a trophy gathering dust.

On the other hand, if it means having blueberry waffles and bacon for breakfast on Sunday instead of purple rice and hotdogs (as was the case in Nha Trang), then I suppose that being a relic will be worth it.

The Power of Peace
Jan. 15, 2008
On a Midnight Bus

The average Malaysian earns $3,500 per year. Yet he dines for pennies each day, and a visit to a doctor's office runs about 50 cents under his national health care system. Government-sponsored housing is available, and there is a pension for the elderly as well as half-price on transportation and other services for seniors.

Malaysia's highways look spanking-new, and the freeways hum with towering, immaculate long-distance buses, most of which are air-brushed with striking designs. The cities are also filled with state-of-the-art local buses, many of which appear to have rolled off the assembly line yesterday.

It's no paradise -- workers' rights are non-existent and there's the crackpot Islamic hegemony and Shari'ah courts to deal with. It's claimed that the factory workers are little more than wage slaves. But still, you have to wonder how this poor country has managed to create such a visionary infrastructure. Could it be the power of peace?

A 12-hour bus trip takes me overnight to the island city-state of Singapore, alleged to be the most boring city in the world, but also the cleanest and safest. All of the above ring true.

Talk about serendipity: on the bus I meet a traveler named Rob, 51, a physician from the Netherlands. He too is on a trip around the world, with much the same outlook as me. His wife also stayed home, and she -- like Jeannette -- is also a daycare provider. Their birthdays are only one day apart. Small world. Same-same, but different.

Over dinner in the Little India enclave of Singapore, Rob tells me of his experiences in Africa and allays my reservations as I relate some of the conflicting stories I've heard about the continent. He describes Uganda and Malawi as lovely places -- poor, and stricken with an HIV/ AIDS rate of 25% of the population, but blessed with friendly people and incredible beauty. Far better than northern India, Rob says, adding that if I could handle Nicaragua, then Africa should be no problem. I resolve to go, someday.

Curiously, Rob is the fourth European I've met on this trip who can't wait to emigrate from his native country. Europe is getting too mate- rialistic, they all say -- all anyone cares about is keeping up with der Jones's. People aren't happy in Europe unless they have the newest car, the biggest TV, or the latest styles.

"In Africa, you're happy if you've got a chicken," Rob notes. I've heard this same quote so many times about the residents of various Third World countries that it's starting to sound like an aphorism. And come to think of it, I'm quite happy with a chicken for Sunday dinner myself.

Rob is an experienced backpacker, but he too found northern India to be quite bleak with its ominous poverty, hustlers and crowds. We reflect on the contrast between spotless Singapore and dingy Delhi, which looks like the end of the world. Both are in Asia, yet are planets apart. Why the difference?

I put the blame on the cruelties of colonialism, the cost of war, and the follies of ideology and religion. Malaysia had a fairly benign time under British rule and Singapore evolved as a cooperative trading port, benefiting the Chinese, Indians and Malays alike. The country's multiculturalism forced Muslims and Buddhists to get along, although there are still issues of racism here. And there's been no war since World War II to suck the bones of this place.

As the jungles of Malaysia glide by my window, I wonder what America would be like if every president didn't feel obligated to thrust us into one war after another to feed our military-industrial machine. Parts of our major cities already resemble Third World countries; we drive on crumbling highways and our mass transit is often sub-par to even Malaysia. We simply don't know what we're missing.

The Europeans think we're nuts, and who can blame them? They have six weeks off each year to see the world as it really is, while Americans cower under our media's warnings of a dangerous world and are too constricted by the leash of the week-long vacation to see what's going on for themselves.

Asia offers a model of which way America could swing: the positive, transforming path of peace that has done so much for a poor country like Malaysia, or the downward spiral of broken infrastructure and social ills of India.

A Fine City

End of the Line in a Fine City
Jan. 15, 2008
Singapore

I see at the border of Singapore that the counterfeit DVDs and CDs which are sold everywhere in Asia are *verboten*. Whoops. Also forbidden is the flick-wrist police baton I bought on a lark in Thailand. Oh dear... And again, a friendly reminder that drug dealers receive a mandatory death sentence here -- by hanging. So glad I left that handbag of heroin back in the john at Ho Chi Minh Airport...

Momentarily, it crosses my mind that my bag could get searched. After all, I'm toting a guitar and have a braid down my back -- clearly the marks of an iffy character. But the customs people wave me through as cheerily as Santa's elves and I'm over the penultimate hurdle of my trip.

Singapore is not the sort of place to thumb your nose at the law. A favorite form of punishment here is lashing the bare buttocks of miscreants with a bamboo cane.

In 1994, American teenager Michael Fay went on a vandalism spree which included spray-painting a parked car. When a Singapore court announced that young Mr. Fay would be whacked on the butt with a five-foot bamboo switch, it became a *cause célèbre* in the United States. Some hoped that Singapore would lay it on, while the parents of the tearful teen claimed he'd be traumatized for life by the lashing.

In the end, the 18-year-old high school senior got four whacks across his backside. The incident sparked debate in the U.S. press over corporal punishment as a way of jerking our own bad characters back in line. Then, everyone forgot the incident and went back to misbehaving.

But Singapore turns out to be a fine city despite its bamboo justice.

For instance, there is a $1,000 fine for riding a bicycle on the sidewalk ($1,000 Singapore dollars are about $700 U.S.). There are also $1,000 maximum fines for chewing gum or smoking in forbidden areas, and for feeding birds (those pesky pigeons, don't you know). There's even a $1,000 fine for peeing in elevators, which happens to be one of my favorite things to do.

People here are so well-behaved that they won't even cross a sidewalk when the 'red' man is showing at the crosswalk light, even if no traffic is present. The funny thing is, I walk around for four days and don't see a single cop. Maybe they're all in plainclothes, reading this stuff over my shoulder in the internet cafè and whittling their canes...

***

The Little India section of Singapore is not the exotic backpacker's hangout that it's cracked up to be, but it will do. Bonus: last night a drum-&-keyboards Indian band rocked out with the crappiest, unmelodious 'music' and bad singing I've ever heard until 4 in the morning, keeping everyone in the hostel awake.

Before turning in for the night, I see approximately 1,000 spectators out on the street, taking in a concert at a pavilion that features two Indian singers getting their Vegas vibe on.

Almost everyone in the crowd of Indian expats is male. It's like a night at a disco in Chelsea, Manhattan with a huge mob of men grooving on the tunes, some of them holding hands. Where are all the women? Where are their wives and girlfriends? Home changing diapers or making chapatis, most likely.

Is this for-men-only tendency the result of India's macho society or the result of an unknown gay gene? I conceive a theory that there 100 superstuds roaming India, producing those 130,000 babies each day. The rest of India? Gay as the blazes.

Indoors & Air Conditioned

Orchard Road is the main shopping district in Singapore and is a ringer for Michigan Avenue in Chicago or Seventh Avenue in New York, only broader and lined with jungle greens, palm trees and outdoor cafes. Although it has a reputation for being dull, the town is far from boring: Spectacular rains lash the city each day in a whipping veil; the effect is like strolling through a waterfall. Lightning cracks the sky and you wade through rivers crossing the street. Thank God for Tevas, the rubber sandals I've worn throughout Asia.

Much of Singapore is literally indoors and air-conditioned. You can walk for miles through dozens of shopping malls. The Asians are mad for shopping in a way that the much-maligned materialists of America can't begin to approach.

Utopians who dream of a less materialistic world should spend time with the sons and daughters of communists in Asia who've taken up the capitalist roader's path with the enthusiasm of missionaries. The Asians are especially nuts about their mobile phones, with kiosks everywhere. It wouldn't surprise me if these marathon shoppers were pumped up on steroids to get 'er done.

The most interesting indoor place, however, is the Battle Box -- a bunker 20 feet underground in old Fort Canning, where the British surrendered Singapore to the Japanese on Feb. 15, 1942.

Back then, everything was coming up roses for the Japanese. In December of 1941, they bombed Pearl Harbor and invaded Malaysia, the Philippines, Burma, Hong Kong and Wake Island all in a well-orchestrated swoop.

The Japanese swept down the Malaysian peninsula and were soon at the gates of Singapore, which was considered to be an impregnable fortress -- Britain's "Rock of Gibraltar" of the Far East. But the Japs cut off the island's water supply and captured its stores of food and petrol. British Prime Minister Winston Churchill had already depleted the fort of air defenses and firepower. Hunkered in the sweltering Battle Box, the British generals felt they had little choice but to surrender to avoid the wholesale slaughter of the island's residents. They never lived down the disgrace of surrender, but they did save Singapore from destruction.

Holy Communion

The rest of my time in the Lion City is spent joining the throng of Asia, floating around town like a ghost in my filthy shorts and thin yellow t-shirt from Egypt that's ripped along the seams of the shoulders. I'm not a very good ambassador for America, considering how much the Asians like to dress up.

I drift through Chinatown, Little India, Orchard Road, the waterfront, and a neighborhood called Bugis, named after the pirates who once prowled the Malacca Strait. Did you know that Bugis is the origin of the word "bogeyman," used to scare kids into behaving? Now you do.

I take holy shopping communion with the millions worshipping at the malls and the stalls, taking a last stab at the overpriced food and souvenirs, eating chicken tikka and curried rice with my fingers from a banana leaf plate. Gee, I'm gonna' miss it. My final day is spent filling my bags with last-minute treasures for the folks back home. Fill 'em up, fill 'em up. When in Asia, one must do as the Asians do.

A Slight Adventure

"A good traveler has no fixed plans, and is not intent on arriving."
-- *Lao Tzu*

My ticket home looms as I count down the hours predestined months ago. When you're planning a trip around the world, it's tough to predict how long you should be gone. There are family, friends and career to consider; I did the best I could to weigh the optimum time for heading home, and somehow, mid-January is what came up in the cosmic 8 ball. I find myself reluctant to return, but duty-bound.

Funny, but when you finally achieve the "dream of a lifetime," you don't have the sensation of fireworks going off. But I did hear the faint *pop!* of a champagne cork with the realization that my dream of making it around the world had finally come true.

And what do you do when you achieve your greatest dream? It sinks in that you need to come up with another dream...

Mine has been a slight adventure. I didn't get kidnapped by gangsters or beaten and robbed by highwaymen. Surely, that would have made a better story, but somehow I couldn't manage to arrange it. The worst thing I saw on my way around the Earth was a dog getting hit by a car; and my only confrontations were with larcenous taxi drivers and a few wanky teenagers.

Nor did I accomplish any epic task. I didn't spend four years hiking around the world like Steve Newman, the author of *Worldwalker*, or ride my bike all the way around like Barbara Savage in *Miles from Nowhere*. I didn't sneak into Mecca in the guise of a Afghan pilgrim, as did Sir Richard Burton, or ride a camel to China, like Marco Polo.

Nor was I on any sort of "spiritual" journey, or any kind of trip that might be called high-minded. Apologies.

But I did discover a world that is far safer and friendlier than most Americans imagine. Instead of the boogeyman hiding behind every snack cart, I mostly found smiles and hands raised in friendship.

Yeah, and a few bullshitters and con men, it's true -- like anywhere.

And I did see many of the places that I'd always dreamt of, even if my Peter Pan dreams were cracked. That meant visiting the land of my Irish ancestors and pedaling from sea-to-sea across England and down the Danube -- routes which struck my fancy like a monkey mesmerized by a mirror. My interest in British seafaring led me to Portsmouth to see Admiral Nelson's ship. I went to Budapest because back in junior high school, I'd read James Michener's book, *The Bridge at Andau*, about the Hungarian revolt against the Soviets and the "Butcher of Budapest." I went to India to fulfill a youthful backpacker's dream, and to Vietnam because of the impact that country had on my generation. Silly reasons, but they meant a lot to me.

So call my trip ordinary -- the average adventures of an average man.

But isn't that encouraging news for timid travelers? That overall, our world is a safe and friendly place to visit? I hope that my story sheds some light on the backpacking lifestyle at a certain time in the world, and what a thrill it is to roam free with no idea of what's coming your way. And perhaps to give inspiration to others to hoist a pack and head off down the trail to the great Somewhere.

Wrapping it Up
Jan. 16, 2008
Singapore

As luck would have it, the night before leaving Singapore, I scored the last wish on my list for this trip: a chance to play guitar and sing in a pub somewhere on the road around the world.

Nice guy musicians, Andrew Chen and Busker, let me sit in for a set at the Prince of Wales Pub in Little India. If you're ever down Singapore way to catch their act, be sure to say hi for me.

We don't have much of an audience. Most of the crowd of backpackers are outside on the sidewalk, smoking and talking about all the places they've been and where they're going next. But that's alright -- playing there still put the cherry on my sundae. Memo to Jack Kerouac: no one listens to musicians anymore. The days of hipsters sitting spellbound before prophetic folkies or saxmen playing that 'go-daddy-go' be-bop in smoky bars are long gone. But we still keep playing.

Andy knows some deeply obscure stuff from the mid-'60s -- songs that no one here would possibly know, except for an old obscurantist in my shoes -- like "Song of the Sirens" by Tim Buckley, and "Hungry Freaks, Daddy" a 1966 rant by the Mothers of Inventions that sounds like it was written on the fly under the influence of a dooby:

"Mr. America walk on by, your supermarket dream.
Mr. America walk on by, your liquor store, supreme."

A young Malaysian from KL asks where I'm from and I say I'm wrapping up five months around the world, going back to northern Michigan in the far north of America tomorrow. He launches into his own tale of having just returned from three months traveling around the tip of South America, riding the buses from Rio and Sao Paulo in Brazil to Buenos Aires and then down to the tip of Patagonia where the boats leave for Antarctica, and up the west coast of the continent along the Pacific Ocean to Santiago in Chile and back across the Andes.

The lithium glimmer of a *daemon* gleams in his eyes. The kid is a stone travel freak, just like Ann, Florence, Beerlao Bill, Steve, Andrea, John the wandering Irishman, and all of the other cool people I've met on this trip.

"The coast of Chile is the most beautiful place on earth," he rhapsodizes. "And so few people even know it exists."

It sounds like a fabulous lost horizon -- the last backpacker frontier. I make a promise to go there, someday.

***

Afterward, I sit in the dark of the bar and have a pint of ale with Sir Laugh-A-Lot, thinking back on all the good times we had: riding Dulcinea across Europe and playing little concerts for locals with Tinkerbella on junky old trains and outside hotels in Europe, India and Vietnam. A dog who belongs to the bar wanders over and jumps up on the couch with me; she's a border collie -- a black-and-white version of my old dog Shoney. She puts her head by my lap and it's love at first sight. This is what travel is all about.

For a moment, I forget where I am. This has happened several times on the trip, since the scenery changes so often. Where am I? Oh, yeah, Malaysia. I'm in Singapore at the southern tip of Malaysia... I've wondered off and on what would happen if I simply forgot where I was and never found my way home. I'm sure it has happened to someone.

I'd like to ramble on for another six weeks, island-hopping through Indonesia, touching base in Australia and hop-scotching through Fiji, Hawaii and L.A., but you can only give a mule so much tether and mine ends tomorrow with a flight home. Plus, after following the sun around the world and suffering through eight months of summer, I wouldn't want to miss enjoying the coldest part of the winter in Northern Michigan, where the temperatures can range 100 degrees below those of sultry Singapore. And of course, to see my sweetheart's face again, along with family and friends.

What do you learn on a trip around the world? Things that every child already knows: That Planet Earth is much stranger and more interesting than you might imagine, and that most people are friendly to a traveler, especially if you take care to wear a smile.

By the numbers my trip included four continents, 20 countries, 18 flights, 20 trains, 10 long-distance buses, 700 miles by mountain bike, and countless trips by boat, car, pedicab, tuk-tuk, motorbike, camel, donkey, elephant, and on foot. Uncounted are the thousands of smiles, laughs and memories, good and bad.

There were also more than 100 internet cafès around the world where I wrote the blog that served as the basis for this book, scrounging around the back alleys of places like Cairo, Bombay, Galway, Maamalampurum, Amsterdam, Krabi, Penang and Whitehaven to find them. Going to the well of the internet each day kept my sanity and allowed me to remember all that happened, 'just so.'

"We sure had a good time," I say, sitting in the red dusk of the bar.

"Arrr..., that we did." The old knight lifts a phantom glass to his red beard, slowly nodding his gray head. But Sir Laugh-A-Lot is already starting to dissolve as the last grains of sand trickle through the hourglass of our trip. Someday, perhaps we'll meet again.

There were places I wish I'd seen, such as Russia, Tanzania, Turkey, Borneo and Australia. And then there's Patagonia, the Pyrenees, the Dalmatian Coast, Namibia, Buenos Aires, Barcelona, Tokyo, Uganda, Antarctica and the Olduvai Gorge... It would have been nice to have sailed the Indonesian archipelago on a schooner with red sails, or to have hiked high up into the Himalayas in search of snowmen and Shangri-la... but all that will have to wait 'til later, and the magic words: "Next time."

The End

How to Do It

Planning your trip around the world

The world is a jigsaw puzzle and all you have to do is put it together. Backpacking around the world is a matter of good planning, common sense and picking all of the glorious places you plan to visit:

Paper Work: Obtain any necessary visas from each country you'll be visiting before you leave home so you're not turned away at the border or stuck waiting in an endless line at an embassy overseas.

Many countries don't have visa requirements for U.S. citizens or Westerners, but there are a few: Russia, China, India, Egypt, Vietnam, etc. If it's a place where your country has had unfriendly relations in the past, count on needing a visa.

There are numerous companies on the Web that will walk your passport over to the appropriate embassy or consulate to obtain a visa. You need to send them your passport via registered mail, and expect a wait of two weeks to a month. Warning: don't list your occupation as anything like "writer" or "photographer" if you're going to a police state like China -- they may have reservations about letting you in.

Be sure there's at least six months duration left on your passport to avoid problems crossing borders. When obtaining a visa or talking with customs at border crossings, always list your hotel or tour group as your address or overseas contact.

What's Up Doc? See a physician who specializes in travel medicine to get the proper vaccinations for the countries you'll be visiting, along with preventive prescriptions.

It's essential to visit a specialist in tropical diseases or travel medicine because there are nuances to consider, depending on what part of the world you're visiting. For instance, the strains of malaria you encounter in South America are different than those of Southeast Asia.

Be sure to invest in a travel insurance policy to cover the duration of your trip, including medevac and emergency hospital coverage.

The cost of a travel insurance policy is cheap, compared to the expense of being hospitalized and medevac'd if you get broadsided by a motor scooter overseas. I've used Access America insurance, which can be purchased online (www.accessamerica.com).

Ongoing Tickets: Consider getting ongoing tickets for each country you visit. In the post-9/11 world, some countries require that you have an outbound ticket to prove you plan to make a timely exit.

Even the European Union can be a problem. An Australian friend was almost denied entrance to Great Britain because he didn't have an outbound ticket. He protested that he was planning to catch the ferry to France, but it was a close call. No worries if you've got a Eurail pass, of course.

Make a Budget: It's not as expensive as it sounds: Cost-wise, you can buy a round-the-world plane ticket starting as low as $1,200, which will take you to half a dozen hot spots, such as London, Cairo,

Delhi and Bangkok. The bad news: the less you spend, the less you see, with limited destinations.

Personally, I chose an itinerary that would take me to many of the places I'd always dreamed of seeing. The bedrock of my trip cost $5,000 for all the flights around the world, including three tours with the backpacking company, Intrepid Travel (www.intrepidtravel.com), which provided 45 days of native travel and lodging through the rough spots of Egypt, India and Vietnam.

Camping and staying in cheap hostels and guest houses kept other costs down. I planned a budget of $66 per day ($2,000 per month) -- going well over that in Europe but spending less in places like India and Malaysia.

Younger travelers should look into deals such as the International Student Card, Youth Travel Card, and Youth Hostel International, among other student discount schemes. The International Student Travel Confederation is one place to start: www.istc.org.

Fly Free: to many destinations by racking up frequent flyer miles on an airline credit card.

I have a friend who has accumulated more than 90,000 air miles by making absolutely every purchase over the past few years on her Visa WorldPerks credit card. That includes the $8,000-per-semester pay-ments for her son's college education. The caveat is that she pays off her credit card bill faithfully every month. Most of us don't have that kind of discipline, so exercise caution if you take this approach, or you won't be traveling anywhere.

Pack Light: synthetic travel underwear and t-shirts are expensive, but their fast-drying wash-and-wear qualities make it possible to get by with two pairs of each. Take few clothes in general, since you'll find plenty to catch your eye in foreign lands, and you won't be a real backpacker unless you've got the local beer brand tee-shirt, eh? Don't even dream of not taking a sweater and a windbreaker; even steamy places like Egypt and India can be chilly at night, especially when it rains or you're up in the mountains.

Virtual Security: Create an email account to serve as an "electron-ic safe" which you can access from anywhere in the world. Place scans of your passport, visas and extra photos of yourself in email messages which can be accessed in emergencies. Include important documents, such as plane itineraries and hotel reservations. I also kept copies of my credit card numbers in code in my email account, along with the phone numbers to call in the event that my cards were stolen.

Chain, Chain, Chain: Make sure your wallet has a chain on it and keep it in your front pocket or in a waist pouch, which should also be chained to your belt (very important!). Obviously, you'll want to keep most of your cash in a money belt or neck pouch with your passport under your clothes. Use an ATM card to obtain money on the go in doses of $200 or so. Always keep a reserve of emergency cash on your body in case the local ATMs don't work or your card gets stolen.

Money, Honey: Forget travelers' checks: Your ATM card is your lifeline around the world. It's the fastest way to obtain foreign currency at the current rates, with your pot of gold protected back home in your bank.

Be aware, however, that other countries may have ATM idiosyncrasies; often, you'll find machines that accept only cards backed by Visa -- others, only by MasterCard. Try to have one of each, or expect to face a long, distressing search for the 'correct' machine if your card isn't represented by the local ATMs.

In any case, it's a good idea to take along two cards, hidden in separate places on your body in case you lose one, or it gets gobbled by a foreign machine with no apparent bank to complain to.

Also, be sure to inform your bank back home that you'll be traveling overseas for a specific period so they can put a note in your file. Otherwise, they may be tempted to cancel transactions incurred over many months from, say, Togo or Brindesi, especially if they've been unable to contact you to confirm the validity of your withdrawals.

There are reports of crooks being able to copy your card by fiddling with foreign ATMs and capturing an imprint of your card. There's not much you can do about this. A more likely hazard is getting hijacked by muggers and frogmarched to an ATM for a strong-armed withdrawal. No joke: this has happened to a friend of mine living in Sao Paulo, Brazil three times.

Be aware that some ATMs may not have instructions in English -- practice mastering the cues/steps of a machine back home before leaving on your trip.

Ironically, ATMs are available in communist Vietnam, but rather hard to find in hypercapitalist Japan, where only cards from the local bank may be honored and the instructions may be in Japanese. Ditto in Cuba, where citizens of the United States are enjoined from using their credit cards or ATMs. This means packing $1,000 or so in cash on your body, and hoping you don't get rolled in Havana.

Where You'll Be Staying: Unless you're a multi-millionaire or are planning a $200,000 round-the-world cruise, chances are you'll want to stay in some variant of a hostel, pension, guest house or ryokan on your extended walkabout. Especially in the more expensive countries of Europe, Australia, North America and Japan.

Hostels are primarily dormitories where you bunk with 4-10 people of both sexes and all ages and nationalities. The more people who are in the room, the cheaper your bunk. Most hostels also have a few private rooms for couples at double the dorm rates.

Pensions, guest houses and Japanese ryokan are private homes which offer rooms for rent with a shared bath and shower. Rates may be a bit more than a hostel, but these can also be more interesting because you're living with the natives, so to speak.

Most of the above, along with the cheapest hotels, will be found in the area around any railroad station. Sometimes, railroad stations have an office where rooms can be reserved in the surrounding neighborhood, but if not, try walking a few blocks around the station and you're likely to find something. Bear in mind that the sign for a pension, guest house or hostel may be no larger than the lid of a shoe box.

How You'll Be Traveling: On the train, most likely. When you travel around the world, one of the first things you notice is how abominably behind the times the United States is when it comes to rail travel, especially when it comes to bullet trains, which hit speeds of well over 100 mph.

Many countries offer a smorgasbord of rail pass options: BritRail, Eurail, Japan Rail. Each have their own websites where the options can be weighed on which pass will best suit your needs.

But even with a rail pass, train schedules can be fiendishly complicated and you may even get lost in some of the mammoth train stations of the world (Kyoto and Osaka come to mind). There are two ways out of this dilemma:

1. Stare at the train schedule for an hour or so, taking in all of the details regarding the various train lines, numbers, tracks, names, and military time signatures (ie: 8 p.m. = 20:00). Eventually, it will start to sink in.

2. Better yet: Ask a lot of questions at the ticket counter, where chances are someone will speak English and put you on the right track/ train to your destination with a reserved seat. Ask, ask, ask, and ye shall receive.

In fact, if you're the "typical man" who doesn't like to ask directions, make sure that's the first attitude you ditch when you hit the road. You need help, bro, and asking around will save you a world of grief. Most people will be honored to help you, Mr. Exotic Traveler.

There are also likely to be many times when you'll catch local buses. Again, assume nothing about the schedules (for all you know, they apply to some other bus line) and ask for help. Don't ever take it for granted that you're on the "right" bus.

Ease into Your Trip: with culturally-familiar countries such as England, Ireland, the Netherlands or Australia. Don't make a mad-house like India your first stop.

For the more difficult countries on your itinerary, consider a back-packing tour group such as Intrepid Travel, GAP Adventures, or those listed in the back of magazines like *Outside* or *Men's Journal*. Often, you'll see 10 times as much with 10 times less hassle by going with a group; not to mention a chance to make lifelong friendships with people from around the world.

Think Small: You have to prepare more for the things you can count on than on the unexpected. These include things like bug bites, diarrhea, vomiting and a lack of toilet paper when you need it most. Be prepared and pack the remedies. The last thing you want when your bowels are exploding is to have to wander the streets in search of a pharmacy. You may not make it, mate...

Get out of Town: You can hop-scotch around the world via a few notable capitals: London, Rome, Athens, Delhi, Bangkok, L.A., New York -- in fact, these are the spots you're likely to visit on the cheaper round-the-world airline tickets. But don't deny yourself the places in between. Plan on train or bus side trips for exotic destinations and memories that are off the beaten path.

Book Ahead: for hotels and hostels. Obviously, you'll want to book your rooms in advance in the more difficult countries because the alternative may be wandering the streets at night. It's wise to get advance bookings anywhere because often, rooms are all booked up in popular destinations such as Dublin, London or Amsterdam.

Your best bet for backpacker-friendly deals are at the downmarket websites like www.hostelworld.com, which has contacts at 17,000 hostels worldwide. Most of the upscale sites such as Travelocity, Ex-pedia and Hotels.com will steer you toward expensive digs at "bar-gain" rates of $100 or more.

Log Out: on your email or Skype account whenever you use a hostel or internet cafe computer. This will prevent the next guy from reading your mail, or worse.

I met a backpacker whose family received a frantic email from her to send $20,000 to a foreign address, saying that she had been hospitalized and needed immediate help. It was a scam -- the ID crook had simply looked at her email file and noticed a family name on her address list. Fortunately, her husband back home smelled a rat and was able to track her down and discover that she was indeed alright.

Safety First: Common sense is your best protection on the road. As in, resist doing anything that's patently stupid and don't go where you shouldn't oughta' go.

For instance, don't get shit-faced drunk and go racing your rented motor scooter after midnight like two young Aussies did in Hanoi. After they untangled one guy from a fence, his family had to come to Vietnam and pay thousands of dollars for his hospital care, along with paying for the scooter and other damages before he was allowed to be released.

In general, it's a bad idea to get drunk or high in any foreign land because it puts you out of control of your situation. Pleasantly buzzed is fine, but getting blasted puts you at risk for even simple hazards, like falling down and getting hurt on substandard sidewalks. Also, consider that there may be dodgy types lurking in the bar who are experts at slipping date-rape drugs in your drink, or willing to "treat" you to 100-proof alcohol. Keep your substances under control.

On the other hand, sometimes a little "liquid courage" can put a different light on culture shock. Don't get shook up if a place seems too strange and foreign for comfort. Sometimes a timely beer can ease your nerves enough to put things in perspective. `Perhaps it will become clear that the locals aren't really scowling at you -- those grimaces are their way of smiling...

Otherwise, simply grab a cab and make it your escape module from an unfriendly neighborhood. The port of Tangiers in Morocco with its horde of hustlers and thugs waiting at the end of the dock comes to mind here...

Speaking of Cabs: one could write a book on this subject, but in general, trust no one who isn't connected to an official service.

The average taxi driver in any country sits in the hot smog of gridlock traffic all day -- every day -- fuming at his rotten luck for being at the bottom of the karmic totem pole.

Cynical and aggrieved, he may want to know how much money you make and if your life really is like an episode of *90210* back in the States. Alas, these qualities tend to produce their share of chiselers who feel entirely justified for 'getting their share' by cheating you. True, there are also many angels driving cabs, but... watch your back.

• Always opt for the official cab service and obtain a written rate when passing through an airport to avoid the higher-priced freelancers, who'll be bugging you as soon as you walk through the lobby.

• In many countries, metered cabs are not always a reality, so get the rate beforehand. (Check at your hotel or hostel to see what the fare should be and refuse the cab if it's a ripoff.) Repeat the rate once or twice before accepting the fare. Then -- no need to overdo it -- but make a show of using the correct denomination to pay so there's no chance for the cabbie to switch out a lesser bill and claim you cheated him.

• Try to use official, marked cabs when possible, and remember that different cultures have unusual practices in transit, such as picking up other riders heading in the same direction. Don't freak out if you're riding through Tijiuana and the cab driver stops to take on a family of six going in the same direction.

Take it Slow: whenever someone approaches you with a request that sounds fishy. If you drag your feet and ask a lot of questions, chances are a con artist will get nervous and disappear.

Once, at the airport in Beijing, an official-looking woman wearing a blazer and a badge approached my wife and me and said we could pay her a $120 "exit tax," rather than standing in line. Suspecting a scam, but not wanting to be rude in case she was for real, I dragged my feet, played dumb, and suggested we go to the airport office to discuss the matter. She promptly disappeared, and it turned out there was no such tax.

Con men and women -- including some in quasi-police uniforms -- are on the lookout for bewildered travelers. Insist on going to an official venue -- a police station or government office -- to get a second opinion when you're asked for money.

Get Lost... Not: It's easy to get lost in the cities of the world, of which 20 have more than 10 million people. Many city streets were built along the paths of twisting medieval lanes and alleys from hundreds of years ago, so it's no wonder it's easy to get lost.

You can put your faith in a GPS system and hope it works in the hairball of streets that twist through cities like Osaka or New Delhi, or simply pack a compass and a guidebook.

There's something to be said for going 'old school' by packing a compass rather than depending on Global Positioning Satellite technology (assuming it even works overseas). A GPS system may offer the 'correct' route, but it could be through an ugly or dangerous neighborhood or along a busy road -- the instrument has no way of knowing. Also, will the language it provides coincide with what's on the street signs? With a compass, however, you augment your own senses with a guidebook map and a knowledge of your general direction.

Speaking of guidebooks -- you'll groan at the thought of lugging along the thick tomes by *Lonely Planet, The Rough Guide,* or *Fodor's*, but rest assured, that brick is likely to pay for itself many times over with the information it imparts. Study and learn, Obi-Wan...

Save money by buying your guides at used bookstores along the way -- they're common throughout Europe and Asia -- and trade in your old guide or leave it at a hostel for someone else to use when you move on.

Keep it Simple: Don't buy any gift you can't place in the palm of your hand. Presents from exotic lands are well-intended, but they eat up space in your pack and weigh you down, limiting your options. I made the mistake of buying heavy, bulky marble boxes in Vietnam, which made it difficult to travel on. Too many presents or souvenirs can turn Holly Golightly into Burdensome Bertha.

Don't Go: if you're not really into it. But of course you already are, or you wouldn't be reading this book. Happy travels.

What to Pack?

Packing for a trip around the world that will last for months is no easy task. Space is limited and hauling a lot of gear is a hassle that gets old fast.

My trip was complicated by the fact that the first six weeks involved bicycle camping across Europe. This required two sets of gear, and it all had to fit on a bicycle and look trim enough for me to keep my self-respect. I packed the following, some of which may be helpful for your own expedition:

1 Stirling City Sport mountain bike, circa 1986
2 panniers
1 front pack
1 2-man dome tent
1 ground cover
1 sleeping bag
1 Kelty 'suitcase' backpack
1 ThermaRest mattress
1 book light
1 Titanium stove (palm size)
1 Titanium cup (for cooking & drinking)
1 spoon/fork set
1 Leatherman scissor/knife utility
1 water bottle
1 bicycle tool kit & extra tube
1 bike pump
1 20-ft. nylon cord
4 bungi cords
1 international electric plug converter
1 leather waist pouch w/chain
1 moneybelt
2 pair Smart Wool socks
1 cotton t-shirt
1 synthetic/cotton blend t-shirt
1 pair North Face synthetic pants
2 pair synthetic wash & wear underwear
1 lucky travel hat
1 funky cowboy hat
1 pair cycling gloves
1 pair ski gloves
1 'breathable' raincoat
1 pair rainpants
1 pair cycle shorts with pockets
1 fleece sweatshirt
1 clothing compression bag
1 pair Teva sandals
1 pair mesh-top running shoes
1 toiletry kit
1 backpacking felt towel
1 LED headlamp
1 booklight
1 first aid kit w/ Ibuprofen, Cipro antibiotics, anti-diarrhetics, anti-malaria pills
1 credit card LED light
1 write-on-anything pen
1 notebook
1 Crafter acoustic 1/2-size travel guitar
1 harmonica rack
1 "C" harmonica
1 Intellitouch guitar tuner
1 book of favorite songs
2 pack locks
1 sunglasses
1 bandanna
1 roll toilet paper
1 tube sunscreen
1 tube mosquito repellent
1 roll of duct tape
1 digital camera and charger
1 Skype-enabled Nokia N800 Internet tablet and charger
1 pair earbuds
1 box of Nature Valley Maple Nut bars
1 box of Maxwell House filter coffee bags
1 jar instant creamer
-- various guidebooks/novels

Keep in touch:

www.planetbackpacker.net